Silly
Birthday July / 97

Enjoy

your friend
Carl

FROM PILLAR
TO POST

Anne Ammundsen

MINERVA PRESS
MONTREUX   LONDON   WASHINGTON

ISBN 1 86106 103 X

First Published 1996 by
MINERVA PRESS
195 Knightbridge
London SW7 1RE

Second Impression 1996

Printed in Great Britain by
Antony Rowe Ltd, Chippenham, Wiltshire

FROM PILLAR TO POST

For Nina and Marc

Preface

In *From Pillar to Post*, I have endeavoured to give you, the reader, a glimpse into my life as an army daughter and a diplomatic wife.

I grew up in post Second World War Britain, and my father's job took us to many parts of the world at a time when travel was far less common than it is today. I have attempted to give the reader a brief view of those times in Germany, Egypt and Malaysia, against the backdrop of living with a domineering father who, many times, shaped the course of my life.

I have made far more than my fair share of mistakes, too, and this book is written for my children Nina and Marc in the hope that they will one day be able to avoid the pitfalls I have plunged into – mostly headlong. A number of skeletons have clattered out of their cupboards on these pages, both in the interest of accuracy and honesty.

My peripatetic lifestyle will bring the reader along with me to the Middle East and the Pacific, New Zealand and Europe. It will highlight the joys and sorrows of life lived moving from pillar to post.

Anne Ammundsen
New Zealand Residence
Riyadh

Acknowledgements

My thanks are due firstly to my family for their forbearance when I was preoccupied in writing this book, and in particular to my husband, Graeme, for his patience and assistance with the computer. Without his help I would never have completed this task.

My sources of reference have been principally my photograph albums, along with work records. In addition my thanks are due to my father for providing, a long time ago, a list of his army postings which enabled me to piece together the jigsaw which was my childhood.

Historical and geographical facts have been checked in the *Encyclopaedia Britannica*, originally purchased for my children, but which has had as much use by me in recent times, as by them. But most of all, it has been my memories, related here with as much accuracy as I have been able to muster.

My thanks are also due to staff of the British Embassy in The Hague, who were most helpful in checking past events both in the Army, Navy, and the Foreign and Commonwealth Office.

Contents

Chapter One
Camp Follower

Today is the day we have been waiting for since the twelfth of December 1986. Looking back over those years makes me realise just how much has happened to change the world. Britain has had a hurricane; the world has had Black Wednesday; the Iron Curtain has come down; the Iron Lady has had her day; Germany has been reunified; Kuwait has suffered Saddam Hussein; peace at last looks possible in both the Middle East and Northern Ireland, but the former Yugoslavia is a festering sore on the world's collective conscience. None of this could have been foreseen when Graeme and I walked into the study of Mr Barker, the Headmaster of Sevenoaks School, on that grey December day so long ago. Indeed, who would have believed that the town of Sevenoaks would not have seven oaks standing proudly on the Vine (one of the oldest cricket grounds in England) within such a short time of our visit there? Who would have believed that Michael Fish would be not only a household name, but a name engraved on the nation's hearts?

After we had seen around the school and discussed our hopes and aspirations for the children's education, Mr Barker wished us farewell and gave us his assurance that both Nina and Marc would be registered for entry into Sevenoaks in due course. He wished us good luck with their education in the meantime (which was needed since they were at school in Tonga then) and said that he would be in touch periodically up until the time of the entrance examination. Which is today! Now, I wouldn't want to give the impression that we have thought of little else since then, indeed we expected it to be much like any other day, just rather more important. What we didn't expect was that Nina, who being the eldest must take the exam first, would be ill when the time came. Last night she was running a temperature and complaining of a sore throat and headache – all the classic symptoms of the early stages of flu. Today there was little we could do but take her to her school to sit the exam. Today was the day when I knew I must start something challenging enough to take my mind off Nina. Today, Anne Ammundsen requests the pleasure of your company for a stroll down Memory Lane.

My first recollection was when I had my third birthday in Bad Oeynhausen in Germany. I had been given a plastic bead necklace and promptly lost it when I was taken for a walk in the woods with the dog. I was distraught. I thought I would never have anything so beautiful ever again in my life. Imagine my joy when the dog, Britta (a German short-haired pointer), found it and brought it back to me held gently in her mouth. I went back to Bad Oeynhausen in 1991 and even managed to find the house we had lived in then. It was such a strange feeling to be standing there nearly half a century later. We took a photograph of Nina outside the house. She was standing in just the same spot I had been photographed in when I was ten and had been taken back to see the house by my parents. Nina was also ten then and we looked very alike. The photograph of me was a little black and white one, and the one of Nina was huge by comparison and in colour. I took the two pictures to a photographer and they turned Nina's photograph into a medium-sized black and white one, and blew mine up to match it in size. The result was brilliant.

After we had taken the photograph of Nina outside the Bad Oeynhausen house, we rang the doorbell to see if anyone was home and would allow us in to see around. A bemused German lady answered the door and I think she thought I was a commercial traveller trying to sell photograph albums. Once she recognised the photographs of her house, obviously taken long before she knew it, she became interested and asked us all in. We delved into the album and quickly realised that very little had changed. The small fir tree in the front garden was about the only exception and this now towered above the house. Although I had spoken a little German before I spoke English (I had had a German babysitter) I can remember almost nothing of that language and so I was relieved that her English was really quite passable. She explained that her husband had been in the German Navy and had served in U-boats in World War II. After the

War ended she had got a job working in the NAAFI (Navy, Army, Air Force Institute) canteen and had learned her English that way. When I lived in her house it had been a British Army married quarter and my father had been a Major serving on the staff of HQ BAOR (British Army of the Rhine) at a time when Germany had only just been defeated and the country was in ruins. And here I was taking tea with this hospitable lady and her husband in a prosperous and reunified post-war Germany. It was a pleasant journey back to the past.

The past for me had started in Maidstone in 1944 when Kent was being bombarded with Hitler's flying bombs (the so-called doodlebugs) and at that time my father was with HQ 21 Army Group in Normandy and Brussels. After my birth my mother took me to live in Broadstairs with her parents until early 1945 when my father was sent to the Staff College in Camberley. Once his studies began, my mother and I were banished to the far corner of the house at night in order that my father did not have his nights disturbed by a crying baby. It was while we were at Camberley that I was christened in the Staff College Chapel and my mother's sister, Barbie, was one godmother and the other was Marjorie, the wife of Major General Cyril Lloyd, who was my godfather. Cyril had been one of my father's teachers at school and had also been with him in Brussels when I was born. When my father had completed his time at the Staff College, in July 1945, he was sent to Bad Oeynhausen and it was not until September 1946 that my mother and I joined him there. I was nearly two by then and had hardly seen my father other than during the six months at Camberley. We were to stay in Germany until March 1948 and that year and a half was to be the longest we would have in one place for many a long year.

1948 was spent moving about all over the place. Between March and April my father went on a parachute course in Aldershot and on completion he joined the 3rd Parachute Regiment which was stationed in Germany. So we went back with him, this time to Itzehoe from April to August, and Hildesheim, from September to October. While my father was on his parachute course my mother and I were with her parents in Broadstairs, and we went there again in November and December, when my father left Germany once more to attend a company commander's course at Warminster. By this time I had had my fourth birthday and was becoming very close to my grandparents.

The following year was a little more settled and I was living in my first proper home in England in Clanricarde Gardens, off the Bayswater Road, while my father was the Adjutant of the 10 Paras (TA) in Rochester Row. I suppose it must have been some time during this year that I began my very chequered education, but there are no records to verify this. In any event I must have missed much of it through frequent bouts of otitis media. No quick fix antibiotics in those days, or grommets to drain the fluid from the ears – just weeks in bed listening to 'The Archers'! There was no television to relieve the boredom of being sick. We moved again at the beginning of 1950, this time to Tressillian Road in Brockley, as by now my father was at the Territorial Army Centre in Charlton. Having my fifth and sixth year in London gave me plenty more opportunities to see my grandparents and the bond grew closer and closer and they seemed to represent all that was good and stable and secure. Then we moved for the third time in England at the beginning of 1951, this time to the Kings Road, Chelsea. It was unfortunate really, because yet another move was to come about in May that year, this time to Egypt. My father went ahead of us and so my mother and I flew out to join him a short while later. I was six and a half by then, with no front teeth and a pudding basin haircut, but neither of these drawbacks could dampen my excitement about going on an aeroplane. At that time this was not the everyday occurrence that it is today, nor was it the comfortable ride that it is today, but the adventure was something which today's children can only read about! For almost two years Egypt was to be my home although we did manage to clock up another three addresses during that period of time – the Families Camp El Ballah, the Families Camp El Kirsh, and finally moving to Ismailia during my father's tour of duty with HQ Canal North District.

Egypt is a kaleidoscope of memories. None of them connected and all of them chronologically muddled. I learnt about chameleons and how they change colour; I learnt about sandstorms and how the sand cuts your face and gets into every nook and cranny of your house. I came to understand that there were different smells and different ways of life. I saw the Great Pyramids and rode on a camel; I saw donkeys being used as beasts of burden and their backsides beaten raw; I heard the sound of the faithful being called to prayer from the Mosques. I saw the convoys of ships sailing down the Suez Canal and the Gulli Gulli men at Port Said who seemed magical to me because of their tricks and their exciting wares. I learnt that a hot country can be very cold and discovered that there was water which could be drunk and water which could not. One day my father discovered me pouring 'bad water' into the garden from a gin bottle that I had found. Rather foolishly my parents were in the habit of keeping purified water in empty gin bottles in the fridge! I learnt about electric shocks from a faulty table fan and about breast feeding from a neighbour with a new baby. I was given regular salt tablets which I found utterly revolting and was thrown into the Suez Canal and told that I could swim. I was given an enormous bicycle and was told that I could ride it – or that was how it seemed to me when my father let go of the back!

It was while we were in the family camps in 1952 that my mother's father died. She received a telegram. She was given the choice of going back for his funeral and not being able to return to Egypt because of 'the troubles' arising as a result of the Abrogation of the Treaty, or remaining with my father in Egypt. What a terrible decision to have to make. She finally decided to stay and so was unable to pay her last respects to a wonderful father. I was very sad, and suddenly England seemed an awfully long way away. King George VI died that same year, and for some strange reason that affected me badly too – I suppose as a child I couldn't believe that Kings could also die. I discovered what illness was, having caught some disease which was never diagnosed but which caused me to be put in a hospital isolation ward for weeks on end. I could only see my parents through a pane of glass and wasn't at home when the cat had kittens. I learnt about the law of the jungle and how some are more equal than others when, at school, I was not allowed to walk beside the daughters of the Brigadier because my father was only a Major. But how wonderful the NAAFI shop in Moascar was. It seemed like Harrods after so long in camps in the desert. Moascar was the Army barracks in Ismailia and by the time we arrived there we had acquired an Egyptian houseboy whom my parents nicknamed 'I see all I know all', since that was about the extent of his English. One day I came across him in the garden playing with himself. It scared me dreadfully and I felt very threatened.

In February 1953 we sailed back to England from Suez on the troopship T.T. *Empire Ken*. This was tremendous fun and seemed much more like a holiday than a journey although we all suffered greatly going through the Bay of Biscay, that notorious stretch of water which can lay low even the hardiest of sailors. One of the greatest thrills upon our return was Queen Elizabeth II's Coronation and being able to watch it on television. For most people television was an entirely new phenomenon and we were lucky that my father's parents owned a set, so the family gathered round to watch this great spectacle. The fact that it was in black and white, the screen small and the reception poor by today's standards did not occur to us then. It was simply incredible to be able to watch something of this kind in their home. Prior to this we had only had the Pathé News Reels at the cinema as a media by which to watch the moving images of events around the world. Television is so much a part of our lives today that it is hard to remember a time when it was not so. We had returned from Egypt where we had seen one of the wonders of the Ancient World, to live again in England and experience one of the wonders of the Modern World.

Now that my father had been posted back to his Regiment, which was at that time stationed in Tidworth, we had to settle down in our new house which was a married quarter in Perham Down. This house had the most magnificent view over the Downs, but my overriding memory is of being colder than I had ever been in my life before. Getting dressed early to go to school, with no heater in my room, was something I had never experienced in Egypt in spite of the fact that I had known some cold nights there. While we were in Perham Down we acquired a beautiful black Labrador to whom we gave the unoriginal name of 'Nigger'. This was before the days of political correctness and racist connotations which would probably deter a person nowadays giving such a name to a dog! He was a lovely animal, and a good gun dog. Nothing pleased him more than to be out on the Downs retrieving rabbits which my father had shot. We were only in Tidworth for fifteen months though and one of the hardest things about leaving was having to say goodbye to our beautiful Nigger. We gave him to another officer (who was serving at the Regimental Depot) when we left and we heard that he died soon afterwards of a liver disease.

So in May 1954 the Regiment was posted to Minden in Germany and the business of packing up and moving was upon us again. We were not there for long, only seven months, so I recall little of that period in my life. However, one of the first things we did was to go back to the Bad Oeynhausen home to see it again (when that photo of me had been taken) and we also went to look at the houses we had lived in, in Itzehoe and Hildesheim. For a long time I had been getting frequent bouts of otitis media and tonsillitis and while I was in Germany I had both my tonsils and adenoids out. In the end I had seven operations to remove these organs since they kept growing again. I'm told this can only happen if they are not removed properly in the first place! My principal memories of Minden are, therefore, of being in hospital and my mother visiting me with huge bowls of whipped condensed milk. I loved it so much that it almost made the operations worthwhile. I don't remember hours of listening to 'The Archers', so perhaps that programme could not be received in Germany at that time? One trip which did thrill me was being taken to Hamelin to see the home of the Pied Piper. This seemed like a fairy tale come true to me and I also enjoyed a holiday spent in the beautiful Black Forest.

My father's tour of duty with his Regiment came to an end in December 1954 and we moved back to London to a basement flat in Dartmouth Terrace, Blackheath. For the next two years my father was working at the War Office but we still managed to move three times, on each occasion to another address in Blackheath. It seemed as though we were in perpetual motion but I was thrilled to find that our second move took us to The Old Coach House, in Langton Way. It was full of character and I loved it. We had our first television there and I became a great fan of Muffin The Mule, The Flower Pot Men, and, of course, Sooty! We also had a cat, called Mr Matthias (I have no idea why), and a grand piano on which I would bang away at the keys and hope that all within earshot would assume I could play. While we were there I was taken to see the film *The Man Who Never Was*, and it frightened me dreadfully. To get up to my room at night I had to climb the stairs which lead to a dark landing above and behind me. On this landing was a wooden chest and I convinced myself that the Man was in there! I also found myself confronted with the problems facing those who are getting old. My parents had become friendly with an old man who lived nearby and he often came to sit and watch our television – the chair was nearly always wet when he left.

By this time I was ten years old and had attended twelve schools in the five or so years since I began my education. I had missed the vital grounding which is normally achieved in those early years and, more than that, I had not learnt how to settle because I was always a 'new girl'. My parents recognised this problem and decided to put me into boarding school. I was sent to Baston, in Hayes, Kent (a famous old-girl being Margaret Thatcher's daughter, Carol). It was a nice school and I gradually settled down and started to learn although I was very behind my contemporaries. It began to be part of my life and I welcomed the stability and continuity it afforded me. It also meant that I was in one place long enough to make friends and although I lost touch with them there are one or two whom I remember well to this day (a Thai girl called Pimulpun Kitasanka, in particular). But my parents decided they wanted something different for me and I was moved again when I was twelve. The decision was made with the best of intentions, but I knew that they were making a mistake and I cried copious tears when I left Baston. 1955 and 1956 were the only happy school days I experienced.

During this time I began what was to be many years of orthodontic treatment. My teeth presented a sufficient challenge for me to be accepted by Kings College Hospital and have my case directed by the well-known Professor Shilling. While this was a great honour it did mean that I was a sort of guinea-pig and there as much for the benefit of the students as for the future improved appearance of my mouth. If the reaction of dentists over the years is anything to go by, some fairly new and as yet untried methods were employed in the course of my treatment. I had eight teeth out and many different varieties of braces – even a monoblock to wear at night which didn't make talking after lights out very easy! Today's children look upon braces as a fashion accessory which is almost a 'must'. This is an ideal attitude, but in my day this was not the case and I was very self-conscious about my appearance. When I was at Baston there were times when we went to the local church service and the last thing I wanted the choirboys to see was my brace! So I would remove it and place it in a handkerchief in my pocket. One day, during a hushed moment in the service, I needed to blow my nose and quite forgot that my brace was in my hanky. As I rushed to get it to my nose the brace flew across the aisle and landed in front of the altar right under the noses of the choirboys! I was utterly humiliated and didn't know how to face them afterwards when we were in the habit of talking to them over the hedge in the far corner of the playing fields.

Although we didn't know it at the time the dawning of 1957 marked a watershed in the lives of our small nomadic family. In January we moved to the third of our homes in Blackheath, which was just a bedsit for my mother to live in because my father was posted to Korea to rejoin his Regiment, and I was moved to my final and fourteenth school, Farringtons in Chislehurst. I went as a boarder in the middle of an academic year at the age of twelve. There was only one other new girl arriving at the same time as me and we were both teased unmercifully. Unfortunately for us, we didn't have much else in common, otherwise we might have survived it better and been able to give each other support. In one fell swoop I had lost the school I loved, the house I loved and the father I loved. I was a very unhappy child, having just reached puberty and believing that my world had fallen apart.

Life seemed to hold some chance of improvement when we got news of the Regiment's transfer from Korea to Gibraltar in August 1957, and it was with the highest of hopes that I flew there, with my mother, during the summer holidays of that year. The prospect of seeing my father again seemed to be the chance I needed to heal the wounds. However, the Regiment had been moved from Korea to Gibraltar by troopship, as was the custom in those days, and during this voyage my father had fallen for the wife of a fellow officer on board. She had sailed on with her husband, leaving him in Gibraltar to meet us there. That day is engraved on my memory as no other. I pushed my way off the aircraft, ahead of others before me, brandishing my tennis racket and running across the tarmac into my father's arms. I never knew what happened that day, because I was told to stay in my room (we moved into a married quarter in Moorish Castle) but I knew that my mother was a brokenhearted woman when she joined me there that night. Nothing was ever the same between my father and me after that, and over the years to come my parents told me that they were only staying together because of me. That was probably true, but my father was an ambitious man and he knew that a divorce, in those days, would have marked the end of his career. He is married to that 'other woman' now, and has been for many years, but his career came first and he didn't leave my mother until it was over.

I could not have been in Gibraltar long on that occasion, probably only two or three weeks, because it was soon time for me to return to the school where I was so unhappy and to leave my parents to sort out their lives. I flew once more to Gibraltar for the Christmas school holiday, but before I could get there again for Easter my father was transferred to command the Regimental Depot at Chichester in March 1958. Once they were in Britain it did, at least, mean that my parents could take me out for half terms and exeats. However, on one occasion an outing which had been intended to be enjoyable caused me much humiliation. My father had taken me to see St Paul's Cathedral in London, where the Whispering Gallery had been quite an attraction, but when he suggested that we climb the ladder to reach the top of the dome, I was not at all sure this was for me. No doubt the view from the summit would have been most worthwhile but my fear of climbing the rickety ladder, followed by a hairpin turn to climb into the turret, could not be overcome. Once we reached the front of the queue he tried to persuade me up. I didn't want to do it but he would not take no for an answer. A humiliating scene developed, in front of the waiting crowd, but my fear won over his persuasive tactics and I had to descend back down the ladder when I was only halfway up! In spite of this unhappy occasion, I was glad to have my parents back in England and their presence at school functions, such as Speech Day, helped me to settle a bit better at Farringtons, but I never found happiness at the school and my academic abilities were not probed since they found me an odd ball.

I had arrived in their midst, virtually uneducated, at the age of twelve and there was little they felt they could do for me. My parents were told that I should give up all but those subjects which might lead to the acquisition of an O level pass, which meant subjects which required learning a set two-year syllabus. So, my education, the first and only education I ever received which didn't come to an abrupt halt, consisted of Geography, History, Biology, English Language, English Literature, and Art. I had dreadful trouble with English Language since I had never had a grounding in the subject, but I was very fond of the English teacher and wanted to do well for her, Miss Hall being the only teacher at the school who inspired me. The other person I had great respect for was the Head of Music, Miss Newing, and to this day I cannot hear Trumpet Voluntary without thinking of her playing it on the organ as we filed out of Chapel.

Farringtons was my way of life until the summer of 1961 when I left at the age of sixteen, coming up seventeen. They were, overall, turbulent years and I became a rebel. I rebelled at the way I had been treated both by the girls themselves when I arrived and by the teachers who made no effort to understand me. I did some stupid things, which even now I cannot imagine my reasons for, and one of them was to try and dye some red shoes brown by simply lathering them with brown shoe polish. As if that stupidity was not enough (I had ruined a pair of shoes I really liked) I then proceeded to the staff bathroom to wash the brown polish off. I made the most unholy mess and the final insult was to use the staff hand-towel to wipe both my shoes and the surrounding area clean. I had not meant to be insulting to the teachers, at the time I was far more worried about what my mother would say when she saw what I had done to my shoes, but my actions were as inexplicable and inexcusable then as they are to me now. I was in trouble – *big* trouble – but that always seemed to be the case. What I discovered was that the more trouble I was in with the teachers, the more the girls started to accept me and I appeared to have found a way through to them at last! I became their ringleader, their spokesperson and I always got the can. The words of the simply ghastly Yorkshire matron have rung out to me down the years: "It'll all come back on yer – never fear!"

It's funny, isn't it, how it always seems to have been summer when one was a child? Funnier still that the summers always seem to have been better than any summer one has known as an adult. But sunny or not the time at school seemed an eternity and I thought each term would never end. This is in stark contrast to my own children who seem to think, like me now, that time flies past. I remember endless summer days playing tennis; revising in the school grounds; being given a small area in which we could plant our own garden; stealing fruit from the kitchen garden; watching the gardeners mow the grass and that simply wonderful smell after they had done so. Then there were the weekly walks to Chislehurst, in a 'crocodile' two by two, to attend the Sunday service at the Methodist church. They seemed dry and lifeless occasions. I was finally inspired enough to be confirmed, however, but this was only because we had Confirmation classes from the dear, kind Mr Budget from the Anglican Church, St Nicholas's, where I was confirmed and, years later, Nina was christened.

The interminable terms did end, of course, and it was then that I would go down to Chichester for the school holidays. During this time I had both my fourteenth and fifteenth birthdays and was becoming very self-conscious and shy in the company of older people. There were some very handsome young Subalterns at the Chichester Depot and little did they know that I developed a 'crush' on several of them. I had always been led to believe that my destiny was to become an Army wife and I was doing some subtle 'scouting about'. But I admired them from afar since I was much too shy to speak to them when I did have the chance. My parents thought that this problem would be eased if I came with them to cocktail parties, but it only exacerbated the situation and I clung to my mother's side. In May 1960 my father was transferred to Northern Ireland to command his Regiment. They were stationed in a town called Holywood just outside Belfast.

By now I was nearly sixteen but the Subalterns there did not hold so much fascination for me and I found, instead, that I was glad to be accepted into the local community during the school holidays and achieved this by joining a tennis club. There were some nice social occasions that resulted from this and I welcomed the chance to get away from the stifling effects of an all-girls school. I discovered for the first time, too, that boys were not so scary after all and I found myself falling for a nice boy called Peter. He was the son of a millionaire, who had made his money manufacturing carpets, and my father did not consider him a suitable boyfriend for me. I was so sad to be forbidden to see Peter again – he had shown me a good time and was very sweet and kind.

One day I arrived in Holywood for the school holidays to be told that the cat had died. I was dreadfully upset not to have been able to say goodbye first. My parents had had a very bizarre experience over the cat's death for, when the batman (a sort of military valet), had brought in the dead animal which he had found in the garden they, too, were very upset and had a sad little burial ceremony for him underneath his favourite tree. A couple of hours later he nonchalantly strolled in for his dinner! Whose cat had they buried?! The next day the batman did the same thing, once more bringing in the dead cat. The scene of the day before was repeated, but this time all concerned believed that Whisky (he was black and white) would once again turn up for dinner. Sadly, he did not, and as the days passed they realised that poor Whisky really was dead.

My school days were coming to an end and that happy day dawned in July 1961 when I flew to Northern Ireland for the last time. I was lucky enough to be there in August that year when the Queen made a visit to Ulster. It was a great thrill to be at the official functions and to see her so close up. I remembered her Coronation so well and couldn't believe that I was now virtually face to face with her. After that excitement was over, it was time to think about my future and it had been decided that I should do a secretarial course at St James's Secretarial College in London. A suitable ladies' hostel was selected and off I went into the big wide world!

Chapter Two

The Interim Years

The hostel my mother selected was opposite Sir Winston Churchill's house in Hyde Park Gate and we sometimes saw the great man. Even to my post-war generation he was revered and adulated and I considered it a great privilege to be able to see his house just across the road from my window. I was so happy to be in London and living in such a lovely area of that city too. I came to know London well and began to regard it as home and myself as a Londoner. My roots had never grown anywhere and so this seemed as good a place as any to put them down.

I made some friends, both at the hostel and at the college, and set about learning in a far better environment than I had experienced of late. I took to it all like a duck to water and thoroughly enjoyed both my studies and my freedom. The city seemed to have so much to offer and I found myself enjoying it in a hundred ways. I discovered the joys of the theatre and many a play was viewed from the gods. I became particularly friendly with a Rhodesian girl called Jacquie, who introduced me to her set of Rhodesian and South African friends. It all seemed very sophisticated and exciting to me and I felt I wanted to emulate her in every way. Neither of us had 'homes' to go to, though, and so we both welcomed our mutual friendship with a sweet girl to whom we gave the very undeserved name of "Odd". She used to invite us home once in a while and we very much enjoyed her mother's home cooking. I think her surname must have been Robinson, because I remember her every time I hear the song *Here's to you, Mrs Robinson*!

It wasn't long, however, before my parents moved from Northern Ireland and my father continued to command the Regiment in its new base of Shorncliff in Kent. At first they moved into a married quarter at the barracks but in March 1962 they moved into Underhill House, Shorncliff. This was, without a doubt, the most beautiful house we ever lived in. Part of it dated back to the time of Charles II who had sheltered in its stables when he fled to France in 1651. Everything about the house was marvellous – except the ghost. Whenever the batman was there alone he carried his gun around with him lest he be confronted by it! However, nobody told me about either the ghost or the batman's reaction to it, probably to spare me any worry on those occasions when I was alone there at night. I would sometimes go down to Underhill House for the weekends from London and occasionally my parents would have to attend some function and leave me there by myself – I was, after all, seventeen by then.

The ghost story, as I learnt much later, was well known in the district and dated back to a time when the butler had murdered the parlour maid. This heinous deed had, apparently, been committed in the room which was now my bedroom! One night, as I lay there about to fall asleep, I heard a thud. It was distinct and unmistakable. I tried to think of a rational explanation and immediately thought that my thick, felt dressing gown had fallen off its hook on the bedroom door. I turned on the light to check, and, to my horror, saw that the dressing gown was still hanging in its place. There was nothing out of place and there was no explanation for the very distinct sound of something falling which I had, without question, heard. My imagination had not been running away with me before I'd heard this noise, but it certainly was afterwards and I had never been so pleased to see my parents as I was when they returned that night.

And so life continued, in a very pleasant fashion, for six months with my studies in London during the week and summer around the corner for weekend visits to Underhill House. Looking back it doesn't seem possible that it was only for half a year, but it was and it was a tragedy that we couldn't have gone on like that at least for a bit longer. My father was posted once more in the September of 1962 as GSO1 to HQ 17 Gurkha Division, Seremban, Malaya. My secretarial course was not yet over and we had to decide whether I should remain in London on my own to complete the course or whether I should go to Malaya with my parents. The obvious answer would have been to complete my course and then join my parents but the Army did not pay for the movement of dependant children once they reached the age of eighteen and in my case this was due to happen in October. My father told me that if I was to be with them during their two year posting I had to go now or not at all. It was the first time in my life that I was faced with some pretty tough decision-making. Should I stay in England without a home to go to for two years, but at least finish my secretarial course, or should I abandon my studies before they were completed and sail halfway round the world to a new life? Although I finally decided on the latter I always felt that I should not have been put in that position and that a compromise should have been reached.

The last troopship to sail for the Far East was the T.T. *Oxfordshire* and it left Southampton on the eighteenth of September bound for Hong Kong. It was a historic event in the movement of military personnel around the world and the passing of the age of sea voyages was a sad reflection of the times. It had many advantages over air travel. Personnel arrived fit, well and acclimatised. Air travel in those days was very slow and those who flew to the Far East would arrive exhausted and not yet acclimatised. Any time 'gained' by flying had to be made up by slowly getting used to the steamy heat encountered in the jungles of Malaya. Not one to miss out on the last chance to go by sea, my father had insisted we do so. However, this had not gone unnoticed in Malaya where he was needed the 'day before yesterday'! His new Brigadier never quite got over the length of time it took him to arrive and so their relationship had got off to a bad start before we ever stepped onto Malaysian soil. But none of this was on our minds as we said our farewells to friends and family who came to see us off at Southampton that warm September day. Two friends from school, Pene and Lynda, were there, as was my Rhodesian friend Jacquie. To the strains of the Royal Marine Band playing *Rule Britannia* we inched our way out of Southampton harbour and eventually waved a sad farewell to the receding coastline of England as we set off on our big adventure.

And adventure it certainly was! There were a couple or so Regiments on board, plus many other individuals destined for various points east – a cross-section of military personnel along with medical and nursing staff being posted to military hospitals around the world. And we were on holiday, no doubt about that, and it wasn't even counted as leave – what more could we all ask for? So the serious business of enjoying ourselves began once the tear-stained hankies were safely away in our pockets. It was just the most exciting experience for a girl of almost eighteen. First things first, though, and there was no chance of enjoying myself until I found a girlfriend (another Army daughter) of my own age. This I did and Janet and I are still friends over thirty years later. We soon formed a foursome with two very nice Royal Marine officers and in Janet's case this friendship continued to the point where I think they would have been married in Singapore had Charles not met with a tragic road accident and died. For three weeks we all had a wonderful time relaxing on the sun-deck by day, with the occasional game of quoits if we got too lazy, and dancing our nights away. This was my first full-time exposure to such a range of attractive Subalterns and I certainly didn't waste that opportunity. I had a brief flirtation with a nice boy in a Scottish Regiment but they were destined for Aden and so we had to say goodbye to one another all too soon. Before we reached Aden, though, we sailed past old familiar places such as Gibraltar and, of course, Port Said, where we were able to become re-acquainted with the Gulli Gulli men who were still doing the same old tricks and selling the same old wares! It was funny sailing down the Suez Canal where once I had stood watching the convoys sail by and to put down anchor in the Bitter Lakes, which is the main 'traffic lights' halfway down the Canal where ships can pass one another.

We were starting to feel very hot and the closer we got to Aden the more humid the heat became. Once we were anchored off Aden we all thought we were ready to die of heat and so we welcomed the chance to go ashore and visit friends at the RAF base of Khormaksar. Their house seemed like a haven of comfort with the ceiling fans working themselves into a frenzy of giddy speed and it was nice to find our 'land legs' again although we were quite wobbly for a while there. We were only moored in the harbour for a short time, though, while the Regiment destined for a tour of duty in Aden disembarked. I didn't know, as I scanned the ragged hills behind, that Aden was going to change the course of my life and lead, eventually, to the complete breakdown of my family unit. But that was for the future and right now we were glad to be getting away from the oppressive heat.

We didn't disembark again until we reached our destination, but we took on provisions in Cochin, India, where we were treated to the rather strange sight of many small boats in the harbour with men sitting sheltering from the rain under large black umbrellas of the type one was more used to seeing in Whitehall. They looked like so many crows bobbing around on the water. The voyage continued uninterrupted for a few days more and we began to realise that this idyllic way of life was coming to an end. We would like to have remained on board until the ship berthed in Singapore, but we were already late and so we disembarked in Penang and got a train to Kuala Lumpur where we were met by a staff car and driven to Seremban.

We arrived on the ninth of October, less than a week before my eighteenth birthday, so it really could be said that I had arrived by the skin of my teeth. Having arrived courtesy of the British Army meant that I was entitled to a flight home at the end of the posting, but I really could not have been a more borderline case. It wasn't long before I found I could put my scanty secretarial skills into practice and I got a job working in the same Headquarters complex as my father. My boss was the charming Colonel of the Brigade of Gurkhas, Colonel Pulley, and he did his best to put me at ease. However, I was surrounded by senior NCOs who found me a much weirder fish than they had been used to, but we all got on famously in the end. That could not be said of my first day though, when Colonel Pulley called me in for dictation and without warning began "Your Majesty, It is my honour and privilege to present this my second report on the state of Your Majesty's subjects serving in the British Army." My incomplete training at St James's had somehow left me wondering how to write "Majesty" in shorthand and that, together with my surprise at having to do so, left me far behind and the poor man had to start again. We finally completed the letter to His Majesty, the King of Nepal, and I am happy that I have a copy of it still since it was eventually published in the *Journal of the Brigade of Gurkhas*, 1963. What a start to my working life! There was much to get used to, for all of us, but first we had to see the T.T. *Oxfordshire* one more time and this we managed to do by driving to Port Dickson on the west coast of Malaya our first weekend in Seremban. There we stood on the beach waving like mad to our friends on board as they sailed by en route for Singapore. We had told them we would be there and we hoped that they had their binoculars trained on the beach and could see us! As the ship sailed out of sight we felt the cold chill of the passage of time. It was 1962 and it was the end of an era.

But the swinging sixties were upon us, even in that far-flung corner of what had, until five years earlier, been part of the British

Empire, and the influence of the new era was upon us too. Many of the popular songs of the time, particularly *A Summer Place* and *Raindrops Keep Falling* remind me of my early days in Malaya. We settled into our new way of life which consisted of an early start to the working day in order to benefit from the cooler temperature in the early morning and so, after a light breakfast of pawpaw sprinkled with lemon juice followed by a malaria prophylactic tablet, I set off to work with my father. The day may have begun early, but it finished early too and the later part of the afternoons were ours to relax and enjoy ourselves. We often went to the Sungei Ujong Club and enjoyed a swim and a bit of sunbathing, or a game of tennis if it wasn't too humid and hot, but the one thing we came to rely upon was the rain which always seemed to arrive punctually at four in the afternoon, just as we sat down to enjoy our tea on the verandah. It was a deluge, but it didn't last long and soon the grass was steaming as the sun reappeared to dry up the sodden earth. It was a comfortable routine and a thoroughly enjoyable lifestyle which incorporated the essential ingredients of both work and play, and Church Parade on Sundays.

On one rather important such occasion my mother had acquired a nice new dress, in navy and white, with a matching blue hat accompanied by navy shoes and handbag. While sitting in church, with her legs crossed, she noticed that she had put on her black shoes by mistake. She was annoyed with herself for this mistake, but her annoyance turned to horror when she noticed later that her other foot sported the required navy shoe! She extended both feet to inspect the anomaly, at the same time drawing my attention to it by giving me a gentle shove in the ribs with her elbow. For a woman who took pride in her appearance the ill-matched shoes were very out of character and the humour of it struck us both in unison. We both shook in silent mirth until the end of the church service when it was a great relief to be able to laugh out loud. My father had been astonished at our behaviour and considered it to have been quite out of place.

We saw a lot of Malaysia while we were there and came to love the country and the people. We travelled north, south, west and east and saw some of the most beautiful beaches in the world. The east coast was quite spectacular and on one visit there we were privileged to witness a turtle coming in to lay her eggs. There was no control over the theft of turtle eggs in those days and they were frequently stolen since they were much in demand as a culinary delicacy. We visited rubber plantations and saw how the sap from the trees is 'tapped' and enjoyed the cultural diversity of the country. Port Dickson was a favourite weekend retreat and I had the chance to learn how to water-ski which I found utterly exhilarating. Another time we visited the Cameron Highlands and discovered a different world up there altogether. It was so cool and so beautiful but the journey up to the top was the most hair-raising car journey I have ever experienced on account of the steep, winding, unprotected roads. We often went up to Butterworth near Ipoh and on one occasion managed to see rather more of Penang than we did when we had first disembarked there. The roads were not very good in those days and so journeys took a long time but that did not seem to stop any of us from making the most of our time in such a beautiful country.

But not all was well. I was finding my job difficult on account of my lack of confidence and I suppose I must have taken my frustrations home and soon my father was becoming increasingly exasperated by me and wishing he had left me in London. Three months after we arrived we moved house again (something we did with monotonous and sometimes unnecessary regularity). We lurched from one crisis to the next, but tried our best to enjoy ourselves in between arguments. Certainly I felt that by eighteen I was a grown woman and entitled to a life of my own with a free choice of friends to spend my time with. However, my father viewed things differently and without exception took a dislike to any man I became friendly with. The one he took the greatest exception to was the son of the Brigadier with whom he had got off to a bad start. Wasn't it ironic? – there were the two fathers at daggers drawn, and their offspring quite besotted with each other. A touch of Romeo and Juliet, if you like! Warwick was not living with his parents since he too was in the Army and was with his Regiment in Malaya, but naturally he spent quite a lot of time with them and this was how we had met. We had a great time, which mostly meant being part of 'the young ones' at the Sungei Ujong Club. However, my father thought that his worst nightmare might come true if this relationship was allowed to continue and one day he saw his opportunity to split us up.

I had developed another of those strange illnesses that nobody could diagnose (a pyrexia of unknown origin) and I finally became hospitalised. What I had not realised, as I lay somewhat listlessly in my hospital bed, was that I was losing stones in weight. It was all quite painless and there have been many times over the years when I have thought how I would welcome that PUO back into my life if I could just, once more, lose that kind of weight so easily! I finally emerged from hospital and had the shock of my life to realise that the dress my mother brought me to get changed into was several sizes too big! Actually, I looked like a skeleton, but it was the beginning of what were to be my 'Slim Years'. I very much welcomed this new image and was even more delighted that it entailed an entirely new wardrobe!

Upon my discharge the doctors had commented that I would probably benefit from a change of climate and that a spell in temperate conditions would help me to recover more fully. My father saw his chance, and before I had had time to consider the implications, I found it had been decided that I should go to Hong Kong. I was given forty pounds and told that I could get an indulgence flight to Hong Kong from Singapore (which was basically a free flight on a military aircraft) and that I would be able to find a job once I got there. I had no accommodation arranged, although I was told that I might get a room at a hostel there when I arrived. So I was packed off to Singapore to wait patiently at Changi Airport until such time as I was given a place on an aircraft. Friends put me up while I waited, which was over a week, and during that time I was able to see Warwick in Singapore. We were both rather bemused by the speed of events overtaking us but neither of us knew how to get off the roller coaster which was taking us to our final emotional farewell.

The day dawned when I was informed I could leave on a military aircraft going to Hong Kong that day. Twelve hours later I emerged into a night made bright by the illuminations of a steaming, teething exotic eastern city. After the quiet life in Malaya, I was definitely suffering from culture shock. On completion of formalities at the military wing of Kai Tak airport, I got a taxi to the Star Ferry to get across to Victoria. I had all my worldly possessions with me, and what with all those new clothes I had had to get, this amounted to several suitcases. I took them, one by one, to the ferry, worrying all the while what would be happening to the ones I had not yet collected, but eventually I and all my possessions were safely aboard. It doesn't take long to get across the water and so I was soon doing the same thing in reverse on the other side! I really must have made quite a spectacle of myself, particularly at that time of night. Finally I got another taxi and with some trepidation asked to be taken to the Helena May Institute for Young Ladies (yes, in the sixties it did still exist!) and it was with an enormous amount of relief that I was told that they could give me a room. The charge was modest, which was just as well since I had limited funds until I could earn my living. The next morning was the fifteenth of October, 1963, just over a year since I had stepped off the T.T. *Oxfordshire*, and the dawn of my nineteenth birthday.

I felt pole-axed from my experiences of the day before. The flight on the C-130 Hercules had been very uncomfortable although the twelve hours had included a stop in Saigon on the way. I was hot, dirty and tired and the first thing I needed to do was to unpack and get my clothes pressed so that I could look presentable for interviews. I found an amah who said she would do this for a small fee, and so began the process of trying to find employment. I walked the streets of Hong Kong looking for likely looking organisations and businesses. I tried everything and everyone, including the offices of MI6. I knew some of the girls from the Secret Service, having met them socially in Malaya, and although they were very kind and understanding of my predicament, they were not needing locally engaged staff at that time. And thereby hung my problem: Hong Kong was teeming with the wives and daughters of military personnel who were only too happy to find work to keep them occupied since they were all lucky enough to have house staff. They did not need to earn enough to keep themselves and wages were geared according to the demand. I, on the other hand, had to earn enough to pay for all my costs, including accommodation. I was young and inexperienced – hardly a catch in those days, although I was clutching a very nice testimonial from the Brigadier in charge of the Headquarters in Seremban (Warwick's father)!

I plodded on, like this, being turned down right, left and centre for all the jobs with decent salaries and I became very unhappy. I was missing my mother and Warwick, too, of course, and all the old familiarity of my job with the Brigade of Gurkhas. Nor was I fully well from my illness. But one day my luck appeared to change when I applied to the Hong Kong and Shanghai Bank. They actually seemed interested in my application and told me that although the job they had in mind had been offered to an officer's wife, they thought that she would not be taking it up. She was thinking about it and would let them know at the end of the week. I was in with a chance! It was short-lived though and I didn't get the job in the end. There was nothing for it but to go back to Malaya but I was very fearful of my father's reaction. However, before I left there was something I had to do. My father's brother had been serving in the Indian Army during World War II and had been killed at the hands of the Japanese while with his Regiment in Hong Kong. I took a posy of flowers to his grave and bade farewell to an uncle I had never known.

By the time I managed to get on a military indulgence flight back to Singapore I had only small change left in my purse. I remember nothing more about my return, or how I got back to Seremban, because my mind was too full of what I was going to tell my father. My mother secreted me back into the house and confronted him for me. The rest is a blank! The threads of life were slowly resumed and events started to overtake us once more for another move was scheduled for January 1964. I started to pick up some of the threads of my pre-Hong Kong life, but Warwick was not one of them. Another nice man started to date me, an officer with the Royal Corps of Signals, but again he did not meet with my father's approval and was sacked from the post of 'boyfriend' after taking me to a party in Kuala Lumpur which had gone on all night. My father saw red and 'carpeted' us both – it had been innocent fun but we were not believed.

Before I left Seremban I was persuaded to go on a jungle trek although I had some misgivings about this since it involved hours of walking. The day commenced very early one Sunday morning and we were all kitted out with the proper Army gear. However, the smallest jungle boots were simply too big for me and quickly caused blisters to form on my feet. We walked on and on, and I had no option but to walk in socks only in spite of the danger from leeches. We finally reached the aboriginal settlement which had been our destination, but by then I was too exhausted to take much interest and lay down on one of their beds and slept. After this break everyone was refreshed, but soon the heat and limited water supplies, coupled with dreadfully sore feet took their toll once more. When the group stopped for a break by a jungle pool, I knew that I had to continue or I would never be able to walk any further. I walked on alone, in the belief that there had only been one path which we had followed all the way. I couldn't get lost, could I? I walked on for a couple of hours and began to realise that I had, in fact, done just that. The noise of the jungle became deafening and I could only think about all the dangers which were out there. Tigers, poisonous snakes, leeches, aborigines who were unfamiliar with Westerners, and above all, no water! I thought that my number was up and that I would never get out of the jungle alive. Eventually, after many a wrong turn, I came to something I recognised which in turn led to the start of the jungle trek. Some Malay people saw my distress and took me to their kampong long-house for some very hot sweet milky tea. Nothing had ever tasked so wonderful in my life before. At last I was reunited with the group I had started with and returned home, very much the worse for wear from my experience. I burst into the house in a very weepy condition and explained what had happened. My father put his head back and laughed – a great belly-laugh. I couldn't believe it! – I had been in considerable danger and he found it *funny*.

The move to Kluang at the beginning of 1964 was the chance of a new start, but it never really took off and I have none of the fond memories for Kluang that I have of Seremban. I got another job, in HQ Malaya Area, but was utterly bored by it and cannot even remember whom I was working for. However, one thing which was an improvement was that we were much closer to Singapore and this meant that we could go down there for shopping expeditions which were thoroughly enjoyable. It also gave me the chance to go and see Janet, my friend from the T.T. *Oxfordshire*. I went for the weekend and stayed at her parents' house, which was a married quarter on a big estate. She arranged a very nice programme of events for my visit and I envied her being in such a cosmopolitan and vibrant city. The first evening was spent at a restaurant in Singapore with her boyfriend and a blind-date for me. We had gone in separate cars and met up for our night on the town. It was all very exciting to a country bumpkin from Kluang – and I revelled in the bright lights and exotic smells surrounding me. We had a good time but eventually had to call it a night and return to Janet's home. My escort duly returned me, and I expected to find the key under the mat in case I got back before Janet. I looked but couldn't find it. It was by now the small hours of the morning and, to my surprise, getting rather cold.

We waited for Janet for about an hour but eventually decided that there was nothing for it but to wake up the amah to request to be let in. She was most charming and told us to help ourselves to a warm drink and something to eat if we were hungry. We were relieved to be inside and did, indeed, make ourselves at home. While we were sipping our coffee I started to gaze around the room and began to see little things which I had not noticed before. The standard lamp was not where it should be, the gramophone had been moved, and other things seemed strange. I started to look for things I was certain about, like the mirror halfway up the stairs, but it was not there. The penny had finally dropped and I had to confirm my suspicions by checking the cap badge on the Army officer's hat in the hallway. Yes, it was true, *we were in the wrong house*! I couldn't help laughing, in fact I became almost hysterical with mirth – there we were, drinking coffee in a complete stranger's house at about three in the morning. No wonder I had been unable to find the key! My poor escort became very agitated indeed and visions of imminent court martial swam before his eyes. We collected our cups, washed them up and beat a hasty retreat. Next door we found a key under the mat and I let myself in. Janet asked me what on earth we had been doing and I told her I'd explain tomorrow. After a few hours sleep I woke to confront the next day and the need to return next door to apologise. The lady of the house had been informed by her amah that 'Missy' and her boyfriend had been unable to get in last night and that she had opened the door for us! Memsahib was not at all amused and can you blame her? She was mustering the silver when I rang the doorbell to come and offer my rather pathetic excuses for what had happened.

All good things come to an end and in January 1965 HQ Malaya Area was transferred to Borneo. My father's departure from Kluang left my mother with some decisions to make since families were not allowed to go to Borneo. For many years she had suffered with Ménière's Disease and this condition was not getting any better for her so she decided to move to Singapore where she could be near to military medical facilities and also on the spot for the occasions when my father could get over from Borneo. I had got itchy feet the year before and felt that I had been stagnating in Kluang for too long. I had decided then that it would be better for me to return to England alone. We had heard about another hostel in London, this time in Lexham Gardens, and so arrangements were made for me to leave from Singapore in July 1964 and go to stay with my grandmother until I could get accommodation arranged and a job lined up. I had one last shopping spree in Singapore and bought a lovely new dress to travel in, along with matching shoes and handbag. I was thrilled with my purchases and particularly excited about my dress which was made of a new (to me, anyway) man-made fibre called polyester silk. It had beautifully sharp permanent pleats and somehow made me feel quite the international traveller and ready to take on anything life might throw my way. Thus attired in my new gear I embarked on a twenty-four hour flight to London and felt a thrill of excitement to be about to make my own way in life.

Chapter Three
Flatting, Freedom And Fun

The flight had been long and tiring, but very exciting too with a stop in Bombay and another in the Gulf before reaching England. It was wonderful to be home after nearly two years away and I couldn't wait to see my grandmother again. She had moved from Broadstairs after my grandfather died and was now living near Maidstone. I had missed her a lot and she gave me a wonderful welcome with a spread of all the things she knew I loved to eat whenever I visited her. I would have liked to stay on with her, but she was eighty-two years old and getting frail. I was conscious of this frailty and so, when I heard her calling for me to come quickly, I feared the worst and flew down the stairs at high speed. When I got there I saw her sitting in front of the television and on the screen was an item about some girls from my old school, Farringtons, who had just produced a cookery book called *Pot Luck* which they had put together in aid of the Freedom from Hunger Campaign. It took me a moment or two to realise that that was why she had called me and my relief knew no bounds! I was glad that I had seen the item and it was strange too, since only the day before I had been a long way away from England and had it been on then I would have missed it.

I returned to my unpacking and then asked my grandmother if I could wash some clothes. She said that the task would be easier if, when I had done so, I used her wonderful new electric spin dryer with which she was very pleased. It sounded a good idea to me and I duly filled it with my travel clothes, which included my lovely new dress. Oh dear, I was neither familiar with polyester, nor with electric spin-dryers and I was simply horrified at what the latter had done to the former when the spinning died down. My new dress was a crumpled ball which was unrecognisable from the item of clothing which had given me so much pleasure and confidence. It was a lesson to me, and I have always had the greatest respect for spin dryers since but that didn't help me then as I gazed in misery at something which I would never be able to wear again.

I had little in the way of warm clothing so I lifted my spirits by getting some things suitable for the British climate. The next task was to arrange for accommodation in London and I found that the Lexham Gardens Hostel would accept me. I then got in touch with my godfather, Cyril Lloyd, who at this time was the Director General of the City and Guilds of London Institute in Portland Place. I asked him if he could give me a job to tide me over until I knew better what I wanted to do. He agreed to let me work in his office, under the guidance of his personal assistant, until I was feeling more confident and more in touch with the demands of working in London.

Thus equipped with clothes, a job, and a hostel to go to, I kissed my grandmother goodbye and went off to London to seek my fortune. Oh, the optimism of youth, the irresponsibility of youth, the single-minded determination of young people to have a good time. I doubt if I was unique for a girl of my time and I had all three qualities in abundance. But the hostel was not as nice as the one in Hyde Park Gate, and I decided that I must try to find a flat as soon as possible. Luckily I was sharing a room with two very nice girls who felt, like me, that it would be better to have a place of our own. So Judy, Jean and I went off flat hunting together and soon found a flat we really liked. It was a maisonette over a flower shop in Gloucester Road and seemed ideal for our purposes. We needed a fourth girl to help with the rent and so Judy asked a friend of hers to join us. We lived there for two years and I have some of the happiest memories of my life during those years in London. When Judy's friend, Penny, left to get married we decided to ask Janet to join us for by then she had also returned from Singapore. The very best of my memories of the Gloucester Road flat were during the time that Judy, Jean, Janet and I were there.

We seemed to be laughing all the time. We were young and carefree and none of us was dedicated to our careers, since they were regarded as a means to an end – the end being to have a good time, find a boyfriend, and get married. Career women were few and far between in our circle, and we girls had no ambition other than marriage and children. It was what was expected of us. It was how we had been raised and we didn't question it at all. But since having a good time was the first item on the agenda we set about executing it to the full. We all got on very well and so suffered little aggravation or irritation with one another, although we were all very different and some of our priorities were pegged differently. Three of us came from a service background – Janet and me with fathers in the Army, whilst Judy's father was in the Navy – and Jean was the only civilian with a businessman father. He had, therefore, been chosen to sign the tenancy agreement with our landlord and be responsible for paying the rent. We in turn paid our share to him and, as far as I know, never gave him a day's worry!

So we were all set and raring to go. We soon fell into a pattern of living and although the household chores were rather down the line in terms of what we wanted to do, they did get done, even if, eventually, we decided on a roster system to ensure that somebody did pay regular visits to the laundromat across the road to wash the sheets. The times I really enjoyed the best were the weekends when we would sleep in late, eventually surface for brunch (I'm sure we must have invented that meal) and then have a lazy afternoon either looking round the shops or visiting friends in flats nearby. Then, if we were lucky, there would be a party to go to on Saturday night when we would dance the night away until the small hours of the morning. Sunday was for recovery and was taken at a very slow pace, with a few gentle chores attended to before preparing for work again the next day.

Sometimes we would be the ones holding the party and on one such occasion we had prepared a huge shepherd's pie to serve to our guests. The kitchen was on the top floor and the dining-room on the floor below and I was the one bringing this huge hot dish down the stairs. I was wearing stiletto-heel shoes at the time. The inevitable happened and I stumbled and dropped the dinner all down the stairs. Everyone heard the racket, together with my screams, and as I lay there surrounded by mushy minced meat I saw all these faces appear round the door. There was nothing left in the dish, except one of my shoes! For a moment or two we felt panic-stricken about what we were going to give our guests for dinner, but the moment passed as we opened a bottle of wine and set about finding what we had in the fridge. It was probably tomorrow's brunch, since it consisted mostly of sausages and eggs, but soon we were enjoying the meal and the company and thinking nothing more about the shepherd's pie which had met with such an untimely end.

I was settled into my new way of life by the time my parents returned from Singapore and Borneo. In April 1965 my father was posted to the Ministry of Defence in Whitehall (although we still tended to think of it as the War Office), and they had decided to rent a house in Bromley. We had become familiar with Bromley while I had been at school in Chislehurst nearby, but it did seem strange, somehow, that they should be living there now. They had been miles away when I had been at school there, but now that it was no longer relevant, it was their home. In March 1966, almost a year after returning from the Far East, they bought their first home – in Chislehurst itself. It was quite an event for my mother. She was fifty-four years old, had been married twenty-one years, and had moved thirty-two times. Now, at last, she could use her creative talents with a free hand to make their house their home. It was to be their own house for another eight years, although they had to move away again for some of that time. I'm sure, as she saw the huge carpet laid in the lounge, she would never have dreamt that the time would come when it was taken up and cut into two equal halves — his and hers. I think that she must have believed, when she and my father bought the house in Chislehurst, that it heralded a degree of permanence in their lives and indicated that their future would be together. She must have thought that all those threats to leave her over the years, and all the terrible rows and physical violence, would be a thing of the past. They finally had their own home, their silver wedding anniversary was around the corner and they could look forward to retirement in each other's company.

By the time my parents returned to England I was already about to leave my third job in London. I had flown the nest of my godfather's office, grateful for the experience it had afforded me, but for reasons which I can only guess at now had decided to work for Rawlplugs in Cromwell Road. I think I had decided to work close to the flat, thus avoiding travel costs and enabling me to lie in bed a little longer in the mornings, but I had not bargained for the utter boredom of dealing with Rawlplugs all day long. One day the tedium got to me to such an extent that I fell asleep at my desk. I knew the time had come to leave. I got a new job with Service Advertising in Knightsbridge which was only just down the road from my flat and found myself in a very fast and arty world. Very different from Rawlplugs and certainly not boring, but my service background made me feel very out of place amongst all those Bohemian advertising types. It made me nervous and I didn't feel on the same wavelength at all – I also found myself acquiring a woman boss and that, to me, was the bottom. When I did go, Alan, for whom I had been working, gave me a book of poems which he had kindly inscribed:

To Anne to say thanks for all the work and sorry to see you go. Best wishes. Alan L.

I was very touched by this kindness and I felt guilty that I was leaving. At the time I was beginning to think that I should find another job, Janet was also working for an advertising agency, S H Benson in Kingsway. She told me that one of their directors needed a new secretary and I began to think that I should apply. I was running before I could walk, but I couldn't see that then and Peter, the director, seemed impressed with me at the interview especially when he discovered that he had been in the same Regiment as my father. It was decided then. I would have the job and we would be able to reminisce about our long lost army connections! What a fool I was to think that my experience was adequate for a job of that calibre and how foolish of Peter to employ me for reasons of mutual army connections. It wasn't long before I found myself out of my depth and it certainly worried me. I redoubled my efforts to do well, but my confidence, which was beginning to falter, was taking quite a knock. Peter finally found his opportunity to 'fire' me when one of his fellow directors retired. As a result of this a senior director's secretary became redundant, which could not be allowed, and so it was suggested that I take a job with one of the back room boys while she took mine! I doubt if they expected me to accept their offer but I think Peter felt guilty when the day of my departure dawned and he came into my office with a small gift – a book of poems he had written and which he had inscribed with the words:

Farewell souvenir of a cruel boss! Peter H.

I was collecting poetry books faster than I could find shelf space for them.

I decided that it would be preferable not to get another permanent job and that temporary work might well be the answer in order to gain more experience and see what type of work suited me best. For the next year I did just that and ended up having a wide range of experience. Beginning with George Weston, a firm of estate agents, I then moved on to the Red Cross; followed by Michell & Partners, a firm of architects; another advertising agency called Rex Publicity; British Oxygen; The London Probation Service; The Gas Council; yet another advertising agency called Muse Gallagher Jones & Smail; a firm of solicitors by the name of Trower Still & Keeling; then Screen Process Supplies Ltd; a firm of surveyors by the name of George Belbin & Co.; followed by the import/export merchants Booker Merchants; then ITA, the independent television people; followed by Donald Cook canned foods and finally back to the import/export world of Booker (Nigeria) Ltd. If nothing else, I was back on the familiar ground of moving about all over the place which seemed to be my lot in life. But none of it seemed to be 'me' at all. I hadn't found my niche in life yet.

Some of my friends were settling down though. They had passed through the having a good time phase, to finding a boyfriend and now my mantelpiece started to fill up with wedding invitations. One of my class-mates from Farringtons, a girl called Jenny, was the first to tie the knot and one of her bridesmaids was her sister's daughter, who was a miniature version of herself. It was a happy occasion and several old school friends were there too. Another wedding was that of one of the Brigadier's daughters from Ismailia – the one who, together with her sister, had not allowed me to walk beside them when my father was a Major in Egypt! Anne had turned into a very beautiful woman and her wedding in Scotland was a 'high society' occasion. Along with several other weddings, invitations to many twenty-first birthday parties started to arrive in the post and so I never seemed to be short of a party to go to. Nor were we ever lacking in ideas or excuses for a party and even an election presented us with the opportunity to get a group of friends together. When Harold Wilson led the Labour Party to victory in 1964 we were in Trafalgar Square watching the results come through. To my astonishment I saw a hearse draw up and dozens of men dressed as undertakers pour out and proceed to dive into the fountains! Little did I imagine that I could know any of them but as they approached I realised that the son of my father's commanding officer in Gibraltar was amongst this group. Ian was now at the Britannia Royal Naval College in Dartmouth and had come to London to celebrate with some fellow cadets. They really were a spectacle and I didn't know whether I should own up to knowing one of them, or not. However, Ian spotted me too and so our group of girls joined in with their fun, although we drew the line at leaping into the fountains. At the end of the evening we all piled into the hearse and went back to our flat for a party. It was nice to meet up with Ian again (we had last bumped into each other at a nightclub in Singapore when I was spending my farewell evening with Warwick) and this chance encounter lead to an invitation to the Passing Out Ball at Dartmouth which was a very special occasion. Ian also managed to come to my twenty-first birthday party which commenced with a reception at the Combined Services Club in Pall Mall (which was my father's London Club) followed by dinner and dancing at our flat.

Our close-knit foursome at the Gloucester Road flat was coming under threat from predatory boyfriends, though, and Janet was the first to leave us. She had met a delightful Royal Marine officer in Singapore and they had become engaged in London after they had both returned to England. Alan was a frequent visitor to the flat and we all became very fond of him but upset when their marriage deprived us of Janet's company. Judy had a friend from work who was interested in filling her place and so Sheila joined our little group. We were all saddened when, in 1965, Sir Winston Churchill died and we joined the long queues of people snaking round Parliament Square to pay their last respects to the greatest statesman in living memory at his Lying in State. It symbolised the passing of yet another era and we all felt the loss of a great man. I had planned to be amongst the crowds at his funeral but was unable to make it on account of acute stomach pains the night before which resulted in the girls calling for a doctor in the middle of the night. It was my appendix complaining, not enough to be removed, but enough to cause me to miss this State occasion.

In January, 1966, Jean and I took ourselves off to Switzerland for a skiing holiday in Andermatt. It was the first holiday I had been on which I had paid for and organised myself and this gave me a good feeling of independence. We had great fun and it was very exhilarating but I don't think either of us fully mastered the sport in the time available to us. However, it was very worthwhile in that we both came back to England feeling really fit – a feeling which remained with us for quite a while, much to the chagrin of the other girls in the flat who couldn't understand why we were so bright and cheerful so early in the morning. Shortly after our return the rent on our flat was increased and we decided that it was more than we could afford to pay. We started flat hunting, although with some sadness since we had been so happy in Gloucester Road. It was decided that the process of choice would be thoroughly democratic and simply be based on a majority vote. A flat was found in Brompton Road, but although the others liked it, it didn't have the same feeling of 'home' to me and it lacked the character of our maisonette. I was beginning to feel that the best of the 'flatting' days were over and that I had better take a long hard look at where I was heading.

Although I had worked in London for two years I had not found a job to my liking and I began to feel that what I had missed was the service background in which I had grown up. The commercial and business world were 'foreign' to me and consequently, too, the people who worked there. I began to be drawn to the idea of joining the Foreign Office which I felt would afford me not only the chance of seeing some more of the world, but also the likelihood of finding the people more of my ilk. I set about applying, although I wondered what my chances of success might be. It was a slow process but eventually I was called to attend an interview and test. There was another girl going through the same process and the two of us were shown to a room where we would be given the shorthand and typing test. We were both very nervous since everything hinged on this test and it was not designed to be easy. No sooner were we under way than the other poor girl with me burst into tears and fled the room. This obviously put me off my stroke a bit and I had the feeling, afterwards, that I was accepted more on the basis of having kept going, rather than actually passing the test! I offered a silent prayer of thanks to the girl who had not been successful. I was in for another wait before I knew the outcome, however, and during this waiting period decided to go down to Chislehurst to stay with my parents. I filled the anxious weeks by working on a temporary basis with the Abbey National Building Society and started to go with my parents to some of the army functions I had missed during my time in London. We were honoured by two royal functions as well, one of which was a Garden Party at Buckingham Palace. This was a fascinating experience and we were afforded the opportunity not only to see the Queen, but many other members of the Royal Family as well. The glimpse inside the Palace as we walked through to the gardens was also a rare treat and we all felt duly honoured to be present. The other royal occasion was a parade in Canterbury at which HM Queen Juliana of the Netherlands was present in her capacity as Colonel in Chief of my father's Regiment. It was a splendid occasion, which I thoroughly enjoyed since I love military parades with their martial music and sharp lines of soldiers marching in unison.

I was still waiting to know if I was accepted by the Foreign Office when I took another holiday with Jean, this time to Florence and Elba, to help pass the time. For Jean it was a sentimental journey since she had been at a finishing school in Italy and wanted to go back to see it all again. For me it was new ground, although I had been taken there as a child, and I revelled in the wonderful sights we saw in Tuscany. We exhausted ourselves sightseeing, especially since it was so hot, and were rather glad of the peace and quiet of Elba where we just lazed in the sun and swam. While we were away Judy was married to her boyfriend, David, and Sheila was one of her bridesmaids. When we returned to London Jean was now the sole remaining member of our flatting foursome. We had all gone our own ways and for me there was news that I had been accepted by the Foreign Office.

There were still more interviews to be attended, though, but finally I got to the stage of waiting outside the office of the head of the secretarial division. There were other girls waiting there too and so I jumped to the conclusion that they were, like me, new recruits. I should have realised that this was not the case when I saw them talking amongst themselves, but the penny had not dropped. I was on new ground and feeling very unsure of myself but these girls, who seemed so friendly amongst themselves, did not try to include me until some while later when one of them decided to make an effort. She leaned across and asked me where I had come from. I wondered about this question and felt unsure of what my answer should be. Did she want to know where I lived? Did she want to know about my journey to London? I wasn't sure, so plumped for Charing Cross! There was stunned silence at this reply, followed quickly by muffled laughter and a communal dismissive look which said it all. I had committed a *faux pas* and become a 'marked' woman — they were not going to forget that one in a hurry! After I had been called into Miss

Lofting's office I was told I would be doing a two-week training course prior to commencing work. This passed pleasantly enough and without incident and before long I was transferred to the main typing pool in the Foreign Office. Although there was a great sense of pride in having got this far, I was by then twenty-two with a few years work experience behind me and being in a typing pool was not my idea of job satisfaction. However, I could see the sense in getting some practical experience and generally finding my way around. On my first morning, when I reported to the typing pool, I saw that the girls I had met two weeks earlier were there too. They were disposed to be rather more friendly this time and, knowing that I was a new girl, decided to show me the ropes. Their idea of putting me at ease was to tell me what had happened only a week or so ago when they had come across another new girl. "She was a complete idiot," they said; "When we asked her where she had come from she replied 'Victoria'"! I was the one who was stunned now, but decided that these girls should not be allowed to get away with this sort of gossip which had clearly been going the rounds for the past fortnight. I took a deep breath and said, "If this story is going to be repeated again, why don't you make it accurate – it wasn't Victoria, it was Charing Cross!"

Fortunately I was not in the typing pool for long. Although I had laboured under the impression that it was the Foreign Office I had joined, on a salary of fourteen pounds three shillings a week, it was to Zambia Department that I was posted, in what had been the Colonial Office but was now the Commonwealth Office. I felt a little disappointed, but quickly discovered that I was far too busy to have time to think along those lines and knuckled down to trying my best to be a good employee. There was a lot to get used to. Ian Smith, the Prime Minister of Rhodesia, had made a Unilateral Declaration of Independence the year before and this had created a situation of hardship for Zambia, which depended on Rhodesia for coal and manufactured goods. It also lost its vital rail link to the sea for its copper exports. With Tanzania, Zambia was one of the so-called 'front-line' states which supported the nationalists during the war which ended with the creation of an independent Zimbabwe. Our department was busy and I found myself working longer hours than I had been accustomed to as a temporary secretary. I was often called in for dictation by the various Third, Second and First Secretaries and generally found that they and the rest of the staff were too busy to be very friendly. I felt rather isolated – I was new and therefore knew nobody and even now I was within a department, people there were just too run off their feet to have much time to make me feel at home. There was one particularly attractive young diplomat, with dark good looks, who unnerved me dreadfully and I found I had a hard time keeping my hand steady when I took dictation from him! I began to think I must be more of a liability than an asset, but at the same time I tried hard to hold onto my pride in working for the Office. Because of UDI having been declared in Rhodesia, the work was very interesting and I found myself learning a lot about the country from which my friend Jacquie hailed. I had seen quite a lot of Jacquie after I got back from Malaya, during my flatting days, but now that I was working in an environment which encompassed her country, she was no longer living in London having returned to Rhodesia to get married.

I continued working in Zambia Department for six months and after that length of time expected to hear that I was to be posted overseas. I went to see Betty Wheate, who was in charge of such matters, and told her that I would like to volunteer for service in Aden. She looked at me in astonishment since she had not expected anyone to be volunteering for duty there, but I think her surprise must have been tempered with relief since it made her job that much easier. I had given a lot of thought to where I would like to be posted and had decided that I wanted to be back in a place where I could meet military people. I had missed them more than I realised and wanted to be back amongst 'my kind of people', so I came up with the idea of going to Aden. On reflection I cannot tell why I asked for Aden in particular, but I expect I was aware that the more glamorous postings which were open to both diplomatic and service personnel would be unlikely to be offered to such a new recruit into the Diplomatic Service.

In April 1967 I went to Heathrow to board a plane to Aden. My parents and Jean came to see me off on what should have been a journey of a lifetime but which in fact was a journey to hell and an experience which was to shape the course of the rest of my life.

Chapter Four
The Galloping Major

Disaster struck immediately – my luggage did not arrive with me but got sent to Nairobi instead, and it took some considerable length of time before I was reunited with it. When my cases finally arrived they were severely damaged and had various items of clothing dangling from the edges. But the worst horrors were to be found inside when I discovered that a bottle of face protection tonic had broken and the contents had united with that from a smashed packet of soap powder to form a gooey wet concoction which had seeped its way into my possessions, in some cases completely removing the colour from the clothing. Oh dear, what an awful beginning. At least, I thought then, I would ultimately receive my sea baggage, which would help, but in the event I did not even get that. When the ship arrived from England my crates were not unloaded because, by then, the 'troubles' had escalated to such an extent we were likely to be evacuated. It was felt that the best policy would be to send the crates back to England where at least they would be safe. It must have only just made it back there because by the middle of the year the Arab/Israeli 'Six Day War' resulted in the Suez Canal being closed. I gazed at the ship carrying my crates and wondered if I would ever see them again. What I didn't know then was that it would be ten years before I could unpack them.

My lack of possessions made an impact on the accommodation I could be offered since I was not, now, going to have any pots or pans or bedding. I was therefore placed with some girls from the Ministry of Works who were in an established flat. It seemed to me as though, once more, I was not going to be with the people I had originally joined to be with. I had chosen the Foreign Office, not the Ministry of Works! That is not to say I wasn't made to feel welcome; they were pleasant people and kind and helpful to me and I was glad that because I was in the MoW compound I was allowed to eat my meals in their Mess. So I didn't need any pots and pans after all. However, all these events did make it difficult for me to feel settled but I found that things improved once I became more familiar with my work at the High Commission where I was appointed as secretary to the British Consul. My spirits soared to dizzy heights when I finally bought my first car, a little Fiat 500, for which I paid one hundred pounds!

I had learnt to drive while we were living in Shorncliff, before going to Malaya, but when I took my driving test at seventeen, I failed. Once we were in Malaya I took another driving test and was successful this time and I gained quite a lot of driving experience during the two years I spent in the Far East. However, this test was not recognised in Britain and I had to take it again once I arrived back in London. I decided not to take any chances the second time and had a week of lessons which paid off and finally I held a British driving licence. Now I had my own car and this made me much more independent in terms of getting to work and generally being responsible for my own affairs. I gradually got to know people although I found that there were few women around since all service families had been evacuated because of the security situation. Basically the only British women in Aden at that time were nurses, and secretaries at the High Commission. My cousin, Brian, was there too, working at the British Bank of the Middle East which was nice for me as he was able to introduce me to some of his civilian friends.

So now I was established at work, installed in a flat, had my own car and was beginning to meet people. My life began to fall into a pattern of daily living and I felt as though I was becoming part of the small expatriate community. I began to meet some of the officers in the various regiments based in Aden at that time and even, on one occasion, met Lieutenant Colonel Mitchell who commanded the Argyll and Sutherland Highlanders – better known as 'Mad Mitch'! One day the girls I shared a flat with decided to give a party and a number of people congregated in our beach-front flat to dance the night away. Towards the end of the evening a dashing officer made advances in my direction and, since he was obviously a very popular man within the group of people there, I felt flattered that he should be spending time with me. I asked one of the girls who he was and she told me that his name was Don and he was usually the life and soul of any party in town. She also told me that he was married and to beware of him. I was rather disappointed by this news. However, I was on my guard now, and somewhat indignant when he tried to kiss me good night and in a rather high-handed fashion told him, "I don't hold with kissing married men"! There are certain things which get said in one's life which are of limited significance at the time the words are spoken but which, in the light of subsequent events, take on a meaning which prevents the words ever leaving one's subconscious mind. Such were these words of mine that night. I was on the edge of a precipice and I could either be saved or I could fall to my doom. My instinct was to climb to the moral high ground, that safe place one can escape to when the going gets tough. I made it that night, and I was safe. For now, anyway.

But Don was not a man to take no for an answer and he pursued me whenever the chance presented itself. He was thirty-four years old, to my twenty-two years, and he had a fatal charm, a way with words, and he knew how to handle a woman. My resolve to resist his advances weakened with each successive encounter until the time came when I finally succumbed to the inevitable and we became an 'item'. All through these encounters I tricked myself into believing that we could have a good time without anybody getting hurt and that, furthermore, we could be discreet and neither the army command nor my bosses would be any the wiser. I was foolish, of course, and became infatuated by a man who treated me as though I was the most important girl in the world and that his mission in life was to transform me from a naïve girl into a woman of the world – according to his mould. He taught me a million things and I grew up very quickly, although a lot of his teachings did not sit comfortably on my shoulders at all. I was mesmerised by all this attention; by the way he screeched up outside my flat in his Jeep with his beret at a rakish angle, always with the words that he was on duty very soon and we must snatch these moments together while we could. The moral high ground had lost its grip on me and I was sliding over the edge.

Life took on a whole new meaning and Don became my *raison d'être*. We grabbed the most unlikely moments together which revolved around him and his military commitments. There was a war going on and soldiers were being killed and his soldiers were very important to him. He was at his best with animals, children and his 'men', but often had difficulty with his senior commanders. He was an intellectual at a time when the army tended to be suspicious of intellectuals. He also spoke Arabic fluently and had a high regard for the Arab people, and these qualities were useful in Aden at that time. I think he was probably a good soldier, and in any event he was certainly a caring company commander and the welfare of his men was high on his agenda. The deeper the involvement between us became, the harder I found it to be without him for any length of time, and on one occasion I drove out to the desert encampment where his Regiment was based. How I got through I cannot imagine, and I must have been a sight for sore eyes once I got there – this was well before the days of women soldiers serving alongside their male counterparts in active-service conditions – and the men would not have seen a woman for months.

To get there I had had to drive along Ma'allah's 'murder mile' which was a long stretch of straight road which led out of the town of Aden towards military encampments and the RAF base of Khormaksar (which I had visited when we were on our way to Malaya). 'Murder mile' had previously been the area where service families had lived before their evacuation but now it was deserted. There wasn't a soul in sight as I drove down the road, fast because I was scared to be so alone. In the distance I saw an Arab appear from a doorway with a crate of bottles on his head. He proceeded to cross the road and as he did so I put my foot on the break. He was halfway across the road when he spotted me and to my utter astonishment he turned back the way he had come, thus putting himself right into the path of my car. All my instincts were thrown awry and I didn't know which way to take avoiding action. As I proceeded to veer to the right, he turned once more and came back into my path. How I missed killing him I will never know, but God must have been with me and Allah with him, for we both survived unharmed. The casualty was his crate of glass bottles which were smashed on the road. He was lying on the ground and I was shaking from head to toe while sitting stunned in my car. Before I could blink an eyelid I was surrounded by angry Arabs (where had they come from in such a deserted landscape?) who proceeded to rock my car from side to side. I didn't have time to wonder what would happen next because within seconds this angry mob was being dispersed by a military patrol who had arrived in their armoured vehicle and soldiers with guns were checking on the 'crate man' and telling the angry mob to disperse. As quickly as this mob had appeared from nowhere, they now melted away and once more the street was empty but for me, the soldiers and the 'crate man'. Once it had been established that no one was injured we were told to be on our way. I proceeded, much shaken, to my destination and the feeling of comfort to be in Don's arms was greatly enhanced by this experience.

We were all living life on a day-to-day basis and fighting and death was around us. My job as secretary to the British Consul brought me into contact with the fighting that was going on which resulted in some of our brave soldiers being wounded, or worse. Some of the photographs I saw of what was going on were horrendous to see. The secretaries were rostered for duty outside working hours and one day, as I was basking in the sun and enjoying a swim, I was called up to Government House where our High Commissioner, Sir Humphrey Trevelyan, required an urgent communication typed for dispatch to Whitehall. I had never had any contact with the great man himself although he was well loved by those who knew him. He had been called out of retirement, as a former diplomat of outstanding achievement, to be 'Our Man' in Aden to lead that country to independence. His wife was a cripple and he was often seen, when time and duty permitted, carrying Lady Trevelyan down to the sea from her wheelchair for a swim. I was somewhat surprised at the rather 'Heath Robinson' arrangements for typing at Government House as I was given a ropy old manual typewriter atop a small, rickety piece of furniture and told to get the work done as quickly as possible. Somehow I completed this task but I don't look back on it as the highlight of my diplomatic career!

After spending only a short time in the MoW flat I was moved to a small house which I was to share with Sir Humphrey's secretary, Fleur. Fleur was a lovely person and a real 'class act' who was at the pinnacle of her career with the diplomatic service, and I was very happy indeed to be able to share accommodation with her. It was rumoured that Sir Humphrey had only agreed to come out of retirement if Fleur could be his secretary! We actually had a lot of fun together, and Fleur, in spite of being considerably older than me, was always ready to join in with whatever we younger ones had planned. Nor was she judgmental and she accepted Don into her life too as readily as she had accepted me. Soon after I moved in, a third girl joined us. She was to be married to an RAF officer and thus become the last British bride in Aden. How she managed to do this at a time when families had been evacuated escapes me now, but it must have been a question of who she knew, rather than what she knew. On the latter point she did not score highly and, to Don's mind, her betrothed even less well, for he called them "Sub-human and Child-bride"!

One day I came back from work to find a big commotion going on on the verandah and the house swarming with journalists and photographers. They had come to do an article on our young friend who was shortly to be married. The reality of the situation was that her mother had sent her trousseau from Paris and it was all quite magnificent. The Press did not like this though and decided that it would make a better story if she had had to struggle with coping in difficult times. It was decided that she should be making her own wedding dress with material purchased in the Souq. She had been photographed down town looking at materials, and now she had a white sheet crumpled up in her sewing machine which was outside on the verandah. Anybody who knows Aden will vouch for the fact that that is the last place anybody in their right mind would tackle such a task given the extreme heat outside. Rather one would place a sewing machine strategically under a fan and hope to keep cool enough to complete the task! I sat back and watched this farce, not daring to get involved, but when they had finished I mentioned to 'Child-bride' that it might have been more realistic if she had removed the black cotton from her sewing machine before the photographs were taken. "Oh, that doesn't matter," she said, "it won't be noticed because the pictures are in black and white!" When Don heard this story he renamed them "Sub-human One and Sub-human Two". He could be very cruel at times.

I don't know whether it was because I spent a lot of time sunbathing in those happy days before we were told that everything enjoyable in life is bad for us, but I developed a skin disease. Unluckily for me, it was only on my face and it gave me a very blotchy look. There was no specialist in skin diseases in Aden and I had to make do with some soothing rather than medicinal fluid to apply to this condition. I was distressed by my appearance and decided that a visit to the hairdresser might help to improve things, and so off I went to have highlights put in my hair. The result wasn't so much highlights, rather a total blonde look, with bits missed out. It was atrocious and didn't suit me at all. So there I was, so tanned I was almost Negroid, with a blotchy red face and this horrendous blonde hair. I looked an absolute fright but there was little I could do about any of it but grin and bear it!

I had had my hair done for a party we planned to give and had purchased some frozen raspberries from the NAAFI shop on my way back from work. These were in a plastic bag on the floor in front of the passenger seat of my car. As I drove home I came to a very dangerous hairpin bend in the road as it skirted a jutting rock. I slowed down to encounter this blind corner but after completing my turn was instantly confronted by a stationary vehicle parked in the middle of the road. There was no possible way of avoiding this vehicle, which was a taxi that had stopped to pick up a fare. My little car buckled under the impact, but once more my God had gone with me and there was no loss of life or limb. But my car was badly damaged and again some gallant soldiers appeared like the Genie of the Lamp and bore me off before an angry mob could appear. My car remained at the scene of the accident until arrangements were made to remove it, but friends who passed it on their way home were alarmed at the quantity of 'blood' seen dripping onto the road! My raspberries didn't make it into the trifle that night. The taxi driver took me to court over this incident, but he was proved to have been in the wrong for having stopped at that dangerous point in the road. The worst of it, for me, was the loss of my lovely little car which was taken up to the Crater district of Aden where the Fiat agent tried to put it together again. He was hampered in this task on a number of fronts. Firstly he did not have all the spare parts needed, and secondly he did not know when a vessel would get through with the cargo of spares required. When he did finally mend it and it was due to be collected, Crater had been taken over by the dissidents and not even the gallant soldiers who kept coming to my rescue could help me then!

I hadn't seen a lot of my cousin Brian on account of my involvement with Don but we did meet occasionally, and one day he told me that a friend of his had an empty flat Don and I could borrow if we wanted to have a break together. We both had some local leave due to us and decided to take this flat for a few days. It was extraordinary that we should think we could be 'on holiday' together in the middle of Aden in the middle of a war, but this is what we thought we could do. It wasn't entirely successful, and by the end of the allotted time I had decided that this whole affair should end and tried to creep out of the flat early one morning. Just as I was opening the door Don woke and heard me leave. He was like a child about to lose his favourite toy and would not let me go. My resolve weakened once more, and I lost what could have been another chance to get out of this mess.

The background noise of fighting was always with us and loud bangs did not startle us any more. Aden was the focus of a struggle between two rival nationalist organisations – the Egyptian supported Front for the Liberation of Occupied South Yemen (FLOSY) and the Marxist-oriented National Liberation Front (NLF), both vying for eventual control of the country. It was as a part of the NLF-ruled People's Republic of Southern Yemen that Aden achieved its independence on the thirtieth of November 1967, and became the national capital in 1968 of what was known as South Yemen. While Aden was still a British colony the British forces did their best to keep the peace between these warring factions, but the fighting continued and one afternoon I heard a particularly loud bang. We three girls were at home in our little house which, like my original flat, was within the MoW compound. We came dashing out of our bedrooms where we had been taking a nap during the worst heat of the day and with one accord looked towards the town centre expecting to see signs of fighting. We could see nothing untoward and eventually wandered back to our rooms. Very shortly the telephone rang and an army friend was on the line asking, somewhat breathlessly, if we were all right? Well, of course we were, but we wondered what the loud bang was? "That was a mortar bomb," he said, "it landed in your compound and that is why I'm ringing to find out if you are all right!" Oh, help, we all dashed to the other side of the house to look in the opposite direction from before, and, sure enough, our next door neighbour's house had been completely demolished. Army personnel were already there sorting through the rubble, but mercifully nobody had been injured. The bomb had been intended for Government House, on the hill above us, but none of the bombs hit their target and some landed harmlessly in the sea. But how close we had all been to extinction and how unsuspecting we would have been had it come.

Military manoeuvres continued and security was tightened up even further. Now we were subjected to a curfew which was, of course, to enhance our safety but it certainly cramped our style too and it became difficult to have any life outside of work. One good thing happened though and that was the retaking of Crater by the Argyll and Sutherland Highlanders, who had simply marched back in behind their commanding officer, 'Mad Mitch', accompanied by the drone of the bagpipes. I think it must have been the 'astonishment' factor which caused this to be so successful, and not only was Crater back under British military control, but not a shot was fired in anger in the process! Now I was able to get my little car back, but it was really too late to enjoy having it once more since it was definitely time to think about evacuating all but the most essential staff, and the girls were first in line for moving out.

I was told that I was to be posted to Lesotho, in southern Africa. Normally this news would have delighted me no end since I had always wanted to go to that part of the world. Not only that, but it would have enabled me to visit my friend Jacquie too and to live and work in a very beautiful part of the world. Nevertheless I was very torn, but not really in a position to refuse. However, there was the matter of my skin disease which I felt required a professional opinion. When I suggested that I should go back to London so that this could be seen to, I was told that that shouldn't be necessary since there would be good doctors available in Lesotho. I wasn't so sure, though, but more than that I didn't know how I was going to be able to part from Don. He encouraged me to pursue the line of going back to London for medical attention, and finally I was told that I could do so. I thereby lost another chance to do the right thing and end my affair with Don. How often I have regretted this foolishness. I was offered a way out and I turned it down.

But now the practicalities of leaving had to be attended to and I made a visit to town to buy some suitcases to replace those which had been damaged on my arrival. I bought three beautiful Samsonite cases for an absolute song. They have served me well over the years, only once going astray, never getting smashed, and are still going strong after thirty years or so and more trips round the world than I can remember. I was given a number of items from surplus Army stock which would otherwise have been left behind when the troops withdrew and my three cases were crammed full of things like glass tumblers and electric kettles. I regarded these items as my 'war loot', and, like my suitcases, I have them still, although the glasses have dwindled in number over the years. And so the day for leaving dawned, and somehow or other Don and I left on the same plane. Perhaps it was this fact which caused me to be forgetful enough to leave my washing on the line!

We flew from RAF Khormaksar to a military airfield near London, and I remember little of the flight other than the fact that both Don and I realised that we were going to be faced with the reality of his marital status all too soon. He made me promise that I would not watch him greet his wife and that I would go through first in order to avoid this happening. As I emerged from the formalities of returning to the United Kingdom I entered the Arrivals Hall and saw a line of people waiting. I had seen photographs of Celia and so it was not difficult to recognise her, but the shock of passing by this stranger, knowing who she was, yet knowing she did not know me, was acute. I felt sick and yet wanted to look back. I kept my promise, though, and walked out into the cold night. Nobody knew I was returning and it was an odd feeling being a stranger in my own country with nobody to meet me. I had wanted flexibility of movement and felt that anonymity was the only way to achieve it. I had to sleep somewhere that night, all the same, and so I got a taxi into town and went to Jean's flat – the one in Brompton Road which Judy, Jean and I had moved into originally. She was surprised to see me but offered me a bath to soak in and a couch to sleep on. I was thankful for both, but very sad and alone when I eventually fell asleep that night.

The next day I took stock of the situation. I was going to have to report into the Foreign Office for further instructions, and this I did. I was told that I should make an appointment to see the Treasury Doctor about my skin disease and that I was to be assigned to Security Department and should report for work in a few days time. But I had nowhere to live and so I knew that I was going to have to get in touch with my father to arrange to come home, initially at least. He was still working in Whitehall at the Ministry of Defence, and I met him for lunch in a pub. He must have realised immediately that I was in love because he broached the subject very quickly. After all, he had raised me to be an Army wife, and I suppose he wanted to know if I had been successful in finding a proposed Army husband. The story came tumbling out. I couldn't help myself although I knew that I was taking a risk telling him so much. When I had finished I said to him, "I want you to promise faithfully that you will do nothing. Nothing that will hurt us or harm our careers." He gave me that promise, and I began to relax.

I went to see the Treasury Doctor. He told me I had acne! I couldn't believe it. I had suffered from acne for years and knew that it was not the same at all, but he insisted that that was what it was. Eventually I saw my doctor back in Chislehurst who referred me to the St John's Skin Hospital near Leicester Square, where eventually they diagnosed sarcoid, a rare and untreatable disease. In order to make this diagnosis they had removed a part of the inflamed skin for examination and tests, but they never explained that I would bear the scar from this biopsy for life. I'm quite sure I would have settled for the acne diagnosis if I had realised that the price of enlightenment was such a permanent reminder of the condition which caused it. Anyway, at least I was vindicated on medical grounds, even if not on any other.

My next task was to sort out my ghastly 'streaked' hair, and this I did by having my hair dyed back to its original colour of mid brown. They got the tone wrong and made it much too dark which suited me just as little as the blonde! I bought a hair-piece and wore it until my hair had grown out naturally! Fortunately this was quite common in those days and lots of people wore a hair-piece from time to time, so I did not feel too self-conscious about it any more. I then went down to Chislehurst to try and sort myself out before I was due to start work again shortly. My mother also saw that I was in love and although she was distraught at the news that the object of my desire was already married, she offered me love and understanding.

Within a short time I was ensconced in my new department, this time learning the ropes in the world of Security Department. This appointment had made me wonder if my involvement with Don had somehow gone undetected by my bosses in Aden, although at no time had I deliberately tried to hide it. But at least I was where I thought I wanted to be, namely in London rather than southern Africa. I wasn't all that happy to be living at home again, after the years of freedom I had enjoyed since leaving Malaya, but my mother tried her best to calm the waters which were becoming increasingly troubled between my father and me. A storm was brewing, all the same, and my ship was about to founder.

Chapter Five
Walking Wounded

We had got back to England in September 1967, just in time for Jean's twenty-first birthday party. It was a splendid occasion and her parent's had pulled out all the stops to give her a lovely party to look back on. For me, though, it was awful. All the friends from the flat were there: Janet with her husband Alan, Judy with her husband David, and Jean with her boyfriend Richard. It was like Noah's Ark, everyone came two by two, and then there was me – alone. I had been driven to the occasion by Don who had to wait for several hours outside since he was not invited. It was difficult to have a good time and it made me realise that I was going to lose my friends if I continued with my illicit relationship. But the cat and mouse game we had started to play added fuel to the fire of our passion and the more we were hounded the more we sought refuge in each other's arms.

The lies had begun. Don's mostly, but mine too to some extent. In order to be together he had to find excuses for not being at home and he didn't tell Celia the truth. I couldn't see then, what became clear later, that if he could lie to her with such ease, then the time might come when he could do the same to me with equal alacrity. My twenty-third birthday was coming up soon and in order to be together for a whole weekend, in Worthing, we both had to extract ourselves deceitfully. Although it was wonderful to have each other for two whole days, it was a sad and unhappy weekend and Worthing seemed an awful place to be. We had to play that corny old chestnut of being 'Mr and Mrs Smith' and we spent most of the weekend trying to work out just how we were going to achieve our end, which was to be together properly. It was far from easy. Don was married to his second wife and had custody of the three children from his first marriage, together with a baby daughter from his second. It was a ghastly mess but the worse the problems, the more determined we became.

We had barely been back three weeks before my father broke his promise to do nothing. Since he was working at the Ministry of Defence he had little difficulty in obtaining the private and confidential personal file on Don, under the pretext of considering him for a job in his department. Thus armed with much 'ammunition' he proceeded to rampage up and down Whitehall seeing as many senior officers who knew Don as he could. His aim was firstly 'information' and secondly to use that 'information' to bring about the end of our relationship. It was a fearful campaign, a psychological war, and he had many cards up his sleeve. Throughout the fourteen months which elapsed between my return from Aden and his departure from Whitehall he proceeded to carve up my life, my career, my relationship and in so doing, Don's too. His campaign was plotted with the military precision one would expect of an Army officer and his attacks came from all sides. Having done all he could on the 'military front', he then tried the 'emotional front' and I was told that he even went to see Don's wife to ensure that she knew what was going on and that she would be fighting to keep her man. He then tried the 'spiritual front'. My parents' house was opposite the Vicarage and so, one day, Don was invited to our house to meet this man of God. Stephen, the Vicar, then took up my father's cudgels with a vengeance and got us both down on our knees, (on the very same carpet which was destined to be cut into 'his' and 'hers') and got us to pray to God for forgiveness for our sins and to pray for the end of our affair.

The military, emotional and spiritual campaigns never ceased. They went on day after day. I knew I should get away from it all but somehow lacked the ability to think beyond the hour I was living. I ached for the next post to arrive with a letter from Don, or the next phone call to tell me that we could meet, albeit briefly. I was too emotionally tied up to see my friends, and wanted to keep every spare minute 'free' in case Don found time for me. I was very lonely and unhappy and my health began to deteriorate. I was often to be found at the doctor's surgery requesting either sleeping pills, or tranquillisers, or both. It was my port in a storm, it was the only place where I could get any help. My father's final line of action was his 'medical front' and his *coup de grâce* was to have me struck off my doctor's panel. I never quite knew what he said to the doctor, or how he managed to do this since the medical profession usually honour a patient's confidentiality, but one day when I was in a particularly distraught state I went to the doctor only to be told that my father had spoken to him and he was not prepared to treat me any longer. I was dumbfounded. Now I had nowhere to turn. A terrible row ensued, which was still going strong the next morning when we went up to London by train to our separate jobs in Whitehall. My father left me in tears at Charing Cross station and I had not managed to compose myself by the time I reached the Office.

The girls I worked with in Security Department were a good bunch and we had become friendly. They did not really know what was going on in my life, but had guessed at much of it. They were very kind and supportive that morning and their concern made the tears flow faster. At this point the Head of Security Department walked in and, naturally enough, wanted to know what was going on. I was told to go and see him once I had composed myself. Soon I found myself sitting in his office being given the 'third degree'. It took him no time at all to get the whole story out of me and he was clearly uncomfortable with the knowledge that a member of his department was in a potentially 'compromising' situation. I tried to explain to him that this could hardly be the case since everyone involved, plus most of Whitehall, already knew the full facts. However, he was convinced that he had the makings of a potential security leak on his hands. The fifties and the sixties had been bad decades for British security, with the Burgess, Maclean and Philby affairs, and the whole matter of security was a very touchy subject.

The next thing was to decide what to do with me. The secretarial appointments division put on their thinking caps and came up with the suggestion that an overseas posting would be the best plan. This way I could keep my job with the Diplomatic Service, Security Department could breathe easily once more, but best of all I could be given another chance to break off my relationship with Don. It was certainly food for thought since the last thing I wanted was to lose my job which I really enjoyed. I felt that the Office had been very fair to me and done the best thing all round, according to their sights. But it wasn't what I wanted at all. It had all come about because of the state I was in as a result of my father's actions. I was being precipitated into making a decision which would affect my life – a decision I was not ready to make. The pressure was on now, though, both from the Office as well as my father, and Don and I felt helpless to do anything about the tide which was turning so fast. I was posted to Vienna and I had little choice but to accept. At least they had been kind to me in offering me a nice posting. It was quite on the cards that I be sent somewhere no one else wanted to go. I was terribly ill at ease, though, while I made my preparations for departure to Vienna. I ordered a duty-free car, a little red Mini with a left-hand drive, and my father said that he would drive me over to Austria in it! He was happy. At last he had got his own way. I was to be banished from London and the separation would bring about the end of my affair. His campaign had paid off, and he went out of his way to be a good 'victor', helping me in every way to get ready to leave. But I didn't want to go. How would I get on in a new country and a new job I didn't want? I was busy trying to get ready and so had little time to think about it all, but one day when Don and I met, we both felt that we couldn't bear to part. It was three weeks before I was due in Vienna that I handed in my resignation. I felt sick when I got a letter back (curiously dated 20 April 1968) saying:

> With reference to your minute of 17 May,
> your resignation of your appointment in the
> Diplomatic Service is accepted. Your last
> day of service will be 30 May, 1968.

And after a paragraph concerning the Official Secrets Acts, it went on to say:

> I have been asked to thank you for your
> work since you joined the Service and to
> wish you every success in the future.
> Signed B. E. Wheate.

I had relinquished the one job which I had really loved, the one thing I had really felt was 'me'. I had been so proud to have been part of it all and now I stood on the steps of Queen Anne's Mansions, just a 'has-been'.

How could I have given it all up for a man who was not free to be mine? But wasn't I asking him to make even greater sacrifices? Now

I was really in a mess. My father's wrath knew no bounds. Several battles had been won by him, but now the tables had turned and I had proved that he could not completely rule my life. The latest 'victory' was mine, but it had cost dearly. My health was deteriorating fast and I lived a life where nothing but Don mattered. I held myself in total readiness for his 'call'. I went nowhere and I did nothing unless it was with him. Then the day came when I got the 'call' and I was not ready. He had been making plans to leave Celia, taking with him his three elder children, and eventually found a house which he planned for us to live in. It was the most delightful place, a little house called 'Kettle Cottage' near Borough Green – a real 'love nest' if ever there was one – but when he asked me to move in with him and look after his three children, I knew that my state of health was so low that I could not do so without a complete break first. I arranged to go to Shrubland Hall, a health farm in Suffolk, for a week in the hope that this would put me back on my feet. What none of us knew was that I was so ill that being put on a diet of carrot juice tipped me over the edge. I became feverish to the extent that a doctor had to be called to see me. I was then 'built up' with good nourishing food and lots of personal attention from the proprietor. She was a kind person and I developed a personal friendship with her which lasted quite a long while afterwards. She was a great believer in the ancient Chinese 'oracle' of *I Ching,* and one day got me to 'consult' it. It was quite emphatic in its advice to give Don up.

I was still unwell when my week at Shrubland Hall was up, and my father had to come and collect me from London. I had not told him what I was planning to do, and in the event he never had to know because by the time I got home I was too late to move in with Don. Celia had moved in instead. I couldn't believe that all our plans were on the point of coming to fruition, eight months after we got back from Aden, and now they had crumbled about us because I had been too ill to go when I was called. I lay awake at night crying and crying. I was so lonely and it seemed to me that I had nothing left to live for. Our battle was over and it was lost. I was in a very disturbed state of mind when I got up in the small hours one morning and went to the garage to take my father's car. I drove to Kettle Cottage to be with Don. Along the way I noticed that the car had little petrol in it and I stopped at the next garage, although I had no money with me. The attendant must have realised the state I was in for he let me have a gallon, for free! I drove on and when I got to my destination, Cathy-like, I knocked on the window of the ground floor study which was Don's bedroom. He must have been astonished to see me, although he didn't show it, and we drew comfort from being in each other's presence for a little while. I returned to Chislehurst and put the car back in the garage. My father was waiting for me in the hallway. He was anger personified. He had guessed at what I had been up to, adding various embellishments of his own, and I had never seen him so angry in my life. He had been up in the night to visit the bathroom and had noticed that my bedroom door was open. On investigating he found that I was not there, and when he had looked for me he realised that the car was also missing. He had waited up to greet me. The row which ensued from this was so ghastly that it resulted in my being thrown out of my home, in truly Victorian fashion, never to darken his doorstep again.

I rang my school friend Pene, the one who had come to see me off at Southampton. She lived nearby in Shortlands and had bought her own house there. Pene was one of the few friends I had left who was not married and having babies. She was an air hostess and was living life in the 'fast lane'. It didn't take her a moment to decide if she would help me or not. She dropped what she was doing and came round in her sports car to pick me up and take me back to her house. If ever a girlfriend was a knight in shining armour, this was the time when Pene was one to me! It was just the tonic I needed, and I immediately felt better to be out of the Chislehurst house and away from my father. It heralded a mildly tolerable period within an otherwise ghastly phase of my life. I had been doing temporary work in Bromley after I left the Foreign Office, and had found myself working at Barclays Bank, Farnborough Hospital Management Committee, Norwich Union Insurance Society, Cosmos Travel Agents, Vidor Batteries, Oakbridge Development Company, and finally Charringtons Heating where I had quite often spoken to Enoch Powell on the telephone! In spite of this diversion it had all been terribly boring after the jobs I had had with the Foreign Office, and I had only worked in order to make a living, not for enjoyment at all.

Pene's house was right opposite Shortlands railway station and this made it much easier to work in London, so I transferred to Agencies in town. Not that this made things any better since it only served to remind me of how I had once commuted to Whitehall, and I was also bored when sent to work for the British Sugar Corporation, Moorfields Eye Hospital, and finally Container Fleets Ltd. Only the latter provided some element of comradeship since I ended up being there for several months in the end. So life with Pene took on a slightly brighter hue, although I was still deeply unhappy both in my situation with Don and in my working and family life. My poor mother, who had so disagreed with my father's actions, was very sad at the way things had turned out. She was left to bear the brunt of his anger and it had a detrimental effect on her life too. She was not forgiven for having taken my side, and this had had a lot to do with why I had been thrown out – an act which my father thought would break down the close link with my mother. Of course, it had the opposite effect, since we now had to meet illicitly. She came to see me at Pene's house sometimes, and brought with her some things of mine which I had not had time to take when I left. She was always a welcome visitor, although one day there was a woman waiting on my doorstep when I got back from work who was not nearly so welcome. Don's wife, Celia, was paying me a call. I was shocked to be confronted by her but had little choice other than to invite her in. I thought we both needed to calm our nerves and so offered her a drink. We both sat sipping our Cinzanos in silence for a while, and then the talking started. She stayed for a long time and the weird thing was that I liked her and I think, in a funny sort of way, that she liked me too. We were enemies nonetheless but in different circumstances I think we could have been friends. It was very unsettling for us both, though, because we learned of ways in which Don had been lying to each of us.

Now that I was living independently it was much easier for Don to visit me whenever the opportunity presented itself. Although we did not spend a lot of time together, we didn't manage too badly either, and for the rest I relied upon his letters arriving daily, assuring me of his undying love for me and his earnest desire that we should be together properly as soon as possible. And, of course, there was the telephone. I would receive calls from him at the oddest times, sometimes in whispered tones because he was not alone. He kept our affair going with the promise that it would all be all right in the end. For my part there was nothing I could do other than to ensure that I was always available when he needed me. But it was no life for a twenty-three year old. One day he turned up at Pene's house with the two elder girls, Fanny and Claire-Elizabeth. The eldest, his son Simon, was at boarding school and the little one was with Celia. There was a second spare bedroom, with just one bed in it, and we tucked them up to sleep top-to-toe. Pene was marvellous about this invasion and was very supportive to the four of us, and in fact she had quite a way with children, far better than me. But the fact was that this was not the way to do it and even if he had thought that it might work, it was clear that the children could not be taken away from both their stepmother and their school and their things for any length of time. It wasn't long before they all went home, in Don's case to try and work out a different strategy.

He thought that moving to another house might do the trick, thereby enabling himself and his three children to move elsewhere, and that I could then join them. So he set about house hunting and found a lovely place in The Meadway in Blackheath. The plan didn't work, all the same, for Celia moved too. 1968 was slipping by, albeit very slowly, and round about the time of my twenty-fourth birthday my father had hatched another plan to get me out of the country. How he was still exercising such control over me, having washed his hands of me, is something I am unclear about now. But such was the way things were. My mother and I were 'private soldiers' to his 'senior officer' and we more or less had to do as we were told. Me, usually with a fight. However, it was on the sixteenth of October 1968, a month before he left the Ministry of Defence to take up his penultimate appointment with the Army, that I was sent to Belgium to stay with his Canadian Army cousin who was based with SHAPE (Supreme Headquarters Allied Powers Europe) in Mons.

Don and I must have concurred, to some extent, with this decision, because this time I went and Don drove me to Dover to catch the ferry. As I saw the white cliffs of Dover disappear into the distance I had a very different feeling to that which I had had when I set sail from Southampton six years earlier. It was also five years to the day that I had been sent to Hong Kong – that previous occasion when I had been banished to break up a relationship – and my feelings were much more akin to that time.

This latest venture was a disaster. I didn't know the cousins and didn't like them when I did. I disliked their way of life and the food they ate. We had not one thing in common and I regarded them as my gaolers. They in turn cannot have enjoyed my stay either and accommodated me simply to oblige my father. The plan had been for me to get a job with SHAPE and eventually set up on my own in Brussels. It didn't work, not only because I couldn't get a job, but also because I didn't want to be there. I did nothing all the time I was there (other than make a small effort to get a job) apart from reading *The Lord of the Rings*, which Don had given me to pass the time. I hated the book, but there was nothing else to do with my time. One weekend I escaped to Luxembourg to visit my friend Hazel who had been posted to the British Embassy there. She had been a friend from my Security Department days and it was lovely to see her again. However, it brought home to me just what I had given up. I cannot have been in Belgium long, but all the time I was there Don kept ringing me, telling me the latest developments, all in whispered conversations very late at night. What the cousins thought about their telephone ringing in the small hours of the morning, with me quickly answering it, I cannot imagine. They kept their thoughts to themselves, but it was with mutual pleasure that I returned once more to England.

My parents had already left England, my father having been transferred to the American Staff College at Fort Leavenworth in Kansas. On the one hand I was relieved, but on the other I missed my mother desperately. It seemed as though I had nobody left at all now since she had been my only staunch ally, continuing to show me love in spite of all that was happening in my life. I felt desperate. The situation was deteriorating rapidly and still there was no sign that Don and I would be together. I had returned to Pene's house and although this was, to some extent, a safe haven she was often away, doing what air hostesses do, flying around the world. My spirits sunk lower and lower. My friends were all married and having babies now, and even if I had been able to visit them I did not do so for fear of losing a chance to see Don. And now my mother was no longer in England. Pene's latest flying commitment was the last straw, and once again I reached that desperate stage of believing that there was little point in my life.

By the spring of 1969 the strain of the past year and a half had also got through to Celia, and in April she went to live in her home town of Sutton, leaving Don and his three children in Blackheath. It was what we had been waiting for for so long. This time, when I was called, I went immediately. But once we had got our hearts' desire, the house of cards began to crumble. Our first major problem was that the children were distressed by their stepmother's departure and try as I might I could not get through to them — except Fanny. She turned her little face my way and became my friend. Simon was at boarding school, but was a sullen and unhappy boy when he was at home and Claire-Elizabeth, although a lot younger, was much the same. We lived like this for a year and our love for one another survived the storms, which still did not abate. But too much drama had taken place; too much heartbreak for everybody concerned; too many sacrifices had been made in the name of our love. And then there was Don's guilt. The guilt permeated our life. He assuaged this guilt by going to Sutton to visit Celia and help her set up her own home. Now the lies were the ones he told me. But all the excuses seemed genuine and I believed and trusted him. My role was reversed but I didn't know I was being deceived. By Christmas 1969 we had settled down into something resembling a normal family life. The children had accepted the situation a little bit better and Fanny and I were getting along famously. We tried to make it a good Christmas for the children and Don's parents joined us for the holiday period. During the course of conversation they spoke about a holiday they had taken recently and how they had taken a taxi to Heathrow. I went into a state of shock on hearing this. Surely I couldn't be hearing them correctly? Don had told me that he took them to the airport. Finally the penny dropped and I knew that I had simply reversed roles with Celia; she was now the 'other woman' – to be visited clandestinely. That was our only Christmas together.

All Don's protestations of love for me could not overcome my shock at the lie. No relationship can survive deceit and this was the beginning of the end for us. Other factors were beginning to play their part too, and although I thought that we could, perhaps, survive this setback other things also stood in the way. Don was to be sent back to his Regimental Depot and it would have been almost impossible for me to go there with him. In London we could be anonymous, but not amongst his Regimental comrades. Also it was time for Fanny to go off to boarding school, and to lose her meant that I was to lose my little friend. When Don would not allow me to go to the school with her when she first went there, in spite of the fact that I had made all the preparations for her, I knew that this was the death knell of our relationship sounding loud and clear.

I really had no idea what to do next. I had had my twenty-fifth birthday by now and it seemed as though, when I should have been in the prime of my youth, I was in fact on the scrap heap. My 'sell-by' date had come and gone and I was heading for the back of the shelf. My parents were out of the country, and even supposing I had wanted to run home I could not. My friends were all married, except Pene, and I didn't feel that I could go back to that life which I had spent 'in waiting' for Don. I didn't want to live alone, but there were no old friends waiting for my return to the land of the living, nor any new ones acquired over the past three years. I had to have a job which was a way of life; a job which was more demanding than the average job; a job which provided accommodation. I thought long and hard and a few ideas came to me, but the one which kept popping back into my mind was the Women's Royal Naval Service. My mother had been a wartime WRNS officer, as had her sister (my godmother Barbie), and I thought that this might be the answer for me. In early 1970 I applied to join and in time I heard that my application was successful.

On the eighth of April, during our last month together, my paternal grandfather died. I had been very fond of him, although he was a cantankerous old man, and I wanted to be at his funeral. But I didn't want to see my father. I didn't want to tell him that it was all over between Don and me. I didn't want to tell him I was joining the WRNS. I was too upset to contend with his pleasure at my news. And then I thought of my grandfather and what a terribly difficult life he had led. He had been married for nearly sixty years to a 'society' American whom he married when she was only eighteen – eleven years younger than himself. She had led him a merry dance and had brought scant happiness into his life. For all the years I had known him they had led quite separate lives, yet under the same roof. Their home was not a happy place, and the only times they spoke were in terms of mutual dislike. He had become taciturn over the years, and who could blame him, for he had had to contend with a disloyal wife who never lost an opportunity to show her contempt for him. I had loved him, though, and I wanted to be at his funeral. My father had flown over from America and it was going to be impossible to avoid him. Don gave me as much moral support as he could and drove me down to Brighton, but he could hardly attend the funeral with me. I went in alone. Fortunately there was little opportunity for conversation at the church, and as soon as the service was over I slipped out to my meeting place with Don. I had barely spoken to my father.

Once back in Blackheath I had to turn my attention to the unhappy task of packing up. I had nowhere to put my possessions since the Chislehurst house was no longer available to me, and so I bought a Renault 4 car which was spacious enough to hold my various trunks and cartons. In May 1970, just over a year since I went to live in Blackheath, I put my things into the car and drove up to Cambridge to meet Don. He had gone to collect Fanny from her boarding school and I waited in a pre-arranged car park until they arrived. We spent one last day together, just the three of us, and at the end of that day I waited in the car park again while Don took Fanny back to school. He returned and we said our goodbyes. We cried, we hugged, we clung to each other. We had been defeated by circumstances. We had been worn down by events. We had waged a bitter psychological war with my father and still survived to be together. But there were casualties strewn all around us because of our love. That love was leading us down a blind alley, and we were now casualties ourselves. I was one of the walking wounded as I turned to get into my car in that Cambridge car park.

Chapter Six

Never At Sea

I drove in a daze, tears still coursing down my cheeks, to my aunt in Colchester – my mother's other sister, Joan. She was a good person to turn to with a broken heart, for she had had more sorrows in her life than she ever spoke about. She had been married, briefly, to a handsome Syrian gentleman who had swept her off her feet when she served as an occupational therapist in The Lebanon during World War II. She had returned to England before him, but he joined her there only briefly before moving on to America. From there he sent her a letter, addressed in her maiden name, in which he informed her that in accordance with the Koran he had divorced her simply by saying, "I divorce you, I divorce you, I divorce you" the requisite three times in front of a mullah. She had never been able to accept this, coming as such a complete shock as it had, and I think that over the years she came to regard herself more as a widow than a divorcee. She never remarried and had had no children. She welcomed me now and did her best to comfort me. But I was inconsolable – totally distraught and unable to believe that there could be any 'life after Don' for me. I felt as if I had lost a part of me. It sounds so corny, but that was just how it was. For three years I had lived with the sound of Don's voice on the telephone, the comfort of his letters, and, for the past year, his daily presence. Now there was the sound of silence all around me.

I stayed with Joan for a few days and I was grateful to her for providing me with the best comfort she could offer, although I was unreceptive to her contentions that time was a great healer. I couldn't stay long because I was off to join the Navy, or at least the Women's Navy, and time and tide wait for no man (or woman) when they have been called up. I had to drive to Reading to report for training at

HMS *Dauntless*, the new entry training establishment for the WRNS. I don't think that they had ever had a new recruit turn up in her own car before, much less with her entire worldly possessions stashed in the back. I presented them with an instant conundrum – what to do with my car, since there was no recruits' car park and I could hardly leave it in the road since it was so full of things. They coped admirably, although I cannot say the same for me since I think those four weeks at HMS *Dauntless* were the hardest of my life. Most of the girls were young and many had joined straight from school so they had less difficulty coping with the discipline. But for me it was almost unbearable to be marched and bossed about from the moment I got out of bed, in a shared dormitory, first thing in the morning until last thing at night. When we were not in the classroom, learning the ropes (literally), ranks and badges and various other things nautical, we were to be found scrubbing and cleaning. Never have I cleaned so much brass, washed so many windows and floors, and generally scrubbed out as I did during those four weeks. It was all supposed to be good for the spirit. They had to break you down before they could build you up. They were presented with a mish-mash of womenfolk, from all backgrounds and creeds, and their task was to turn us out all the same. A cohesive, disciplined 'herd of wrens'.

There were two other Direct Entry candidates in Warspite Division at HMS *Dauntless* in May 1970. One of them was a girl of my age called Vicky, and another was Lindy. The three of us were destined to become officers by the quickest possible means, which was the Direct Entry scheme. The fact that we would be officers within six months made not a jot of difference then. We were the lowest of the low and we were never allowed to forget it. It was hard, having come from a situation where I had been running a household, and looking after children for the past year, to this. It was dehumanising and I nearly didn't survive. Two factors saved me – one was forming a friendship with Vicky (who is now Nina's godmother), and the other was my car! We escaped once or twice for a drive. It restored our sense of sanity and made us realise that there was a world out there to which we would be safely returned one day soon.

We were kitted out in Wrens uniform, supplied with various other items for our personal use, such as kit bags, and taught how to make beds properly. We were inspected from top to toe, shown how to polish our shoes so that even the Coldstream Guards would have been proud to wear them, and taught how to salute. I'm sure it all had its funny side, but the humour escapes me as much now as it did then although Vicky and I sometimes laugh about the time we went out in my car and got lost while on the way back to the training establishment. We finally returned after the evening curfew and expected all sorts of dire consequences to come our way, like extra brass polishing for the next week – that sort of thing. I don't remember if it happened, or not, but I'm sure the dread of it was enough to ensure we were not late back again. There is no doubt that I have never experienced a longer month in my life, and it was with relief that we were finally passed-out as presentable enough for further training. The only sad thing about my departure from HMS *Dauntless* was the fact that the next stage of training was to be what was called 'port experience', and Lindy, Vicky and I were being split up into quite different Naval establishments around the country. I was going to miss Vicky dreadfully, now I only had my car to keep me going.

I was posted to HMS *Daedalus*, an air station in Lee-on-Solent for my so-called 'port experience', and as I was destined for the Supply and Secretarial Branch of the WRNS, referred to as the Pussers, during my time there I was moved around the various categories which fall under this general heading. For a week I was with stores, another with the catering branch, and some time was spent in the registry. I suppose I must have learnt something, but I was terribly unhappy. I was viewed with suspicion by the other Wrens, who no doubt thought, "Who does she think she is?", but neither they nor I could help the fact that we had little in common. It made me realise how comparatively tolerable HMS *Dauntless* had been. There I had not been alone socially and I became aware of just how much Vicky had helped me get through that experience. I think the reason that I remember so little about my 'port experience' had a lot to do with the fact that my mind was almost always with Don. I did what I had to do in a robotic fashion, just praying for each day to end and to be one day closer to the completion of this part of my training. Finally the happy day dawned when I drove my loaded car to the Royal Naval College, Greenwich, which was to be the location for that part of our training designed to mould us into officers.

We acquired little white tabs on our uniform, which identified us as officer cadets, and we were treated in a much more lady-like manner. But the best thing was that we were all much more of a muchness, and once again Lindy, Vicky and I were reunited. Actually Greenwich was really rather fun. It was stimulating and demanding, and although there were similarities with the training we had received at HMS *Dauntless*, it was all being done in the most wonderful surroundings which could not fail to inspire even the most lacklustre of recruits. Greenwich was the birthplace of Henry VIII and the place was steeped in history. Christopher Wren had built the present palace at the end of the seventeenth century, and since 1873 it had been used as the Royal Naval College for officer training. Between the years of 1708 and 1727 James Thornhill painted the ceiling of the Great Hall at Greenwich Palace, and this was where we ate all our meals on a daily basis. Now this is the stuff of inspiration if ever there was, and just being there lifted our spirits no end and made us feel a great sense of pride in what we were doing. The course work went ahead apace and it was necessary to work hard, especially if, like me, it was some ten years since participating in formal learning of this kind. I did enjoy it, although on my twenty-sixth birthday I had a fit of depression. This was largely due to the fact that I received a book (of poetry, what else!) and a card from Don in which he had written, *"J'espère"*. What did he mean by this? Hope for what, for whom and when? If this cryptic note was intended to lift my spirits, it failed miserably and only served to make me feel that my world had fallen in and that I would never climb back out of the mire. I was convinced that I would never find another man and make a happy family life for myself. I would never have children of my own. I was doomed to be a sour old spinster for the rest of my life and suddenly I felt trapped in a crazy world of overpowering discipline. I wondered what on earth I was doing and ended up, in tears, saying as much to the course officer in her study. She was pretty astonished and didn't really know what to say, other than that I was 'only' twenty-six and I didn't really have to start worrying until I was at least as old as she! Since she was a very beautiful woman in her thirties, I did in fact draw comfort from her words and after a polite sherry went back to my quarters somewhat comforted.

Vicky had another idea, designed to get me smiling again, and asked me if I had ever had a go on the Ouija board. I told her I had, in my flatting days, and she suggested we have a go now. Her choice of venue was the room in which, at one time, Admiral John Byng had been incarcerated prior to his execution in March 1757. He had been sent with an inadequate force to relieve Minorca and had fought a half-hearted engagement with a French fleet and then retired, leaving Minorca to the enemy. Found guilty of neglect of duty, Byng died before a firing squad. The episode prompted Voltaire to retort that the English found it necessary from time to time to shoot an admiral *'pour encourager les autres'*. It was said that Byng's ghost haunted the College, but none of us came across him during our stay. However, it was with some trepidation that we embarked on our chosen pastime and consulted the Ouija board. For a while, nothing happened, but in time our patience was rewarded and Vicky was told that she would marry a man called George, and I in turn was informed that the man of my dreams would be called – and here I lost the information, although I got some of the letters, which included a G, A, R, M and some Es. We laughed, saying that Vicky's man sounded rather boring and mine must hail from somewhere in darkest Africa! While I would hate to give the impression that I am in favour of the Ouija board, since I think it has the potential to be highly dangerous, it might be interesting to note here that fourteen years later Vicky married a solicitor called George and eleven years later I married a New Zealand diplomat called Graeme!

Our training was varied and interesting and, in the main, most enjoyable. One area I enjoyed less was the time spent on the parade ground with the Royal Marines drill sergeant. Although he tried hard to treat us with courtesy, there was always a touch of the "you 'orrible little women" routine. He must have trained us really well, though, because on completion of a diplomatic outing to Philips Electronics in Eindhoven (during our posting in Holland), we were boarding the official train to return to The Hague and the authorities had laid on a brass band to play on the platform as the ambassadors and their wives alighted. As I walked down the platform I found that it was impossible for me not to march in time with the music and, as I did so, make a little skip in order to be on the correct foot – the left one, not the right. I do hope nobody noticed, but for me it was a strange sense of the past coming up and hitting me in the face – or should I say the *foot* – twenty-four years later!

One of the final tasks to be completed at Greenwich was for each of us to deliver a ten-minute speech. We were all nervous about this although we had been given a free rein to choose our subject. Vicky chose 'Mary, Queen of Scots', my choice was 'Malaysia', but the best of all was the one chosen by Caroline, one of the youngest girls on the course. Caroline spoke for ten minutes on 'earthquakes', and her talk was not only informative and enjoyable but she also drew an extremely accurate map of the world in about thirty seconds flat. She had practised this for quite a while, but her efforts paid off brilliantly, and it was no surprise to any of us that not only was her speech the best, but she also passed out as the Top Cadet and walked off with the prize of a Canaletto picture of the Royal Naval College. To us Caroline became a 'marked woman' and we all felt quite sure that the day would come when she would be the Director WRNS. Little did we dream that when the time came there would be no WRNS to be Director of! I was more than a little surprised to know that I came second, but there were no prizes for that position.

In December, 1970, a Passing Out parade was held at Greenwich for the WRNS OTC 3/70. We were now Probationary Third Officers in the Women's Royal Naval Service and we all felt proud of our achievements. My parents had been in America for the past two years, during which time I had had no contact with my father, but his tour of duty there had come to an end the month before the Passing Out parade. Since I had now not only broken up with Don but had also successfully entered the WRNS, I had once more become acceptable in my father's eyes. Both my parents came to the ceremony at the College, after which we went back to the Chislehurst house in which they were now living once more. It had been a busy eight months of training and everyone was glad that a break for Christmas gave us time to recharge our batteries before commencing further training in the new year.

At the beginning of 1971, several girls from Greenwich assembled at the Naval barracks in Chatham for the Supply and Secretarial Course, and so it was with many friends that I was able to commence yet further training there. I was glad that Vicky was with me, once again, and it gave us a chance to cement a friendship which has lasted down the years. There was a lot to learn at Chatham, and, Vicky tells me, I worked very hard during that time, although I do not really remember doing so. It was different being on a course as an officer, and now we were fully integrated into Wardroom life we began to see that life with the Navy could be very enjoyable. There were many visits to other Naval specialist establishments organised and we began to get a more all round view of what we had embarked on, including, on one occasion, a fire-fighting demonstration. Time passed quickly, and before long we were waiting anxiously to know where we were all going to be posted. It seemed they didn't know what to do with me because in the event I was posted to the office of the Director WRNS in the Old Admiralty Building in Whitehall on a 'holding' basis to 'gain experience'. Whether this meant that I had failed the Chatham course miserably, I never knew, but I certainly felt like a fish out of water when I arrived at the office of the great lady herself, since there were no junior officers at all, only WRNS officers of considerable service. The worst of it was that there wasn't a job to do, and I spent most of my time as a fly on the wall trying to be as little of a nuisance as possible. It didn't do my confidence much good either, and the only time I seemed to be of any use was when a new advertising campaign was being launched and a nice new WRNS officer's hat was needed to feature in the advertisement. Well, I was your girl for that, no mistake, since I had just the very thing, hardly worn, especially since I was now back in civilian clothes while working in Whitehall. So my hat was chosen, above all others, as being the most suitable for the photographic session. Whilst it was quite nice to know this, when the advertisement appeared in the press, it wasn't enough to make me feel worthwhile! During my time at Old Admiralty I lived in the WRNS accommodation unit of Furse House which was almost opposite the Gloucester Road flat I had lived in in the mid-sixties. It seemed so strange to be back in my old stamping ground, and once again I thoroughly enjoyed being in London and rediscovering old haunts. After a short while in London I was posted to the Western Fleet Headquarters at Northwood, to be Personal Assistant to the Chief of Staff, Rear Admiral Ian Jamieson. There couldn't have been a nicer Admiral in the Royal Navy, and not only was I so lucky to have him as my boss, but his Secretary, a Lieutenant Commander called Peter Nelson, was just as nice. In no time at all we had formed a mutual-admiration society, and the Chief of Staff's office at Northwood was a very happy one indeed. These two officers guided me through my first job and made it an enjoyable and rewarding experience. Northwood was a hub of activity and there was never a dull moment. A NATO Headquarters was situated alongside the Western Fleet HQ, and so we had a variety of nationalities in the Wardroom which gave it a cosmopolitan and international air. I was starting to feel happy again and began to think that I would, after all, be able to rebuild my life into something worthwhile. I became familiar with my various duties and these included being responsible for a division of Wrens. One evening, while Duty WRNS Officer, a message came through that the father of one of the Wrens had died. It was going to be my unpleasant duty to tell her this and I suddenly wondered if I would do it right. On making enquiries, I discovered she was babysitting, for Peter as it happened, and so the duty Wren was dispatched to take over from her. The poor girl arrived, somewhat nervously, wondering what on earth the Duty WRNS Officer wanted with her, and I took a deep breath before telling her her unhappy news. I gave her her travel warrants and leave passes and made arrangements for her to get home as quickly as possible. I must have got it right because several weeks later I had the most charming letter from her mother thanking me for having broken the news so gently to her. It was a very humbling experience, coming from a lady whose life had just been turned upside down.

I gradually became more and more familiar with the place and all that went on there and began to know some of my fellow WRNS and Naval officers, but there was still a sadness within me which never went away. I tried to look at other men, but most of them were already married and I had no intention of going down that path again. I had one or two brief flirtations, but nothing meaningful and nothing which really enlivened my life. I was still lonely and spent much of my off-duty time by myself. But at least the days were good, and it was with pleasure that I went to work each morning from my 'cabin' in the Wardroom.

In the summer of 1971 I tried to get an indulgence flight to America. A friend from my Security Department days, called Daphne, had been posted to the Embassy in Washington DC and had invited me to stay. Indulging was no longer as easy as it had once been and this time I was not lucky. I had to pay for my air fare which, as I recall, cost eighty-five pounds. On a WRNS officer's salary of forty pounds a week this was not as cheap as it sounds today, but it was well worth the expense and I loved the States. Daphne took me for a wonderful drive down the east coast of America, and I saw many places of interest along the way, including Williamsburg and the Chesapeake Bay bridge. Before we left Washington she took me to the British Embassy to see around and meet some of the people. It's a pity she didn't suggest I call into the New Zealand Consulate General in New York when I went there on my way home, because had I done so I might have met my husband-to-be who was working there at the time.

I'd had a great holiday but I was happy to be back at Northwood again. This happiness wasn't to last though, and soon Admiral Jamieson was due to retire, and with his departure went too my only happy times in the WRNS. His successor was a different type altogether and his reputation as 'the smiling assassin' came before him to warn me of what was to come. The reality of the situation was far worse than the expectation and his 'bite was worse than his bark'. I could do no right, no matter how hard I tried. I never pleased him. Peter was in much the same situation, and his departure from the Chief of Staff's office came even more speedily than my own. Once Peter had gone I was really in a no-win situation for his successor was a high-flyer very much in the new Admiral's mould. When the Director WRNS visited Northwood she called on the Chief of Staff and subsequently requested that I visit her for discussions. I explained my situation and she was extremely sympathetic, which encouraged me, since I think she understood what I was going through. She arranged for my transfer out of Northwood and it was with the utmost relief that my time there finally came to an end.

I was posted to HMS *Raleigh* at Torpoint, near Plymouth. Now this was an adventure in itself since I hardly knew the west country at all. Being a city person I cannot say that I really found it to my liking and those wide open spaces did not do for me what they did for many others. Captain Denman was the Captain of HMS *Raleigh*, the Navy's new entry training establishment (the men's equivalent of HMS *Dauntless*) at that time, and he was another delightful person, in many ways like Admiral Jamieson. I had been appointed as his Assistant Secretary, succeeding Caroline, the Top Cadet from Greenwich. If ever there was a hard act to follow, then it was to succeed her. Not only did I have that fact to contend with but I also found myself working much more closely with the Captain's Secretary than I did with the Captain himself. The Secretary was very sad to see Caroline go, and who could blame him for that, but he did not attempt to hide his feelings and soon made it clear that he found me a very poor substitute. Of course, this did nothing whatsoever for my confidence, especially since I had just had a similar experience at Northwood, and soon I found that my working days were becoming a nightmare of insinuations and innuendoes. I became very defensive in my approach but because of the delicate situation of working, at least officially, for the Captain I felt that I had nowhere to turn for advice or guidance since I could hardly be seen to be critical of my superior, the Captain's Secretary. He found fault with me at every turn and soon I really hated my working environment. Fortunately I got on well with everybody else and had no difficulty in my relationships with all the other senior officers with whom I was also working quite closely. But my life became a real misery and I began to see little merit in working hard for a man who could only throw brickbats my way. Everyone knew what he was like, and many found him as difficult as I did, but only I shared an office with him.

We were always busy and working long hours and never more so than prior to an official visit by HRH The Princess Anne who was to lay the foundation stone for the new HMS *Raleigh* on the ninth of May, 1972. It was an interesting occasion and an honour to be involved with a royal visit. I received an invitation from The Right Honourable Julian Amery MP to attend the official ceremony and afterwards to sit at the same table as the Princess for the luncheon. Heady stuff for a newly confirmed Third Officer WRNS! That was a good day, but they were few and far between, and once the contractors moved in to start building the new establishment we seemed to live in a sea of mud. It got everywhere and soon the old wartime prefabricated huts which were the 'old' HMS *Raleigh* were even more depressing to live and work in than before. How I longed for the splendour of the Painted Hall at Greenwich, or the early happy days in the sophisticated atmosphere of Northwood. I began to feel as if I was in a rather dreary backwater, working long hours, and for what? There was light relief though, and all the other officers at HMS *Raleigh* at that time were great fun to work and socialise with. Flirtations here and there helped to confirm that I could still be attractive to men, but none of those men who came into my life at that time could heal the pain that was still within me. It was going to be a long haul to get over Don, but I would never have believed then that it was going to take ten years. From twenty-five to thirty-five I was out there in the emotional wilderness.

The training establishment worked on a termly basis and closed down periodically during the year, at which time we all took our leave. In July 1972 I was at home in Chislehurst for one such break and was therefore able to attend another Garden Party at Buckingham Palace with my parents. Having so recently had a royal visit to HMS *Raleigh*, I was being rather spoiled to be at the Palace again, but it was a real pleasure and honour to be there once more. When my father returned from America at the end of 1970 he had only one more year to do in the army. 1971 had been spent at the Ministry of Defence building in Berkeley Square from which job he finally retired after a career spanning some thirty-two years. Now he was a civilian but was doing a retired officer's job at the Army Museum's Ogilby Trust, the offices of which were situated in Whitehall. I think it must have felt just like old times really since he was right on the doorstep of his former headquarters of the Ministry of Defence.

While I was at Torpoint I met a Naval Surgeon who was taking a great interest in plastic surgery. He fired my interest in the prospect of having a 'nose job'. Having seen what could be done for Cilla Black I had long dreamt of a more beautiful nose and now saw my chance to make my dreams come true. I got permission to enter the Naval Hospital in Plymouth where this operation was performed. Some friends from HMS *Raleigh* visited me on the day of the operation, and one particular Schoolie (Instructor Officer Branch) thought that I needed cheering up and proceeded to crack jokes. I was soon splitting my sides laughing but in so doing dislodged the broken bones in my nose. I was panic stricken and a nurse was called. She was a boot-faced-old-so-and-so and refused to believe me and furthermore refused to call the doctor who had performed the operation. When he did see me, a day or two later, he confirmed my worst fears and said that yes, indeed, I had managed to dislodge his handiwork. It was, however, too late now for him to rectify the situation. The final outcome was probably overall an improvement, but my nose had a definite lean to port which was a cause of distress to me in later years. If only I had left well alone. If only I hadn't laughed so hard. If only I had managed to get the old bat of a nurse to listen to me when I knew something had gone wrong.

Vicky was curious to know how the whole thing had gone and inspected my face closely the next time we met! She was still in her original job at Manadon and we managed to meet once in a while, which I always enjoyed. Others from our course were nearby too, and one girl (another Anne) became a closer friend in those days than had been the case at Greenwich. She ultimately left the WRNS to marry a delightful Roman Catholic padre and she was destined to reshape the course of my life too, but this was for later.

After I came out of hospital I took a weekend break with my parents who had driven down to the west country for a holiday. On my way back to Torpoint I misjudged the narrow country lanes and managed to drive straight into a grassy bank, thereby buckling my Renault 4 rather badly. It took ages to mend and when I did get it back it somehow never felt the same. I didn't feel safe in it anymore and soon afterwards sold it and bought a shiny red Datsun Cherry. My Renault's departure seemed to represent another step away from Don, but in truth he was still never far from my thoughts.

Peter, my colleague from Northwood, had separated from his wife Pat, a very beautiful Maltese woman, and Pat was now living near Plymouth with the new man in her life. I used to visit her quite often and she would also be welcoming to any man who might visit with me. I think she was beginning to believe that if I didn't get my act together very soon I was going to be left behind. I was thinking that way myself too. Then one day I ran into Ian Glennie, whose father had commanded the Regiment when we were in Gibraltar. Ian was the Naval cadet whom I had come across in Trafalgar Square that election night back in 1964 when he and some friends had driven up from Dartmouth in a hearse. It seemed I was always bumping into him, rather as I had years earlier in Singapore. I was beginning to wonder if there was some sort of destiny at work here when I bumped into him again in Plymouth. We dated for a while, but there was a vital ingredient missing which can only be described as that necessary spark.

When I finally left Torpoint to go to the Staff of Flag Officer Submarines in Portsmouth I was twenty-nine years old. It was difficult, starting all over again in a new establishment, finding my way around and once again not knowing anybody. It wasn't a lively Mess, in fact it was depressingly quiet. Nor was my job anything to write home about. It wasn't a job for a WRNS Officer. Rather it should have been done by a rating, preferably one with experience in submarines. I could contribute nothing of substance as the 'O' Section Officer since the content of the work was technical. All I could do was pass papers around, in the hope that they would end up on the right desk. It was very demoralising. I was beginning to wonder if it was me that was not cut out for service life, or whether there was something lacking in either the training or the career planning. I did make some friends after a while and my immediate boss on the Operations side was a very nice Lieutenant Commander in charge of the Ops Room. Morley did his best to involve me and took me with him on a familiarisation visit to Faslane, the submarine base in Scotland. We got on famously and the best part of any day would be the times I had to go to the Ops Room.

While I was at HMS *Dolphin* I developed a gynaecological problem and was admitted to the nearby Haslar Royal Naval hospital for a routine operation. Immediately upon my return from the operating theatre I was told to get up and return to my establishment. I was still drowsy from the anaesthetic and couldn't believe that I was being told to get up and drive a car back to HMS *Dolphin*. Although I insisted on staying long enough to have a clear enough head to drive, this episode plunged me into another fit of depression and I felt that I was part of a very uncaring organisation. None of it seemed worthwhile any longer and my depression got the better of me. In the event I developed a post-operative infection and this may well have contributed to my debilitated state and my depressed frame of mind.

The cumulative effect was that I decided that I wanted no more of any of it, that life in the WRNS was no longer for me, and I decided to leave. The date of my release was the twenty-eighth of December 1973, on the basis of voluntary retirement. Nearly four years earlier I had run away to join the Navy, believing at the time that it would be the answer to my problems. I had been wrong and it was now time for me to 'pack up my troubles in my old kit bag' and once more head for home.

Chapter Seven

The Desert Calls

The time bomb was ticking away. 1974 had dawned and it was to be the year in which our family finally broke up. It had been weak at the seams for so long and, when I needed the support of a strongly knit unit, it finally disintegrated in front of my eyes. I was fast approaching my thirtieth birthday and clearly had made a huge mess of my life so far. Every time I nearly had it all, it was either whipped away from me or I turned my back on my achievements. I had never settled anywhere and it didn't look as if I was going to learn how to, even though I was long past the normal 'nest making' years. I knew that the traumas which had taken place in my life over the past seven years had taken their toll on me and that what I really needed was a long break away from it all. After spending January and February in Chislehurst, licking my wounds, I then went out to the Oman to stay with friends, Jack and Mary, who had been friends since we met in Malaysia twelve years earlier. In Seremban, Jack had been my father's number two, and his wife, Mary, was a young woman little older than myself. Now Jack was a Brigadier in charge of Dhofar Brigade, the Headquarters of which was in Salalah, running that part of the Sultan of Oman's Army which was fighting a guerrilla war against communist infiltrators from Aden (South Yemen), my old stamping ground. I stayed with them for one month and it was just the panacea I needed.

Mary asked me to bring out some rose plants from England and the variety she chose was the 'Peace' rose. It was quite a tricky journey, which involved travelling via Baghdad, and at one stage I was wandering about Baghdad airport between flights, sampling the revolting coffee which needs to be eaten, not drunk, trying to avoid the ogling eyes of several Oriental gentlemen of dubious intent, and all the while clinging onto several pots of Peace roses. I must have made quite a spectacle! Finally I got a plane to Muscat where I was greeted by an Army colleague of Jack's who kindly escorted me to the military flight which was to take me on the last leg of the journey, down to the army headquarters in Salalah. It really was an eye opener to be in the Oman in 1974. At that time the country was just emerging out of the middle ages into the twentieth century, oil having been discovered in the 1960s. It was one big construction site. And the wealth of the Sultan was obvious when one saw the number of Cadillacs parked outside the palace in Salalah – and they only belonged to the servants! Jack and Mary made me so welcome at Villa Dhofar, their army quarter near the beach. The latter facility could not really be enjoyed because, being a strictly Islamic country, we were not allowed to strip down to bathing costumes and go for a swim. However, there was a service club where we went to enjoy a dip, and to socialise generally with the other military personnel. But the first thing we did was to plant the roses in Mary's front garden, overlooking the sea. I couldn't help feeling that they were doomed from the start in that stark and harsh desert landscape. However, Mary was very optimistic that her fingers were green enough to see them bloom. I do hope they did.

I had a lovely time with my hosts, who showed me great hospitality, and who devoted much of their time to showing me around. We went on trips to Rayzut; to Arzat where we saw frankincense growing (the Oman is the only country in the world to produce gold, frankincense and myrrh, so perhaps it was the home of the Three Kings); Taqa and up the coast eastwards towards Juffa. It was all very exciting and we found ourselves looking round the local Souqs and admiring the exquisitely crafted silver jewellery, and endless brass ornaments. I was tempted at every turn, but in the end only bought a brass Arabic coffee pot which was encrusted with the grime of ages and which I had to spend days and days soaking in Coca Cola in order to finally see the beauty of the form underneath. An outing to the Royal Stables in Salalah was arranged and on another occasion we found ourselves being entertained to lunch on board the Royal Yacht, but, alas, the Sultan was not present! In fact there were several outings of a nautical nature and all of them were thoroughly enjoyable. I found myself not only on the Royal Yacht, but also on a Fast Patrol Boat, and an Arab Dhow. On each of these trips there was a charming host to look after us and everything we did helped pass the time in an entertaining and relaxing fashion. We had trips into the desert to admire the spectacular sunsets and to collect geodes, those magnificent rocks containing a cavity lined with crystals. Mary collected some enormous ones and I wished that I could too, but being mindful that I must get them in my suitcase I was restricted to a couple of small ones. The idea with geodes is that you either cut or break them in half, thus displaying the beauty which lies within. When I got back to England I took mine to a stonemason to be cut in half. One became damaged in the process, but I still enjoy the other which has been displayed on several mantel pieces around the world since I collected it in the Omani desert.

Without a doubt the most memorable of the outings was to go in a Beaver aircraft over to Habarut on the border with South Yemen where the fighting was taking place. Jack had told me beforehand that I could only go if I thought I could get through the occasion without needing to go to the loo, since there were no such facilities for women in the war zone! I wasn't going to miss such an experience for the lack of a loo and starting the day before I was extremely careful about how much I drank. Mary and I were kitted out in sandy coloured clothing in order to blend with the soldiers and Jack set off with his two 'desert rats' in attendance. The flight in the Beaver aircraft would have been enough of an experience, but more was to come when we reached Habarut. We climbed up into the gun positions and sat alongside the multi-national forces who made up the Sultan's Army, commanded by officers from the British Army. We could hardly be recognised as women, being so heavily disguised in our 'uniforms', and there was a look of surprise when we thanked the soldiers for their offer of a shared metal mug of steaming tea – our voices had given us away.

I don't know how long we had been away from Villa Dhofar, or whether it was that shared mug of fly-ridden tea, but the time came when I knew I was going to let Jack down and asked what on earth I could do about the need for a loo. I felt awful, it had been part of 'the deal' and I hadn't been able to keep my end of the bargain! Now there wasn't a dog's chance of keeping our identity as women under wraps as we walked into the desert in search of a bush, with a protective armed guard in attendance. The probing eyes of the enemy watch were on us, from their vantage points in the hills around us, and all in all I felt a complete and utter fool. Poor Jack, he must have wished he hadn't brought me on this particular occasion.

Towards the end of my time in the Oman Jack had to go north to the Jebel Regiment's Headquarters in Nazwa, not far from Muscat. He must have forgiven me for the episode in Habarut because he suggested that Mary and I join him for the long Jeep drive north through the gravelly desert which covers much of the country. The climate is dry and very hot and I don't think I have ever undertaken a more unpleasant journey in my life. We were very quickly covered from head to foot in sand. It got in everywhere. It went right through our clothing and rubbed and itched as we became hotter and hotter. It got in our ears, up our noses and, worst of all, in our eyes. When we arrived we were all totally white, from top to toe. It would be nice to be able to say that it had been a fascinating journey, which I am sure it was, but I am left only with the impression that I never wanted to see another grain of sand in my life after that drive. That night as we soaked ourselves in the shower, being clean again had never felt so good before. We were entertained royally in the officer's mess at Nazwa. They had all met Mary before, but I was a newcomer and was made to feel very welcome amongst all those women-starved males! It did my morale a power of good, in spite of the total lack of unmarried competition, and the whole fairy-tale Arabian-nights atmosphere quickly got through to me and I embarked on a holiday romance with one of the officers there. It was all quite magical, and I was swept off my feet by this handsome man who seemed to think that I was the best thing since sliced bread. It must have been the hot Arabian sun, but I did think, for one brief moment, that I had met the man of my dreams. We had enormous fun and Chris took me around and about and showed me the sights; one day to the deserted village of Tanuf, mysterious in its grandeur and solitude, another time to watch a firing drill at Saiq and yet another day, wandering about in the Souq at Nazwa. Mary and Jack had returned to Salalah, sparing me that ghastly return journey in the Jeep, and I had been sad to see them go. They had truly shown me a good time and I have never forgotten their friendship in those dark early days of 1974. The holiday had done me a power of good and had restored my confidence in myself. But it wasn't over yet and now it was Chris who was showing me a good time as I stayed on while waiting for my return flight from Muscat.

Travel agents didn't exactly abound in the wilderness surrounding Nazwa, but telex messages were being sent to establish the exact time of my flight from Baghdad to London on Iraqi Airways. There was some confusion owing to the fact that Iraqi Airways was about to start its summer timetable on the 1st of April, but finally we got news of when I should arrive in Baghdad from Muscat. Chris drove me to the airport in Muscat, which was another uncomfortable journey, and we left with time to spare to be alone together before I flew home. We had some difficulty checking into a hotel together, but we overcame that problem and made arrangements to meet again soon in London. When I got to Baghdad I discovered that I had been given the wrong information concerning my flight to London and that the flight in question would not be leaving for another three days. I had no alternative but to buy another ticket on another airline.

Once back in London I began legal proceedings against Iraqi Airways in order to recover the cost of the extra air fare. I didn't think that I had much chance of success, but to my astonishment I won the case and was awarded costs. It was a pity that there had to be that episode because it was the only hiccough in an otherwise unforgettably happy holiday. And I was in love, to boot! Shortly Chris would be over in England on leave and we would meet again. But when we did, he didn't look the same, in his London suit, and I gradually became aware that I had made a huge mistake. I couldn't return his affection any more. I saw the confusion in his eyes and the disbelief that I was no longer receptive to his advances, and I hated myself for causing him pain. It had been a holiday romance, without the happy ending.

When I came back from the Oman I had thought that Chris and I might have got married and that this would hardly be the moment to commit myself to another job and, besides, I had absolutely no idea what I wanted to do. So I went back to Chislehurst, once more, and waited for something to turn up. One evening my friend Pene (who had taken me in the night my father had thrown me out of my home) came round for dinner. The atmosphere was somewhat tense, to say the least, and as might be expected a difference of opinion broke out between my father and me. It wasn't long before Pene and my mother joined me in my altercation with my father. Nobody had ever agreed with his actions regarding me, and as much was said that night. He stormed out of the house and none of us knew where he had gone.

As it transpired, much later on, he had gone to his London Club. There he had met up with the husband of the woman he had fallen in love with back in 1957 (on the troop ship back from Korea), and with whom he was still in love. They had met, from time to time, over the intervening seventeen years, and their need for one another was still alive. From her husband he gathered that their marriage was over and that he was about to marry an Australian woman. The husband suggested to my father that he resume his affair once more and told him where to find his old paramour. What a blessing it was for him that my father turned up, like a bolt from the blue, that night. The timing couldn't have been better. They both liked to hear what the other had to say: the one saying that his wife was now 'free', and the other that he was now ready to leave his family and that his career constraints no longer applied.

The rest didn't take long. My mother was told to move as soon as she could find another place to live so that the family home could be sold. She was in shock. After thirty years of marriage she found that there was nothing she could do but accept the situation. She sought legal advice, from a High Street solicitor in Chislehurst, the very one who had won my case against Iraqi Airways for me. What she didn't know at the time was that this very solicitor was in the process of leaving his wife also and had no truck with the needs, or demands, of 'the wife'. My mother had a very raw deal indeed and was bundled out in the manner of old possessions no longer required. Her whole world was crashing about her and she had little to sustain her other than her inner strength. Her essential goodness came out in strange ways and she certainly did not fight for her rights. Nor did her solicitor. She was simply told to move and to divide all the household goods equally. This in itself was totally unjust since, over the years, she had been the one to purchase the household possessions with her inherited family money. My father always pleaded that his Army salary went little further than paying the bills. What was left over would only be enough for him to pursue his sporting activities and so, over the years, my mother bought the boring but necessary items, like curtains and furniture. She now set about dividing it all up. Silverware was carefully counted and put into 'his' and 'hers' piles, thereby splitting up matching sets. She even went to the extent of having the big blue carpet in the lounge cut in half. This was not the action of a bitter and twisted woman. It was the action of a scrupulously honest one, who, in her state of shock, was making unwise decisions.

This was hardly the moment for me to leave home. It was entirely too fraught for me to even think about what I would do with my own life. One day my mother came back to the house to say that she had found a lovely flat in the village, right by the golf course, and that she thought that she might be able to be happy there particularly since it would enable her to continue playing golf without any difficulty in getting to the course. She was mindful that now my father had left, which he had done with all speed, she was without a car. She had had a very nasty episode in America, where her Ménière's Disease had flared up unexpectedly while she had been driving the car. She had become instantly giddy, which is the nature of the disease, and had crashed the car. Mercifully nobody had been hurt, but it had been a salutary warning to her and she had never driven since. Now she would have to rely on buses. Anyway, she told me about this flat and said that she had already got the purchase in hand. The weeks slipped past and I helped her as best I could in the process of packing up her life. On the day she exchanged contracts on the flat, she and I went in to have another look at it. To our horror we found the place swimming in water. We simply could not believe our eyes and we both panicked at what we saw. My mother dashed down the street to her solicitor and asked if the papers she had just signed had yet been processed. They had not, and she withdrew from the deal.

It is always easy to be wise afterwards, but that was the biggest mistake my mother made. It was a lovely, three-bedroomed flat, and it would have been ideal for her at that stage in her life. The water problem was not serious, as it turned out, but that quirk of fate turned out to be a real shame. Had we gone the next day it might have been too late to retrieve the papers she had signed, and she would have discovered that the water pouring down the walls was simply from the person in the flat above who had left the bath running and forgotten to turn it off. Now she was really under pressure to move, and move quickly, since my father saw this as merely a delaying tactic. She rushed into the first flat she saw, which was much smaller and not nearly so nice. It was also situated on a steep hill which, once she was there, presented her with an ever increasing problem in walking to the bus stop. She was nearly sixty-three years old and already having difficulties with her feet. It was a crying shame that the first flat had been lost so unnecessarily. However, the die was cast now and we moved together into the new flat.

I stayed with her there for seven months, during which time I was making plenty of mistakes myself having got an entirely unsuitable job for myself in London. It didn't take me long to realise that my niche was not with Pencol Engineering Consultants, but it did provide me with the curious experience of passing the home of Lord Lucan, on a daily basis; an event which was heightened in curiosity value after he allegedly murdered his children's nanny and apparently tried to murder his wife, only to then disappear never to be seen or heard of again. Some while later I saw Lady Lucan, with her head bandaged, and while I felt guilt at my voyeurism, it was a strange sensation to actually see someone one was reading about in the papers every day.

During the month which elapsed between my leaving Pencol, and embarking on my next venture, I came back to the flat one day to find my mother was out. She had left a note saying that she had had to dash down to Maidstone where her mother was in a nursing home. My grandmother had taken a turn for the worse, at the age of ninety-three, and to my mother's everlasting grief she did not arrive in Maidstone before her mother died. None of the family were with her at the end and all of us were dreadfully saddened by this fact. She had been a wonderful mother and grandmother and was deeply loved by her family. She had been a widow for twenty-three years during which time she had been the stalwart of our family, seeing us through thick and thin and always being there for us. None of us could believe that we wouldn't see her again. During the months which had elapsed since my father had left her, my mother had been careful to explain that she was visiting without him because of this excuse or that. My grandmother never knew of my mother's deep sadness and that was how she wanted it to be. It was dreadful for my mother to lose her mother so soon after losing her husband. And now she was about to lose me too. Almost as soon as my grandmother's funeral was over I left England. It had all been arranged before we knew my grandmother would die, and it was with a real sense of sadness that I finally left my mother alone knowing that she had lost the three people who meant the most to her. Now she really only had her sister Barbie left.

During the time I had been at Pencol Engineering I had been casting my eye over the Sits. Vac. columns of the newspapers to see if

I could find a job overseas. My nomadic life was in my blood and I had itchy feet to travel once more. Nothing very hopeful came up, until one day I saw an advertisement for a job in Kuwait. Although it was now five years since Don and I had split up I had never really lost my need of him. I missed him all the time and longed to be back in his arms. I had not really lost touch with him either and somehow or other was always hearing how he was and where he was. I knew he was in Kuwait. And now I was looking at this advertisement for a job there. The temptation was too great and I applied. From the start it didn't feel right, but I was totally blinded by my need to see Don again and to be near him once more. The whole interviewing process smacked of something not being the way it should be, but I suppressed all my instincts and was simply determined to be successful in my application. And I was. In April 1975, just a couple of weeks after my grandmother died, I was winging my way to the Middle East once more.

When I arrived, late in the day, I was told that I must go immediately to work. I couldn't believe that I was expected to commence work the moment I stepped off the plane, but sure enough, that was what I had to do. I was taken to the offices of the Supply and Building Company and introduced to the boss, Omar Bakhir, to whom I had been appointed personal assistant. He was a Palestinian refugee, as were so many businessmen in Kuwait, and I quickly found that their attitude to work was very different from mine. The hours of work were from seven in the morning until seven at night, with a two-hour break for lunch. I also discovered that the area of Kuwait in which expatriate personnel live is some distance from the city. It took half an hour to get in to work in the morning, an hour to and fro at lunch time (reducing the lunch break to one hour) and another half an hour in the evening. So I was leaving at 6.30 a.m. and not getting home until after 7.30 at night. And all this was being done in the most extreme heat, Kuwait being one of the hottest places on earth. It was not the credo I had been used to in my life with the services, where often it had been necessary to commence work early because of the heat, but always there had been time later in the day to make up for the early start. Now I seemed to be copping it at both ends of the day.

I was never going to survive this pace! And it wasn't as if the work was interesting, because it wasn't. I found the world of importing and exporting deadly dull. I also found the fact that they impounded my passport extremely suspicious. Surely nobody had the right to deprive me of my passport? When I enquired why, I was met with a stony silence, or, at best, the mumbled words that it was 'the system' there. The flat I was allocated was brand new, which was nice, but then again that fact also had its drawbacks because nothing had been tried and tested, and, in a lot of cases, things didn't work. The plumbing gave problems, the electricity gave problems and the new appliances were often out of action. It was so frustrating to find, when I got back tired at the end of each day, that yet another workman had been into the flat and made the most appalling mess trying to fix this or that. I found I was too hot and tired to be bothered getting myself much to eat and too tired to walk to the shops for things I needed. The heat was so oppressive and draining that my life quickly became nothing much besides working and sleeping. I thought things might look up a little when, with the help of those who knew the ropes, I became the proud owner of a little car. But the pleasure was short lived since I managed to have an accident in it driving it back from the office on the first day I got it. It was hardly surprising, really, since not only was I driving on the 'wrong' side of the road to that which was familiar to me, but also I had hardly got my bearings on which road I should be taking. I had actually been stopping at a grocery shop, on the way back from work, when I misjudged distances and crashed the side of my car in! It was still drivable, though, but I wasn't at all happy as I opened a tin of baked beans for dinner on my return to the flat.

I thought it must be time to find Don. I started to make some discreet enquiries as to his whereabouts, but before I knew it the whole office seemed to be taking part in tracking him down for me! He rang me at work and I couldn't believe that the sound of his voice could set my heart thumping the way that it did. He asked me where I lived and said that he would be round that evening. When we met again, after those five long years, it was as if no time had passed at all. It was just as it had always been between us. The pain of losing him was washed away now that I was, once more, back in his arms. I didn't know whether to laugh or cry, but to me it was as if the clock had been turned back and we were just as we were. He wanted to know everything about me and all that had happened since we had last met. I hardly noticed his reticence with me in my sheer joy at being with him again. He started to take over, telling me of all the ways in which I had been foolish, not least of all in parting with my passport. He took me round to his house and got his houseboy to cook me a square meal, which tasted like food for the gods after all those scrappy meals I had made do with in my exhaustion. And then we talked. We seemed to be unable to get to the end of our sentences in such a hurry were we to catch up with each other. It all seemed so right at last and all my misgivings about what I had done in coming to Kuwait seemed to disappear in a glowing feeling of happiness to be back, once more, with the man I had loved for the past eight years. I was thirty now, and Don was forty-two, and I really thought that this time everything was going to work out right and I didn't try to silence the sound of wedding bells which started to jangle at the back of my mind.

Don hadn't told me much about himself though. He had managed to avoid my questions by quickly turning the questioning back to me. I really hadn't gleaned much about his private life, although I assumed that there couldn't be a woman in it since he had so readily taken me back to his house and had, the very next day, included me in a party he was giving there. He had also given a very good impression of a man who had been without a woman for quite a considerable time. How could I know that this was not the case and how could I stop my imagination from running wild when, as I thought, all my wildest dreams were about to come true? Don was gentleness and consideration personified and clearly had every intention of being 'the man about the house' so far as the practicalities of getting things working in the flat were concerned. He had been in Kuwait long enough to know how to get things fixed quickly and who to see about what and it was just what I needed. I had been suffering from culture shock since the night of my arrival when I had been whipped along to start work and had had few waking hours since, when not at work, to try to get my life running along proper lines. Now Don took charge and he worked miracles in no time at all. My happiness soared. He seemed to have all the time in the world for me. I felt totally at ease with him and at ease with the situation we were both in.

Then suddenly the bubble burst. I don't know what triggered it and I don't suppose I ever will, although Pene, who had also been in Kuwait previously (a fact which I had not known at the time) later on talked darkly about a one-armed Indian lady probably having something to do with it all. But the bubble had surely burst and the magic was gone. Now Don was doing his utmost to see me out of the country. He set about getting my passport returned to me with all speed, having issued dire threats to Omar Bakhir in the event that this was not done immediately. He also managed to dispose of my damaged car, but I never got to the bottom of how he managed that either. And, after he had seen me off at the airport, he arranged for my crates to be shipped back to London. The very ones which had not managed to arrive in Aden were now being shipped back from Kuwait, still packed as they had been in 1967.

I arrived back from my Kuwaiti fiasco a couple of months after I had left England. It was going to be another sixteen months before I had enough confidence in myself once more to embark on yet another adventure, but, on the plus side, it meant that my mother was no longer alone and I could continue to share in her life for a little longer. She was already unsettled in her flat and had decided to move and so I was there to help her into the next abode, another flat, but this time away from Chislehurst to nearby Bromley. She was destined to move three more times and it eventually got to the point that, while I was away, I was hardly ever able to visualise her in her surroundings!

For the sixteen months remaining to me, before I finally left England more or less permanently, I did temporary work again. I signed up with Brook Street Bureau and worked in another succession of offices; firstly for a firm of solicitors called Frederick Wills & Co.; then Ward Howell International, who were a firm of personnel consultants; on to the Architects Department of the Greater London Council; from there to the property developers Hartford & Co. and, staying with the property world, on to Mountbrooke Properties Limited. At this point I had a complete change of scene by going to the offices of *The Observer* newspaper, but it wasn't long before I found myself back with the personnel consultancy world of Douglas Llambias Associates, from whose offices I then went to the Estate Agents E A Shaw & Partners. Following these forays into London I had a local assignment for a while, at the Bromley Language Learning Centre, but the call of London came all too soon and I found myself attaining a degree of stability in the pleasant offices of Escombe, McGrath & Co. Ltd, the shipping agents.

During all these assignments I scoured the newspapers for jobs overseas but nothing appealed. While at Escombe McGrath I was given a range of papers by the people I worked with, but still nothing transpired. One week I stopped looking, principally because I was sick of the sight of job ads but also because my boss was away on business and I didn't, therefore, have access to so many papers. During that week my ex-WRNS friend, Anne, who had been working in Plymouth when I was at HMS *Raleigh* and who was about to marry her Roman Catholic priest, had been busy looking for me. She had spotted a Crown Agents advertisement for secretaries wanted by the Solomon Islands' Government in the Pacific. She thought it sounded like me and cut the advertisement out and sent it to me. By the time I received it I thought I would be too late to have much chance but it did appeal and I decided to try anyway.

The process of selection was fairly drawn out, and I gathered later that there had been three hundred applicants for the five jobs available, but eventually I heard that I had been selected to be one of them. Right from the moment I opened Anne's letter sending me the advertisement I had had a feeling of destiny about this application, and, now that I had been successful I was more certain than ever that it was right for me. While my application was being processed I had one more assignment with Brook Street Bureau, which was at the Royal Dental Hospital, at the end of which time I then moved Agencies and signed up with Senior Secretaries. They, in turn, sent me to Arbuthnot Securities Limited, a merchant bank in the City, where I stayed for the remaining three months before I left to get myself packed up for my big adventure.

July and August of 1976 were spent with my mother and generally shopping and packing for the Pacific. Two years had passed since my father had left, during which time I had had no contact with him at all, and it was getting close to the time when my parents would be divorced. As it happened, I was in the Solomon Islands when my mother wrote to tell me that she and my father were no longer married, and it was a strange feeling being so far away from home at such a moment in time. Before I left, however, I had to attend an introduction course at Farnham Castle which was designed to familiarise those people destined for far-flung corners of the world and give them useful tips and advice before leaving. It gave me a chance to meet the other girls selected to go and, indeed, to meet some people who had been living in Honiara for some time. It certainly sounded like an adventure, all right, and I came away with some small misgivings. But I didn't let these dampen my spirits and the feeling of destiny was keeping me riding high.

Friends came round to my mother's Bromley flat to say goodbye and I took the opportunity to record their voices on my new-fangled music centre so that I could listen to the familiar sounds of them speaking to me on the other side of the world! I did this again at Barbie's house, where she hosted a family farewell to me (which coincided nicely with her daughter Sheila's 17th birthday), but I found that everyone was shy of this new device and didn't really want to know what their voices sounded like! However, I persevered, and still enjoy listening to the tape. While I was there, Barbie handed me a letter which read:

> 29 August 1976. My darling Anne, I know
> how fond you were of grandpa and how much
> he loved you, and I thought you might like to
> have this little card which belonged to him and
> which he often used to read to Granny. I am
> sure that none of us will say all that is in our
> hearts today but you know that you will be in
> our thoughts and prayers, and we wish you
> every happiness in your new life. God bless
> you darling, Love Auntie Barbara.

The enclosed card she referred to read:

> And I said to the man who stood at the Gate of
> the Year, 'Give me a light that I may tread
> safely into the unknown.' And he replied,
> 'Go out into the darkness, and put your hand
> into the hand of God. That shall be to you
> better than light, and safer than a known way.'

I treasure Barbie's letter, and the card it contained, and it did sustain me in the years to come. But I treasure it all the more because Barbie died while I was on my way home, at the end of my three and a half year contract in the Solomon Islands, and although I did see her again after she gave me the letter, she wasn't there when I finally went home to introduce the family to my husband-to-be.

Chapter Eight
Into The Unknown

The first leg of my journey into the unknown took me from Heathrow to Los Angeles. In spite of my American heritage I have to say that I don't like the formalities involved in entering the United States, even when one is only in transit. I was treated with suspicion from the moment I landed. A couple of months earlier I had taken the precaution of getting a multiple-entry American visa stamped into my passport, but this didn't seem to make any difference on that day. It turned out that the difficulty arose because I had a one-way ticket from London, to Honiara in the Solomon Islands. As I was on a three-year contract it seemed eminently sensible to me that I had not got a return ticket at this stage. But the Americans didn't view it that way. I was told I must prove that I was on a three-year contract or else I would be deported back to London. The documentation was in my suitcase and the suitcase had not accompanied me to the terminal. After all, I was only in transit while waiting for another flight to Fiji. So my case had to be tracked down and brought to me to unpack and find my contract papers. Even when they saw them they only reluctantly allowed me to continue my journey. Mercifully I did not encounter this difficulty anywhere else I transited en route to the Solomons, and it was wonderful to arrive in Fiji, where I immediately felt the sweet, gentle, hibiscus-scented breeze blow away the jet lag and the irritation of the Los Angeles experience.

It had been a long journey so far and I had crossed both the equator and the date line. I didn't know whether I was on my head or my heels and I was very glad that my next flight, to the New Hebrides, was not until the following day. I was thankful for the chance to shower and sleep at a hotel that night, and when I awoke the following morning I felt refreshed and ready to see around a little, albeit not for long. It was an incredible experience to be in the South Pacific for the first time. Everything was different, and yet it also fulfilled all my images of how it would be. The smells were wonderful, made so fragrant by the exotic tropical flowers, and the people were so friendly and relaxed. Yes, that was really what made it so different. It totally lacked the frenzied, polluted lifestyle so familiar to those who live and work in the major cities of the world. And yet it had its own style of sophistication too and it catered for the needs and wishes of foreigners not to have to forgo modern conveniences. It seemed to me to be a little piece of Paradise, but then again, I have become very aware in the course of my travels that passing through, and living there, are likely to produce two very different experiences of a place.

Soon it was time to board the small plane which was to take me to Port Vila in the New Hebrides. In those days the New Hebrides was jointly administered by France and Britain and it was strange to arrive at the airstrip and be immediately aware of this fact. The police, who were quite in evidence, looked on one side just like British Bobbies, and on the other the image of Gendarmes! I cannot imagine how it ever worked, or how the French and British would have been able to jointly administer this tiny country. There was no time to see anything, other than the airport, but even so it was obvious that there was a clearly defined line of what was under British influence and what was under French. I'm sure that during the intervening years since independence the gentle Melanesians of these islands (now called Vanuatu) have managed to stamp their own personality on their country, but I'm equally sure that there will still be evidence of those earlier strange bedfellows. Port Vila had only been a short stop, and soon we were on our way to Honiara and the real start of my new beginning. It wasn't long before the little plane was swooping down into Henderson Airstrip on the island of Guadalcanal, on which island is situated Honiara, the capital of the Solomon Islands. As soon as the cabin doors were opened, the heat and humidity took my breath away. I had not expected it to be so bad, but just walking from the plane to the Customs shed made me feel like a wet rag. Someone from the Government was there to meet me, as were some of the girls I had met at Farnham Castle, and they took me the short distance into town and to the flat which had been allocated to me. On the way I was astonished to see so much evidence, still around, of the war in the

Pacific. We passed several rusting wrecks of ships and planes which had met their end during the bitter fighting which had taken place between the Japanese and American forces in the Battle of Guadalcanal during the Second World War. It was hard to imagine that they could still be there thirty years later, but little money had been available for the clean-up operation.

The Solomon Islands lie in the southwest Pacific Ocean about one thousand miles from the Australian coast. Today they form an independent parliamentary state within the Commonwealth. The chain of islands and atolls stretches for some nine hundred miles and covers a total area of ten thousand six hundred and forty square miles. The main islands are Choiseul, Santa Isabella, Malaita, Vella Lavella, Kolombangara, New Georgia, Guadalcanal, and San Cristobal. The larger islands have volcanic mountains rising to over ten thousand feet and most of them are thickly forested. There are few animals except wild pigs, large rats, the giant bats called flying foxes, birds such as pigeons and cockatoos, and many butterflies and other insects. The climate is hot, with a heavy rainfall, thus making it very humid. Most of the people of the Solomon Islands are Melanesians, with a few Polynesians on the outlying atolls. The islands were settled at least three thousand five hundred years before they were discovered by the Spanish explorer Alvaro de Mendana de Neyra in 1568. He expected to find great wealth there and named the islands after the rich King Solomon. The islanders grow root crops such as taro and yams for food, as well as hunting pigs and collecting fruit, and they catch fish from their beautifully carved canoes. They have many different languages (I was once told that it came to sixty-seven in all) but most understand pidgin English. Apart from food crops, the only important products of the Solomon Islands are timber and copra (dried coconut-kernels from which cosmetics and soaps are made). Commercial fishing is also a major industry with tuna the main fish caught. Some gold and silver mining takes place. From about 1850 the Solomon Islands were visited by 'blackbirders' who took away natives to work on the sugar plantations in Queensland and Fiji. At this time they were also visited by missionaries who converted them to Christianity. Between 1893 and 1900 the islands were taken under British protection, except the northern group which were under German protection from 1885 and were taken over by Australia in 1914. The islands' total population is about 292,000.

With Britta, Hildershiem — October 1948

With my mother, Cairo Airport — May 1951

Family reunion with both grandmothers, Barbie, paternal grandfather, Joan and my mother — Easter 1953

Revisiting house in Bad Oeynhausen at the age of nearly ten — May 1954

*HM Queen Elizabeth II visits Belfast (my mother and I
are on the far right) — August 1961*

With Warwick at Sungei Ujong Club — August 1963

On my final departure from Singapore — July 1964

21st birthday party continues at Gloucester Road flat — October 1965

British High Commission, Aden (centre left) — June 1967

WRNS OTC 3/70 Royal Naval College, Greenwich — December 1970
(Vicky – back row, 3rd left; Caroline - back row, far right;
me – back row, 3rd right)

My flat in Hibiscus Avenue, Honiara — September 1976

Independence Ball — July 1978

With Graeme at Tambea — October 1979

Nokkundi, Pakistan — last petrol stop before entering Iran
— March 1980

With Graeme on the occasion of our engagement — June 1980

Tony and Shirin help me celebrate my birthday — October 1980

So here I was, in this isolated part of the world, and I was glad to get to my flat after the long journey from London. Everything had been made ready for me, although it was to remain very bare and basic until my crates arrived from England. When they did arrive I was intrigued to see what I had packed up all those years earlier when they had been destined for Aden. Nearly ten years had elapsed since then, during which time my tastes had changed, but it was still fun to have my personal effects around me again and once I was able to place some pictures and ornaments about the flat it started to feel more like home.

I had been allocated a flat below a New Zealand girl who was a Radiographer at the hospital and, since I found that my job was to be to work at the hospital also, as secretary to the Chief Consultant Surgeon and Chief Medical Officer, I was lucky enough to get a lift to and from work with Eileen. She took me in the following morning and so began a completely new way of life which was to have plenty of strange experiences waiting for me. Here was I, straight from the demands of a busy working life in the City of London, where all the modern office machinery was always available, to a little island hospital in the middle of the Pacific where they considered themselves lucky if they had the most basic of their medical needs supplied. It wasn't a run-down shack of a place at all, it was beautifully clean and well run, but it was, nonetheless, very basic indeed. I also discovered that I was expected to be a medical secretary and be thoroughly familiar with all things administrative in this field. Well, I had certainly got a lot of jobs under my belt, particularly in the temporary field of work, but my medical experience was limited to a short time with the Red Cross, Farnborough Hospital Management Committee, Moorfields Eye Hospital and, more recently, the Royal Dental Hospital! These experiences, while useful, had not turned me into a medical secretary, but life is all about learning and so I quickly set about getting to grips with my new duties.

The doctors were really good to work for and did all they could to help me adjust to my working environment and involved me as much as they could in all aspects of the work of the hospital. I found myself watching operations, which made it much easier to type up the notes afterwards, and surprised myself at not feeling faint while in the operating theatre. It was a small, almost family-style business and we all became friends socially as well as at work. The Solomon Islanders were delightful as well, and Lillimay, the girl I shared an office with, was a sweet, shy person who talked a mixture of English and pidgin (the Islander's lingua franca, which is based on English, but which only has a passing resemblance to that language). She had a marvellous sense of humour, and I can still remember the look of shy pleasure when she had got me to the point of hysterical laughter.

Once I was beginning to feel more at home both at work and in my flat, it was time to be more independent in terms of transport. I decided that the conditions of the roads made the purchase of a new car unwise, and so decided to buy a second-hand Toyota 1000 for the grand sum of six hundred and thirty pounds. It was less than two years old and in good working order. I loved the little car and it served me well over the following three and a half years, rarely giving me any trouble. Kind though Eileen had been in giving me lifts in her car, it was nice to be independent in my movements once more. It gave me a better chance of getting to know people and exploring my new surroundings. Driving was difficult, though, since the roads outside the town area were mainly just clearings through the bush covered in broken coral. Swimming conditions were not good either, in Honiara itself, and it was necessary to drive some distance to Tambea before finding sandy beaches and good swimming conditions. There was a nice social club in Honiara, however, called the Guadalcanal Club (or 'G Club' for short), and once I was a member it meant that I could join in the various activities, such as tennis, swimming in the pool there, weekend film shows watched on a temporarily erected screen in the open air and, from time to time, parties and dances.

There was a small expatriate community, mainly involved in government jobs, but some in business as well. The traders tended to be mainly Chinese, but there were some commercial ventures run by Australians and New Zealanders also. The British expatriates were mostly involved in running various government organisations and Ministries. It didn't take long to get to know the majority of them and although they were principally married couples, there was also a small band of singles. We got together quite often and some nice weekend trips were arranged. Sometimes we went on a boat trip to the nearby island of Tulagi, which used to be the capital, and spent the day swimming, snorkelling, and the more adventurous amongst us would scuba dive in a stretch of water known as 'Ironbottom Sound' because it had become the graveyard of so many wartime ships and planes. The Foreign Office girls who worked at Government House were often the instigators of such trips and we were glad to join them on their outings. We took all our provisions for the day, since none would be available in the deserted places we travelled to, and it was fun to sit in the sun on a Pacific Island beach and think how many people we knew who would be glad to change places with us! For at least the first eighteen months of my time in the Solomons the magic did not wear off and I considered myself very lucky to be in such a lovely place, meeting and working with such nice people.

I had not been working long at the hospital when I discovered that I was in for a job move. One of the girls who had arrived at the same time as me, or just a little earlier, had decided not to stay and complete her contract. She was very much in love with a man back in England who, it would seem, was unable to give her the security in their relationship which she longer for. However, absence had made the heart grow fonder, and he had asked her to return to marry him. She didn't need any persuading and had more or less got on the next plane out. This had left a vacancy open to be the personal assistant to the Minister of Finance. Without due ceremony I was whipped away from the hospital and placed in the rarefied atmosphere of the Ministry of Finance. While I welcomed the chance to be more at the heart of government, I was sorry to say goodbye to the friends I had made at the hospital. I was going to miss Lillimay and her ability to make me laugh.

Ben Kinika, a Solomon Islander, was the Minister of Finance, and in him I soon found a new friend. We got on well, and in his eyes it would seem I could do no wrong. Needless to say, I found myself happy to be working for him. The work was very interesting, under the guidance of the Permanent Secretary, Tony Hughes, but the latter was a demanding boss, sometimes requiring hours of work which were hard to cope with in the tropical heat of the Solomons. Tony loved his work and seemed to live for it, in fact it appeared at times as though he was running the government single-handedly. This rubbed off on the inner sanctum of the Minister's office, and sometimes I felt as though this office was carrying the full load of government work. However, it was interesting to see how an emerging nation was handling its affairs leading up to full independence, which occurred in the middle of my tour of duty, eighteen months after I arrived.

But there was still time to socialise, and one of the pursuits I took up in the Solomons was bridge. It began as a social gathering in the home of another New Zealand girl who was the National Librarian. Sally was an excellent teacher and she got together a few of us who were interested to learn. The evenings were fun, and Sally was a delightful host, being also a first class cook she would turn on a delicious buffet for us when we came for bridge lessons. Also there, on those occasions, was the secretary to the Attorney General, an Irish girl of considerable character. Enya was what could be described as a 'hard bitten expatriate', fond of her whisky and cigarettes, but full of compassion and caring for others. She was definitely different from the rest of us, but she tolerated us well and indeed her presence would enliven the occasions. She was a great one for reading the Tarot cards, and often, when the bridge cards had been put away, would get out her worn pack of Tarot cards and start to tell us what the future had in store for us. On one such occasion she told me, with the utmost conviction that she would definitely not be wrong, that I would get my heart's desire 'in a two' (either two days, two weeks, two months, or two years). The first three possibilities passed as ordinary run-of-the-mill days, and I thought, "What a load of rubbish!" However, there had been something about the way in which she had made her prediction which made me write the two year anniversary in my diary, after which I gave little thought to what had been said. Two years later, to the very day she had spoken, I met my future husband at a party to say farewell to the British High Commissioner's secretary.

Life fell into a pattern of work and play, domesticity and chores mixed with socialising and fun. It was an easy life, in the main, although living so far from civilisation as we know it did have its frustrations. Mainly this took the form of not being able to get things one needed when one needed them. We all seemed to be waiting for the next ship or plane to bring us what we wanted, and often it did not arrive, having been offloaded for something more important. Many times it was basics which we lacked, but we all became adept at managing with alternatives available in the local market. The other problem was the smallness of the community and how, after a while, it began to affect people and they seemed to suffer a sort of madness brought about by living in such an isolated and far-flung corner of the globe. Marriages suffered dreadfully, with wives often not having the chance to do more than stay at home and look after the children. Boredom set in and they longed for some excitement in their lives. They got it, one day, in the form of a Royal New Zealand Air Force contingent sent up to do relief work following an earthquake. The earth moved for several people, in more ways than one, on that occasion!

The earthquake had been 7.7 on the Richter Scale and had been quite an experience for everyone. I was sitting at my desk when things started to move and the Solomon Islander working with me, Faye Saemala (who ended up being a Solomon Islands Ambassador's wife) looked scared and wanted to leave the office. In my total ignorance of serious earthquakes I thought her reaction rather premature, but once I heard the stampede of Ministry of Finance personnel thundering down the stairs, I thought that perhaps I had better follow her example. I wasn't a minute too soon, or perhaps I was, because I got crushed in the sheer volume of people rushing to get out of the building. I seemed to be carried down the stairs, rather than running, and eventually ended up face down in the car park outside the building. There I had the extraordinary experience of lying not far from my car as I watched it jump up and down, along with a line of others nearby, all jumping sideways nearer to where I was prostrate on the tarmac. It was frightening. But it didn't last long enough for fear to register. When it was over, the people gradually shook themselves down and slowly began to file back into the building. It had been a big quake, there was no doubt about that, but each of us was too engrossed in our immediate surroundings to imagine what damage had been done elsewhere. Luckily the Ministry of Finance building survived undamaged, as did most buildings in Honiara apart from the Hong Kong & Shanghai Bank, which had its vaults exposed, but the chaos inside the building was something to behold. Filing cabinets, which had been open at the time the earthquake hit, had fallen over and deposited their contents on the floor – papers and files and documents were everywhere. It was an organised secretary's worst nightmare. Being such a newcomer to this type of phenomenon didn't help either, because my first reaction was to clear up. This I did with a vengeance, determined to create order out of the chaos around me. No sooner had I made a creditable start than Tony came in and asked me if I thought my flat would have survived OK? My flat! I hadn't given it a moment's thought. Tony suggested that I stop what I was doing and go to see, but I think I was out of the door before he had finished his sentence.

It was heartbreaking to walk inside and see the contents of my kitchen cupboards, my dinner service and glassware, which had only so recently been unpacked from its ten years in storage, smashed on the kitchen floor. Sugar spilt everywhere together with flour and other dry items. All that had survived was the contents of the fridge since that was the only door which had not flown open. My clearing-up instincts came to the fore once more and I set to to rectify as much of the damage as I could. Once the worst of it was done I returned to work and told Tony what I had found. He said, "You didn't clear it up, did you?", to which I replied that yes, I had. "That's a pity," he retorted. "There are bound to be aftershocks which could cause just as much damage to happen again." He was right, of course, and when I returned home at the end of the day the shaking had created havoc once more. These aftershocks actually continued for a period of three months. It had all been an experience but one which, on balance, I am glad that I had. Sadly twelve people were killed during the earthquake and two thousand were left homeless but given the severity of the earthquake, it might certainly have been worse. The New Zealand helicopter crews were able to rescue those islanders who had become trapped and brought them to safety.

Several marriages which had been in trouble before the earthquake broke down completely after the event. One wife left to go to New Zealand with one of the aircrew and a chain reaction was then in place which ended up more like a wife-swapping session really. Various husbands now spent more and more time with the singles group and, almost inevitably, I found myself entangled with one or two of them. There were moments when it seemed to be serious but on reflection it was more a case of the men being on the rebound. Other men drifted in and out of my life, some for an evening only, but in the main I spent my time with married friends, or in a group. Now that I was at the Ministry of Finance I began to get to know some other people better than I had before, and one couple became good friends. Brian was the Auditor General, and he and his wife Evol (love spelled backwards!) were from South Africa. They were bridge enthusiasts and I would play with them sometimes, although I cannot imagine how they put up with my standard of play when they were such good players themselves. It was nice to relax in their company at the weekends, swimming in their pool which overlooked the Pacific Ocean, and enjoy Evol's delicious meals, which were particularly welcome since I tended to make little effort for myself. One day I decided that I had accepted so much kind hospitality from friends that I must do something to reciprocate. Other friends, Tony and Dodo, kindly offered to let their house be used for the party I planned, and I was grateful to them since my flat was far too small. I decided that it would be a 'Pyjama Party' and everyone who came went along with the theme. If there had been any likelihood of the party getting off to a slow start it was immediately dispelled at the sight of senior officials in their pyjamas! We all had a good laugh at each other, and the whole evening went extremely well.

I was often asked to attend dinner parties, which I thoroughly enjoyed, and none more so than the occasion when the Under Secretary at the Ministry of Finance was entertaining Tarquin Olivier, the son of Lord Olivier. Tarquin Olivier was in Honiara in connection with the setting up of the Solomon Islands' new currency, which would come into place following independence. Having been a lifelong fan of his famous actor father, I was extremely excited at the prospect of meeting him. When I found myself sitting next to him, however, I felt very inadequate for the task of making interesting conversation with someone who must be used to talking with the world's most glamorous people. But that problem paled into insignificance when the next one came along. On entering my flat one evening I became aware that things were not in their right place. Someone had been moving things about in a very strange manner. Although I had a Solomon Islands housegirl who came in for about an hour a day, I knew that Ellen would not have left things as I found them. I was mystified. As the days passed things got worse and eventually I realised that there were teeth marks all over my plastic containers, none more so than my small rubbish bin. Something was in my flat and it was trying to eat its way into my storage containers! When I looked around to find out what on earth it could be I discovered that the 'something' was hiding in the far recesses under the laundry sink. There was a frantic scrabbling sound, but I could see nothing. I didn't feel I could share my flat with whatever it was and that weekend I went to stay with friends. On Monday morning I managed to get someone from PWD (Public Works Department) to investigate. They found an enormous rat, described to me as the size of a cat. It took three men two hours to catch it. It was ghastly to think that I had had this animal in my flat for the best part of a week and there was still plenty of evidence around me of the damage it had done. The disinfectant bottle came out and I scrubbed my flat from top to bottom, but I still had to look at plenty of Tupperware which the rat had gnawed in its frenzied attempt to get to my food.

It had been a salutary warning to me but one which did not prepare me for worse in store. Another evening I was preparing something to eat in the kitchen when an enormous snake, about twelve foot long, slithered into the room. I was transfixed with fear, but not for long, and all I could think to do was to get out of its path. I leaped up onto the kitchen bench and screamed out of the window up to Eileen in the flat above me. Mercifully she heard me, and as we discussed what was the best plan of action I saw more and more of this huge snake slithering on and on into the kitchen, heading for the open bedroom door. Since it was evening time and neither of us had a telephone, Eileen decided that the best thing would be for her to go over to the G Club to find some men to come and help. There were no macho men there that night, not a single tough Aussie or Kiwi who felt inclined to test his manhood against this huge snake invading my space! One of the Solomon Islanders suggested that he contact the 'Snake Catcher', and this seemed an excellent idea to Eileen. She left him to find the man I needed, and returned to tell me what had happened. By this time the snake had entered my bedroom and I had plucked up enough courage to come down off my perch to close the bedroom door. I was shaking with fear and shock. It had been so big and so evil-looking but, thank God, Eileen was now back to tell me that help was on the way. Eventually the 'Snake Catcher' arrived, with little more than a stick by way of 'specialist tools' and we left him to deal with his prey. We were waiting down in the carport outside the block of flats when the man emerged with this huge reptile wound round and round his stick. It was a python and, apparently, not poisonous, but its sheer size had been enough to scare the living daylights out of me!

It was time to take a long hard look at the cause of all these unwanted visitors entering my flat. It didn't take long to realise that they were entering by climbing up the frangipane tree, the branches of which reached over to my balcony. I had always been so delighted that my balcony had been thus enhanced, but now I could not wait for PWD to return and lop the branches down. I was relieved, on my return from work the next day, to find that several metres now stood between my balcony and the nearest branch. Perhaps I was safe at last, but I had to get PWD back many times to lop the branches once more because in that tropical climate the branches did not take long to grow again.

I had been in the Solomons just over a year now and was beginning to feel in need of a break, although I knew it would be another six months before I would actually be able to get away on holiday. But there were public holidays which enabled one to get away for a long weekend and four of us girls decided to take a trip to a real piece of Paradise, called Tavanipupu. A British expatriate by the name of Charles Humphries had bought a property in the south eastern area of the island of Guadalcanal and had turned it into a simply wonderful little holiday retreat. He had built a magnificent house for himself, up on the hill overlooking the sea, and on the beachfront had built two or three chalets for visitors. The sand was pure white, the sea deep and clear. It had not taken long to fly there but it seemed to be off the end of the world and it was the most beautiful sight I had seen since I lived in Malaysia. Nobody was there except Charles and his wife, and the four of us. We completely switched off, spending our time reading, swimming, sunbathing, snorkelling and taking the few days very, very slowly indeed. It was the most beautiful place imaginable and just what we all needed after the small-town atmosphere of Honiara, along with the recent horrors of rats and snakes in my flat. We came back thoroughly refreshed, but it had been hard to tear ourselves away from such a magnificent corner of the Pacific.

The few months I had to wait before going on my mid-tour leave back to England passed quickly enough, and during that time I managed one more weekend visit, to Auki on the island of Malaita. It was interesting to see the second-most-important centre of the Solomons, but it wasn't a patch on Tavanipupu! During those last few months I had been giving a lot of thought to the planning of my mid-tour leave (it was a common pastime amongst the expatriate community) and I managed to put together a very nice itinerary for myself, and as the months turned to weeks and the weeks turned to days I just couldn't wait to leave the islands I had lived on for the past one and a half years. Suddenly it all seemed so small, so insignificant, and above all, so far away. I was beginning to wonder what was happening in the rest of the world. Although there was the BBC Overseas Service to listen to on the radio, the reception was so poor that it was hard to concentrate on the words coming over the crackling airwaves. There were also airmail editions of newspapers to read, but somehow the events taking place in London, Washington, Paris and New York took on an un-reality when viewed from those sleepy islands in the Pacific. Gradually, over time, the rest of the world had slipped away from me and I no longer felt that I was a part of the real world at all. It was definitely time to get back in touch with my roots. I didn't want to end up a beachcomber!

Chapter Nine
'In A Two' Comes True

When the time of my departure on leave arrived I was more than
ready for it. I felt very tired from eighteen months of working, in
tropical conditions, without a holiday. Some of the offices and some
of the residential accommodation had air-conditioning, but it was not
widely available. I had not been one of the lucky ones, and as time
had passed I found it more and more difficult to cope with the climate.
My clothes and shoes had gone mouldy, my books smelt damp, and
there was an overall deterioration in my possessions generally. They
had a tired and limp look about them, which I felt I reflected myself.
I had had the additional problem of the rooster. My flat backed onto a
local smallholding where they produced fruit, vegetables, and eggs,
which were sold locally. The rooster woke me with his loud
protestations that the new day had dawned, day in, day out, without
even a break from the noise at the weekends! I longed for a lie in,
undisturbed by his crowing, and I longed for some cool air to breathe.

On the second of April, 1978, I arrived in Hong Kong, via
Sydney, on the first leg of my journey home. I had gone to Hong
Kong to spend ten days with Vicky, my WRNS friend, who was by
now posted to that lovely island. Although she was working we
managed to spend a lot of time together and thoroughly enjoyed
catching up with each other's news. Vicky was living in, as I did too
while I was with her, and it was lovely to be back in a Naval
environment, and my visit coincided with a Mess Dinner in the
Wardroom, which I thoroughly enjoyed as well. Vicky took me
shopping, in all her favourite haunts, and one of the things I bought
was a jade flower arrangement. I knew I couldn't carry this round the
world with me, so I made arrangements for the store to send it back to
me in the Solomon Islands. Inevitably it arrived broken, and so I took

it to my friend Brian, the Auditor General, who was a dab hand at mending things. The repair work he did has withstood endless moves since then, and every time I unpack it, in a new posting, I think of Brian and his patience in putting the pieces together again for me.

Most of the time Vicky and I were together was spent talking. It was a luxury to have a natter with a close friend and I had missed Vicky during the time I had been in the Solomons. We made up for lost time and seeing Hong Kong again took second place to sitting and chatting. I did find time to revisit my uncle Bob's grave, though, and I was glad that I now had a second chance to place flowers there on behalf of his family who were unable to do so. Unlike my first visit, I was now older than he was when he died, and it was tragic to think that he had been deprived of his life at such an early age. During my visit Vicky took me to a Chinese fortune teller who, as it turned out, made some fairly accurate predictions, one of which was that I would be married in 1981. He also said that I would die at the ripe old age of eighty-seven, so perhaps Graeme and I will celebrate our Golden Wedding Anniversary together after all!

The ten days in Hong Kong had flown past and soon it was time to leave. My next stop was Bangkok. Bangkok evoked images of the exotic East in my mind, and I had always wanted to go there ever since my parents had done so during our time in Malaysia. However, it wasn't really a place to be travelling alone, and glad though I was to have finally made it to Bangkok, the few days spent there were somewhat lonely. I did fulfil dreams of seeing exotic places such as the Temple of the Reclining Buddha and the Marble Temple, along with familiar tourist sights such as Thai Dancing, the Royal Palace, and the floating market (which is literally, as the name suggests, a market where all the stallholders are on boats). The Thai people were really friendly and I was delighted that I had some success in tracing the family of Pimulpun Kitasanka (my friend Pam from happy Baston days). I had hoped that Pam might be in Bangkok, but I was told that she had married an Englishman and they now had a small daughter called Jasmine and were living in London. Pam would have to wait for another day.

At the airport, on my departure from Bangkok, I was idly passing the time while waiting for my flight to Tel Aviv when a young man started to be exceedingly overfriendly. He was obviously a New Zealander, and I was (in true British fashion) quite taken aback by his

'G'day Sheila' attitude! To say that I behaved in a thoroughly snooty fashion would probably be an understatement, but that was, undoubtedly, my reaction to his forwardness. He looked very hurt, which surprised me somewhat, but he definitely had the last laugh. It turned out that he was Neville Hill, who worked for Solair and was my travel agent in Honiara, whom I knew moderately well socially as well as in his official capacity, but whom I had totally failed to recognise 'out of context'. If nothing else, it showed that I had managed to completely switch off from the life I had left behind in the middle of the Pacific Ocean. I was soon to be reminded of it again, though, because in Tel Aviv I stayed with Beverly who had previously been the secretary to the Australian Commissioner in Honiara (but was now working at their Embassy in Tel Aviv), and she was keen to have news of everybody she had known there. Beverly was kindness personified. She gave me a grand welcome with the news that she was taking local leave to drive me around the Holy Land. But first I had to get through the immigration formalities at Tel Aviv, and if I had thought it difficult to get past the Americans in 1976, it was nothing compared to entering Israel in 1978. There was a very long wait while they removed my Carmen rollers from my suitcase to have the security people inspect them for hidden explosives, cameras - who-knows-what?

Once free of the airport, Beverly took me to her flat which was a bright, light and airy apartment in sprawling downtown Tel Aviv. After a refreshing shower and delicious meal I began to savour, with excitement, the prospect of being in the Holy Land. Our week-long tour began the next day, and Beverly took me to all the places I had hoped to be able to see, plus many more besides. We went first up to Nazareth, where the Angel Gabriel appeared to Mary, and to the place of Joseph's carpentry shop and to Mary's well. Then to Tiberias on the Sea of Galilee from where we drove south, seeing much of interest on the way, to Jericho. From there it wasn't a long drive to the Dead Sea, where I experienced the strangest of sensations in being unable to sink into the water, and I came out feeling thoroughly sticky from the concentration of salt. Our next stop was in Bethlehem, to see the place where Christ was born, and then to Jerusalem, where we spent much time seeing all the wonderful historical and biblical sights. The Via Dolorosa (meaning 'sorrowful way', and up which Jesus Christ reportedly carried His cross) seemed a more moving memorial to

Christ's crucifixion than the Church of the Holy Sepulchre, which seemed to be like any other tourist attraction – totally ruined by the tourists! The tour had been brief, to be sure, but since Israel is a small country it is possible to see much of it in a comparatively short time, and this we had done. I felt inspired by the rugged countryside and all the wonderful Christian sights I had seen, and was enormously grateful to Beverly who had made it all possible. It was time to go home, though, and Israel was my last stop before flying to London on the twenty-seventh of April, nearly four weeks after leaving the Pacific.

The whole of May, and the first week of June, were spent with my mother in Bromley. I think I just slept the first week back, so tired was I not only from my working life in the Solomons, but also my travels so far. After that it was time for catching up with friends and family and generally finding out what had been happening in the world of which I had not really felt a part. The other pressing need was to get to the shops. There was very little clothing available in Honiara, and since my things had deteriorated so much, it was necessary to shop until I dropped. Not that I really minded, as it was a wonderful excuse to be able to say that I was fitting in all my shopping for the next year and a half, but it was a pity that it had to take up so much of my time at home. My mother's sister, Barbie, came over to see us, and with her she brought her daughter, Sheila, and Pam, the mother of my cousin Brian who had been with me in Aden. Pam had brought Karima (Brian's fiancée) along too, and so it was good to be able to catch up with some of the family's news. I had no idea it was to be the last time I would see Barbie. She seemed fit and looked well, showing little sign of the years she had battled with breast cancer. Before I left Bromley I had one very special visitor, Ben Kinika. My boss was in London attending a Commonwealth Finance Ministers' meeting, and I was delighted when he managed to find time to slip away and visit me at home. It also gave me the opportunity to introduce him to my mother, who was glad to have met him.

In early June I began my journey back to the Solomons, but it was to be a much slower journey than that which I had made nearly two years earlier. My first stop was to visit Anne in Ireland — the WRNS friend who had put me onto the Solomons job in the first place and who had subsequently married her Roman Catholic priest. I hadn't really known Ken, but he was a delightfully entertaining person, as is so often the case amongst the Roman Catholic clergy. He was now making a living in the wilds of Donegal as a seascape artist. His father, before him, had been an Irish artist of some considerable note, and, in the years since I visited them in 1978, Ken has earned a very creditable reputation for himself and received commissions from as far afield as the United States. Anne was pregnant and they were both as happy as Larry in a life which, for Anne anyway, was far removed from what she had known before. The few days I spent with them passed very pleasantly, not least the time spent listening to Ken and his Irish way with words.

My mother was coming with me on the next stage of the journey and we had arranged to meet up at Heathrow for our flight to Toronto. It had always been a dream of mine to see the Niagara Falls, and this we did together. The Falls did not disappoint us at all – they were every bit as spectacular as we had imagined them to be. Although why my mother had not been there already, during her time in America, I am not quite sure, but possibly her travelling had been curtailed on account of the bouts of Ménière's Disease which had plagued her there. We should have seen more of Canada, having got that far, but the days of my leave were ticking by and I could not spend more time there if I was to complete my schedule. From Toronto we flew to Atlanta to visit cousins in Rome, Georgia. This was the main event of my return trip, and a wonderful opportunity for my mother to have a holiday which she almost certainly would not have undertaken on her own. But as soon as I arrived in America I realised I was going to have to overcome a rather basic problem. How to cash my traveller's cheques? Since I had obtained my traveller's cheques in Honiara I had gone for the simplest option, which was to get them in Australian Dollars. Oh dear, the Americans didn't like them one little bit – about as much as they had liked my one-way ticket to the Solomons, in fact. My mother was able to help me to some extent, but only to begin with. I was certainly going to have to get to the bottom of this problem if I stood any chance of continuing on with my holiday. I quickly discovered that no bank would touch them with a barge pole, and it was such a pity to arrive with the cousins and confront them with this problem so soon. But I couldn't manage without any money, and so it was merciful that Yancey was prepared to cash the cheques into his own personal account, thereby putting me in funds once more. But I had had another eye-opener in discovering the American reaction to dollars which were not of the green-backed variety.

Elizabeth and Yancey were cousins, not only to me (through my paternal grandmother) but also to each other. The three of us were descendants of Colonel Daniel R. Mitchell (1803-1876) an attorney, planter and ferry operator who, in 1834, helped found Rome and gave the city its name. This shared ancestor, who later commanded a volunteer company, the Mitchell Guards, during the American Civil War, is also credited with marking off the city-to-be into building sites and drawing the city's original map. So, here were my American roots, and we were given a right royal welcome by Elizabeth and Yancey and the good burghers of that town in the Southern States of America. Elizabeth had arranged a tightly packed schedule of social events, mainly in the first week when both my mother and I were there together, and I think we must have met everyone who lived in Rome in those days! The hospitality was incredible, and it was definitely expected that all invitations be accepted, without exception, to the point when I almost longed to leave in order to have a few quiet moments to myself. We had never experienced anything quite like it before, that famous southern hospitality certainly had to be seen to be believed. The culmination of dining here with Miss So-and-so and taking tea with Miss Someone-else (all married ladies seemed to go by the title of Miss) was a party put on by Yancey and Elizabeth just before I left to which the descendants of other founding fathers were also invited, along with other relations too numerous to have been able to work out the connection. It was an incredible end to an incredible week. For two quiet English women to be so fêted in this little corner of America had been an experience which neither of us will ever forget. It had been both fascinating, and totally exhausting.

Although it was very sad to be saying goodbye to my mother and also my kind cousins, I was ready for a break on my own by this time, and after a week in Rome I headed off to Mexico. My mother remained in Rome for a further ten days and, she told me later, had a much quieter time and really enjoyed being able to spend time with the cousins in their beautiful home. Meanwhile I was checking into a somewhat uninspiring hotel in Mexico City and wondering if being on my own there was such a good idea after all. However, having got this far I knew I must make the most of my opportunities and set about finding out what tourist attractions I would head for first. A coach trip seemed to be the answer, and so off I set to take in the sights of monasteries, cathedrals, gardens, Quetzalcoatl Temple, pyramids of the Sun and Moon, and the silver works of Taxco. It was all I managed to do, because that night, on my return from the coach trip, I broke a glass in the bathroom. In the process of clearing up the mess I got a piece of glass in my foot, although at the time I thought that I had only cut it. It hurt sufficiently to make sightseeing impossible, and so for the remaining day or two I simply stayed quietly at the hotel. What a shame to have missed the chance to explore more of the relics from the ancient civilisations of the Toltecs and Aztecs. I had to make do with buying a souvenir, passing 'Go' (but not, unfortunately, receiving two hundred pounds from the bank!), and heading for the next square on the board – Los Angeles.

By the time I returned to America, where this time I was allowed to enter the country without let or hindrance (no doubt because I was travelling on a round-the-world ticket which started and finished in Honiara), I became aware that I was going to have to get medical attention for my foot. I was directed to a hospital where the glass was removed and the relief this afforded me was immediate. Being somewhat overcautious I enquired of the doctor whether he thought he had got all of the glass out. I was rather amazed when he replied that he did not know if he had or not. I couldn't understand this reply and eventually had to have it explained to me that had he said 'yes' and had it then transpired that he had not removed all the glass, I could have sued him for some vast sum of money. By giving me that non-committal answer he was saving himself from the nearest lawyer who would have been happy to take him to court, on my behalf, for every penny he had! It was a new philosophy to me in those days and one with which, even now, I have difficulty identifying. Thus glass-free, I ventured forth to Disneyland, where I soaked up yet another, as then alien, American culture – the Theme Park Personified. It was a great experience, and I was not at all sorry that I had decided to do this, although I had wondered if it was going to be too childish an experience on my own. Not a bit of it. Disneyland is for everyone, young or old, and I thoroughly enjoyed the two days I had there. I was beginning to get agitated, though, for my leave was almost over and before I knew it I would be winging my way back to the Solomons. I wasn't at all sure I was happy that this was the case. The misgivings I had begun to feel before I left had taken on an even greater significance while I had been away, and I was wondering how I would cope with a further year and a half in the stiflingly small community which had become my home.

I think if it had not been for the fact that I was going straight back into the independence celebrations week, I might have had even greater difficulty in boarding my flight. Somehow I felt tired out. I had fitted an enormous amount into the three months I had been away, and although all of it had been enjoyable I felt as if I had done too much and was in need of a holiday! Well, that wouldn't do, and before I realised it I was flying back along the same route which had brought me to the Solomon Islands originally. I returned to Honiara on the first of July 1978, the same day as the Duke and Duchess of Gloucester, who were representing the Queen for the official independence celebrations, arrived, and with their arrival the ten days of celebrations began. It really was great fun and extremely interesting to be there for that big event in the life of the Solomon Islanders. VIPs flooded in from all over the place to take part in the many events and for once the Solomons was actually on the map. I was lucky enough to be at the Prime Minister's official reception as a hostess, and it was an experience to be able to mingle in with the various Heads of State and Government who were there for the occasion.

There were street carnivals and colourful floats, dancing everywhere most of the time and cultural shows arranged on the grassy area between my flat and the Ministry of Finance. I had a ringside view from my balcony and I even found I was sharing this vantage spot with people who were climbing the trees in our grounds to get a good view. (Rather them than any more rats or snakes though!) Little work was done that first week back. Everyone was celebrating and that was the main thing we all did at that special time. My Minister, Ben Kinika, had been kind enough to invite me to go to the Independence Ball with him. I had bought a new long dress in London but really felt a bit like Cinderella as I dressed for the occasion. None of the other secretaries went with their Ministers. However, I counted myself most fortunate to be at the main Independence event and wouldn't have missed it for anything. Fancy dancing cheek by jowl (well, almost) with the Duke and Duchess of Gloucester. It was all tremendous fun and there were some very good floor shows – such as the Cook Islanders doing a hula, and the

Gurkhas doing a kukri dance, and many other visiting islanders doing their national dances. The handing over of the Constitution (the official Independence Ceremony itself) went well with one notable exception. The Governor's ADC, who was responsible for lowering the Union Jack, let go of the rope too quickly and the flag came flying down, quite literally, instead of at a sedate pace to the strains of the National Anthem. There was no time to play 'God Save the Queen' – the flag was down before the first note could be played! It was an awful shame, and one which the poor ADC was not allowed to forget in the few remaining hours before he left, because it deprived us all of that single moment in time when a tear should have come to our eyes.

Now that the British Governor had left and the Solomon Islands was an independent state within the Commonwealth, other changes took place. The Australian Commissioner became known as the Australian High Commissioner, and Gordon Slater, the new British High Commissioner, arrived. Hitherto no other country had had any sort of diplomatic mission in Honiara, but now New Zealand was to open up a High Commission, and one day I opened the local newspaper to see, on the front page, an article about the new New Zealand High Commissioner, Graeme Ammundsen, who had arrived on the island. There was a photograph of him, along with a resumé of his past postings. I thought little further about this until a few weeks later when we were introduced. It was not an earth-shattering moment in my life, in fact I thought he seemed rather preoccupied and distant. As time passed I saw him again once or twice, but he soon became involved with Hillary, a Second Secretary at the Australian High Commission, and so I saw little of him socially. With the Islands now independent and the celebrations out of the way, it was business as usual in the offices around the country. Nothing seemed to have changed at all, except the flag! One thing did change, though, and that was the method of producing *Hansard*, the official reports of proceedings in Parliament. Hitherto the various departmental secretaries had taken it in turns to transcribe from audio cassettes and these transcripts were then edited by the Hansard office. We all hated it! The cassettes were of a very poor quality and many of the parliamentarians spoke in pidgin, thus making it almost impossible to understand what they were saying. But at least we were left alone with the tapes to transcribe them as best we could, even if the finished documents did have several gaps in them.

Now it was all to change and we were expected to be verbatim reporters in Parliament. I couldn't believe this when I first heard it, thinking that someone must be getting the wrong end of the stick. But sure enough, it was right, we were now going to take it in turns to sit in Parliament and take down everything everyone said in shorthand. This was a very highly skilled task and not one I felt at all competent to undertake. At no time had I indicated that my shorthand was up to those sorts of standards and I resented the fact that I seemed to have no leg to stand on when my terms of service were being so manipulated. It was an absolute nightmare, not only trying to keep up with who was speaking, but also understanding and writing down everything they said. I was already suffering from post-independence-celebrations 'blues', coupled with my earlier misgivings about spending another eighteen months in the Pacific, and now this – it was the final straw! My frustration turned to depression, which deepened every time I found myself sitting in Parliament desperately trying to get everything down in shorthand. At the end of my stint I would have a whole pad of notes which then had to be transcribed into something which resembled what had happened while I was the reporter.

The other problem was that at the time of Independence an awful lot of expatriates left, many of whom had been my friends. There were still many expatriates working in the Solomons, but they were to a large extent from a group I had not really become friendly with. I was beginning to feel very alone, especially since the social side of my life was now fairly quiet and I had gained nothing from the various relationships I had had. There was still Brian and Evol, thankfully, and after my health had deteriorated to the point of being hospitalised I was grateful for their friendship in bringing my spirits up again. At that time I was also transferred from the Ministry of Finance to the Ministry of Transport and Communications where my new Minister was John Tepaika. He lacked the charisma of Ben Kinika, who I missed greatly, but it was frankly a relief to no longer be involved with the frenetic work ethos of Tony Hughes who believed that everyone around him should live for their work, as he did himself.

But by April, 1979, the end was in sight with only five months to go before returning home. I was beginning to give serious thought as to what route to take, wanting, as I did, to see as much of the world as I could. I did not know whether I would ever have another chance again and so I decided to go home overland, on a bus from Kathmandu. But here I struck a problem. The next bus, after completion of my contract, would not leave Nepal until the end of February 1980. I had to weigh up my feelings about staying an extra half year in the Solomons, or missing out on this chance of a lifetime. I decided to apply for an extension, which was granted. Now that I knew I had the best part of another year in the Pacific I settled down to try to make the most of it.

My decision had been a lucky quirk of fate because on the same day as it was made I received yet another invitation to yet another farewell party for yet another friend. This time Gordon Slater, the British High Commissioner, was giving a farewell party to his secretary, Janice Keil, who was returning to London. The party was on the twenty-sixth of April 1979, and I have the invitation card still. As parties go, it got off to rather a slow start. We had been invited to a barbecue dinner, but hours seemed to go by without any sign of food. The drinks were plentiful though, and they were diligently topped up. But still no food. Gradually everyone's mood changed and food no longer seemed to matter. The dancing began and the drinks continued to flow. The mood got sillier and sillier and there could be no doubt now, on empty stomachs, everyone was becoming somewhat light-headed. I think we did, eventually, get something to eat, but I only remember that, towards the end, Francis Bugotu, the Foreign Secretary with whom I was dancing at the time, thrust me into the arms of the New Zealand High Commissioner, Graeme Ammundsen, with the words that he really must go home now but that he was sure 'the young ones' would be dancing for a while yet. Graeme did not have Hillary in tow that evening, and he no longer seemed so preoccupied and distant. In fact we danced together for what remained of the evening, and when we left we left together. Once outside we bade each other a lingering farewell and drove home in our separate cars, having arrived independently.

We had had an immediate attraction to each other that night and it wasn't long before we were seeing more and more of one another. My flat was situated at the bottom of the hill on which the New Zealand Residence was located. Graeme had negotiated the purchase of the old Deputy Governor's house for this purpose, and it was a delightful old colonial bungalow with a lovely view over the ocean. It would take time, however, before the building work took place to turn it into a suitable Residence, but in the meantime it had plenty of charm and character. We spent more and more time there together, just quietly enjoying each other's company, never tiring of the view and swimming together in the pool. Sometimes we would want a change and would decide to either stay quietly in my flat or have dinner in one of the Chinese restaurants. At other times we would go to the G Club and play tennis or watch a film. My new Ministry building was right next door to the Soltel offices where Cable and Wireless were located. It was that building in which Graeme had set up the New Zealand High Commission and so we were practically able to wave to each other out of the window. Gradually we became recognised as a couple and I would then, occasionally, be invited to accompany Graeme to one of the more official functions he attended. One such occasion was the St Andrew's Night Dinner, which was a splendid function organised by those doughty Scots, who would always ensure that, no matter where they were in the world, their special night would be organised with flair and style. At other times Graeme invited me to some of the official receptions he had to give in the course of his job. I started to move, much more often, in the upper echelons of Honiara society! One day, he decided to host a small black-tie dinner, although such functions were generally rare there in those days. The style of entertaining was mostly of a fairly casual nature, and it was nice to have an excuse to dress up, particularly since it was so rare.

Never has a function ever, anywhere in the world, taken so much planning as did that dinner! Graeme had two house staff, a Solomon Islands married couple. Robert was the 'butler' and his wife Olivet was the 'cook'. Charming though they both were, they were simple Islanders, and both Graeme and I knew that a black-tie dinner was simply beyond their ken. We coached them, we trained them, we explained to them every last detail of what would be required. We set out the details on a minute-by-minute basis. This we did on telex paper, a long roll of paper for each of them, setting out every little detail of the evening. When to boil the water for the vegetables, when to serve them up and keep them warm while the next stage of preparation was taking place. We had already shopped well in advance for the dinner, leaving nothing to chance lest it not be available when needed, and everything had gone into Graeme's deep freezer. Robert had been kept informed, all along the way as to what was being bought for the dinner and what was for normal consumption, to ensure that the precious purchases didn't get wasted on daily meals. At last, all seemed to be in order, the table was set by me to ensure the right items were there for the guests, and all we had to do now was to pray that it was a success.

The guests duly arrived and had pre-dinner drinks. Everyone was in their finery and almost unrecognisable from the usual shorts and shirts we were accustomed to seeing them in, and the mood was just right for a pleasant evening. Graeme and I exchanged the odd glance, from time to time, both thinking just how well everything was going thanks to our telex roll of instructions to Robert and Olivet. We began to relax and thoroughly enjoyed ourselves, until the time came when we were waiting for the main course to arrive. It seemed to be taking an age. We became fearful of what was happening and I went through agonies of wondering which would be the worst social gaffe – to leave the table to find out, or wait for a disaster to finally appear. Graeme was obviously going through the same thought process but finally decided that he had to investigate. I was glad that he had because it relieved me of the need to do so. A few minutes later he returned, with Robert in tow to serve more wine. Clearly we were going to be in for a further wait and Graeme had rightly decided that, rather like Gordon Slater earlier on, it was better to keep your guests well 'watered' if, for some reason, there was a hold up with the meal.

Finally, after what seemed like an absolute age, the meal turned up but it had been merciful that Graeme had gone out to the kitchen. Olivet had cooked barely enough food to go round half the number of guests, let alone all of them, and Graeme found this, to his horror, when he had gone to investigate. They had been fearful of taking everything from the 'special corner of the freezer for the dinner', so instilled were they with the idea that this section must not be touched. We had nearly had kittens at the time, but at least we were able to laugh about it afterwards, and the main thing was that people had seemed to enjoy themselves.

At about this time I was thumbing through some old papers in my desk and came across the diary I had had two years earlier. I noticed that on the twenty-sixth of April, 1977, Enya had made her Tarot card prediction about my "heart's desire coming to fruition in a two". So, all you sceptics out there, never be scathing about the Tarot cards ever again! In Graeme I had found my heart's desire. All the old wounds were healed and those months I spent with him in Honiara were the happiest days of my life.

Chapter Ten
My Island In The Sun

All those who have been in love will know that it changes, not only your life, but your whole attitude towards everyday events. In early April I had been stretching my resources to find the courage to stay longer in the Solomons, by the end of the month it seemed like a Paradise Island in the sun! All the old misgivings disappeared, depression was a thing of the past, and everything in my world seemed rosy beyond my wildest dreams. In no time at all Graeme and I were firm friends, spending almost all our spare time together. It was just as well most of my former friends had left since I would no longer have had time to see much of them. I was even more thankful that I had had a job change and that my hours of work were now the standard hours required of all public servants. Even reporting for *Hansard* took on a new dimension! I couldn't say that I enjoyed it now, but I no longer worried about whether I could do it or not and simply approached it with a view to doing my best and if that wasn't good enough – well, I wasn't a *Hansard* reporter, was I?

On one of my visits to Graeme's house I found him listening to his amateur radio transceiver. He was concentrating on the crackling airwaves (which sounded rather like gobbledegook to me) and he greeted me with the news that he was getting a report over the air that Margaret Thatcher had swept the Conservatives to victory in the General Election in Britain. So began the Thatcher Years in Britain and, whenever I heard a report in later times stating that Thatcher had been in power this long, or that long, I always associated it in my mind with the first time I heard of her electoral victory. It would always give me a jolt and inwardly I would say to myself, "Gosh, can it really be that long?", not so much thinking of her time in office but more how long I had known Graeme. When I lost that yardstick, it was replaced by reports of how long Britain had had a Conservative Government.

Although Graeme had initially been operating the New Zealand High Commission out of a hotel bedroom at the Mendana Hotel, he had, by now, got things fully settled and organised both in the Soltel building and also, on the accommodation side, at the old Deputy-Governor's residence. It was all up and running and fully operational – all that was needed now was an official 'opening' ceremony. He was lucky to be able to enlist the New Zealand Prime Minister for this task, and it had been agreed that Robert Muldoon would officially open the High Commission when he was up for a South Pacific Forum Meeting taking place in Honiara. Although Graeme was confident that all was as it should be, inevitably there were some last minute panics, not least of which was that, only minutes before the important visitor was due to arrive, Graeme discovered that although he had been careful to ensure that the Prime Minister's favourite tipple (Teacher's Whisky) was in stock, soda water mix had been overlooked. The First Secretary was dispatched with the driver post-haste to the Mendana Hotel with orders to bring back a case of soda water immediately. This was fortuitously achieved in record time, and a short while later the driver came staggering up the stairs, carrying what was needed, just moments before the opening ceremony began. The downside of his success was that he had got his shoes muddy in the process and now the new problem was to clear up the mess he had left on the stairs before the Prime Minister arrived! In the event it was a happy and successful occasion, topped off by a very well-attended reception at the Mendana Hotel to which Graeme invited me to join him. Muldoon and his wife Thea were two people I had never expected to meet, so I clocked that up as being yet another experience.

Although Independence had been well and truly celebrated the year before, the Western District of the Solomons had not, at the time, accepted the fact that the Islands were, indeed, independent. During the course of 1979, the District came to understand that there was nothing for it but to acknowledge the inevitable. They did, however, regret that they had missed out on the celebrations and wanted to make up for this fact by staging their own festivities one year later. The Solomons' Government prevailed on the three Commonwealth High

Commissioners to officiate as guests of honour at strategic locations in the Western District.

The British envoy, Gordon Slater, was destined to appear on the Island of Choiseul, although with great foresight he decided to delegate the job to his First Secretary, Bill Stump. In the event, Bill subsequently returned to Honiara with a broken leg, having been violently tipped out of his bunk in a severe gale as he was dutifully making his way on a local island vessel to Choiseul. The Australian High Commissioner, John Melhuish, had the pick of locations — Munda, which was easily accessible by Solair, the local airline. Graeme for his part was asked to go to the isolated island of Rendova. For him this turned out to be a once in a lifetime experience, including nearly being wrecked on a reef at night in a Taiwanese fishing junk taking him to Rendova from Gizo. While still feeling sick from the rough seas he was regaled with the 'confrontation ceremony' of the Rendovan mud-men (fifty or so naked tribesmen), wearing nothing on their bodies but caked mud with white markings, and brandishing spears and axes. Since little English was spoken in this area, one of the mud-men had a notice tied to his back saying "FOLLOW ME" and one tied to his front saying "STOP". If all this wasn't enough, the following day Graeme was resigned to losing his life as he was taken from Rendova to Munda over very rough open sea in a fibreglass canoe powered by a 15 hp Mercury outboard motor. Only the skill of the Solomon Islands' motorman kept the craft from disappearing, with Graeme, beneath the heavy swell.

It was clearly with great relief on Graeme's part that he eventually arrived at Munda, where I was waiting for him. We had rented a tiny island off Munda, from Agnes, for a five-day break away together. Now Agnes is reputed to be the person on whom a character in the film *South Pacific* was based, but whether there was truth in this or not, I am unsure. I do know that there are an awful lot of *South Pacific* stories which do the rounds in that part of the world, and everyone knows exactly where the film was made and who the characters were based upon. The trouble is that everyone's story is different! Anyway, Agnes had a boatman row us over, along with the provisions we had prepared, and when we saw him disappear back across the expanse of lagoon we knew that we would be entirely alone together, on this enchanting little island, until six o'clock the next day when he would return with drinking water and a few other provisions.

We felt as though we had stepped off the end of the world, truly into Paradise. It was an extraordinary experience to be entirely and completely alone, with no sign of human life, other than the two of us. It was utterly quiet and magnificently beautiful, this little dot of an island with nothing about us but crystal clear turquoise sea and white, white sand. There were a few palm trees, which shaded the little hut which passed for our accommodation. This was really just one big room with a sleeping area and a living area which included a little kitchenette. We swam, we slept, we read, we talked, we ate and listened to the radio and when we had done all that, we did it over again. We lost track of time completely. There was simply nothing, other than the occasional need of a drink or a meal, and the position of the sun, to give us any measurement of the day as it passed by. We settled comfortably into one another's lives in a quiet routine which did not have to be measured or gauged to the next appointment or commitment. There was nothing to distract us from one another and even the daily visit by the boatman did not disturb our peace. We lived Adam-and-Eve style for five idyllic days in a little tiny world of our own making. It was very difficult to leave and return to our normal lives in Honiara, but all good things come to an end, and it was with great reluctance that we eventually returned across the lagoon to catch the Solair island-hopper plane to fly back to Henderson airfield on Guadalcanal.

We had got to know each other even better during those wonderful few days and had told one another much more about our lives. I had already known that Graeme had a wife and four children back in Wellington and he had told me something of them all. He had separated from his wife at the time he came to Honiara the year before, but was missing his children a lot. They were to visit him the following month, during the August school holidays, and this he was looking forward to immensely. While I can safely say that it had never been my wish to be involved with another married man, especially another one with four children (I had been there and done that already, although I didn't have the T-shirt to prove it), it was also fairly obvious that I was unlikely, at the age of thirty-four, to find a single man of the right age. His family circumstances did cause a small cloud to appear on the horizon of our happiness. He was still married to Diana, although there was every indication that a divorce would be likely since Diana had, some years earlier, embarked on another relationship and was still seeing the man involved. However, we chose not to dwell on all of this, and endeavoured to give the children a happy time when they came to stay. I managed to find some pretty lace material and spent a lot of time making a 'wedding dress' for Karyn's doll, together with some other doll's clothes, while Graeme took the boys to the airport to fly his model aircraft. We took them swimming at Tambea, for boat rides in the inflatable dinghy and played tennis with them at the G Club. They watched films with us there, and at other times there was always the swimming pool in the garden or a barbecue on the lawn. In spite of all these activities which we did together, I found I was seeing much less of Graeme while the children were with him and, of course, we had no time alone together while they were in Honiara. I began to realise that I had completely abandoned my former life, the life-before-Graeme bit, and almost felt like a newcomer to the town, not feeling that I knew anyone or that I could, out of the blue as it were, suddenly descend on those who I had previously called on quite often. I was becoming totally immersed in him and it was strange not having him to myself any more. Anyway, he had felt it best not to let the children have too much of a story about me to go back to Wellington with, although they would, undoubtedly, have mentioned that Daddy had got a new friend.

Our life together resumed quickly enough and we once more found that we were spending all of our free time together. The weekends were the best and usually we spent these up at Graeme's place. The demands of the Head of Mission job were not so onerous in those days and Graeme rarely got caught up with official functions or duties at the weekend. It was easy, therefore, for us to tuck ourselves away up at the house and just do as we pleased. If he was on the radio, I would read a book or have a swim in the pool and at other times I would accompany him to the airport where he often liked to fly his model planes. The months slipped past, in this cosy way, until we began to realise that it was all coming to an end. We had a taste of separation, briefly, when Graeme had to return to New Zealand for a meeting, but that was not for long and the reunion afterwards made the separation worthwhile. However, more permanent separation loomed, first in the form of Graeme's leave in New Zealand at Christmas time, and, more seriously, in my departure from the Solomon Islands at the beginning of February the following year. It was something else which we decided not to dwell on, preferring to concentrate on the good time we were having, while it lasted.

My thirty-fifth birthday was coming up, and Graeme asked me if there was anything special I would like to do on the day. Since he had such a lovely house I thought that it would be nice to have a party to celebrate. I had been so cramped in my entertaining style over the years in Honiara, on account of living in such a small flat, that I saw it as a good opportunity to invite some friends to a party by way of thanks for the many times I had been to their homes. We planned it together but Graeme left the invitation list for me to chose, and Robert and Olivet managed to produce a nice meal, buffet-style, for the evening. What Graeme managed to keep quiet was the fact that he had made a lovely chocolate birthday cake, by himself, which he had not only cooked unaided but decorated too. It was a loving gesture and one which I really appreciated, particularly when I heard later of the difficulties he had had with the icing.

And so life continued, for a while longer, doing things together and just being happy in each other's company. Every so often a sad note would creep in, when my mind could not help but focus on Graeme's forthcoming departure, but he would generally manage to get me looking on the brighter side of things quickly enough. Before he left to spend the latter part of December and the whole of January 1980 in Wellington he helped me sort out how I was going to get all my possessions into my crates. I had accumulated a number of things in the past three and a half years and they were all going to have to fit into the same number of crates I had arrived with. It was like a jigsaw puzzle, working out which box would go in which space, and there certainly wasn't going to be any room to play with. When Graeme finally left for New Zealand I was like a lost soul. My whole way of life, outside of work, had been taken away from me and I suddenly found that I had hours on my hands with nothing to do. I threw myself into my packing task and was thankful that I had something I could get on with by myself. I had so cut myself off from my friends that I had no obvious place to go to spend Christmas, although I did receive a last minute invitation so that I was not alone on Christmas Day. But I might as well have been. I wasn't cheerful company as I felt I had lost part of me, which, of course, I had. I was also glad that I didn't have much time off work, only a couple of days public holiday, so at least the lonely Christmas period when people were in their own homes was kept to a minimum.

But time was ticking by. Graeme was not due back until two days before I left. I had received lots of letters from him during his absence, and they had been wonderful to get, but it was him I wanted to see again, for more than forty-eight hours. Then one day I got a letter to say that he was cutting his leave short. He would be back a week earlier than expected and we would have my final ten days on the island together. I was over the moon with happiness when I heard this and was waiting up at his house when he returned from New Zealand. We fell into each other's arms the moment he walked into the room and hardly left that comforting position for the short, short time left to us. It was both wonderful to be together again, and ghastly to think that I was leaving and that perhaps fate would be cruel to us and we might never see each other again. We laughed and we cried. We were happy and we were sad but nothing we did could stop the march of time, and at the end of each happy day together we would be one day nearer to the day I left the Solomon Islands. Finally, both of us in a daze, Graeme took me to Henderson airfield for my flight out of the country. We said goodbye a hundred times, each time we said it one of us would stop the other moving and then we had to say it again. Finally I had got Graeme as far as the foot of the steps to the aircraft and, in the end, even into the plane itself. Eventually there was nothing for it but for him to descend the ladder and stand watching as the aircraft taxied down the runway for its take-off. The tears were coursing down my cheeks and I could hardly see him as he stood there, a lonely figure on the tarmac, waving a slow wave of farewell.

From Honiara I flew to Sydney and from there I got a flight over to Wellington. I was beginning my leave there with Eileen, the girl who had been in my block of flats, just above me, and who had helped me not only with lifts to the hospital at the beginning of my time in the Solomons, but who had run for help when I had the snake episode. I was in Wellington a week and during that time managed to see most of the city, generally on tourist bus trips. I went and saw Graeme's head office, the Ministry of Foreign Affairs which was situated at Terrace Chambers on The Terrace. It helped to make me feel a little closer to him to know that I was standing where he had stood. One evening Eileen took me over to Oriental Parade (a wonderful harbourside residential area in Wellington), where Sally was now living. Sally had been the National Librarian (and bridge tutor) in the Solomons and, like Eileen, had returned to Wellington some considerable time ago. It was so nice to see her again, and she enquired of my bridge. I was able to report that both Graeme and I had attended formal lessons and that we were now keen players but by no means yet good at the game. During the weekend, when Eileen was not having to go to work, I prevailed upon her to drive me over to the place where Graeme's wife and children were living. I think she was worried that I might be about to make some sort of scene, but this was not my intention. I just wanted to see it, and once she realised this she drove me over. It was awful to stand outside the house and realise that that had been his home. I was aching with longing for him and thankful that he rang me while I was with Eileen. He was going through the same pain as me but speaking together did ease the longing, momentarily, but the trauma of putting the phone down only served to reinforce the distance which was now between us.

Before I left the Solomons, Graeme got us both miniature tape recorders to enable us to continue talking together. The little cassettes were ideal for putting in an envelope and mailing. At many times each day I would add a little more to the tape and as soon as it was completed mailed it off to him in Honiara. He was doing the same for me, to be posted to each stopping point along my journey home. They were a life-saver to me and I constantly longed for the next to be received, and while I waited I was either listening to his last one or preparing another for him. I was glad that I was, at least, in his country and better able to identify with his roots. It was fascinating to see Wellington for the first time in 1980. It has changed radically since then, but in those days the shops reminded me of London during my childhood. It was like being in a time warp and stepping back to the 1950s. I had always heard that New Zealand was twenty to thirty years behind Britain, and that impression was very much confirmed during my first visit. February was a good month to be there as this is regarded as the best summer month of the year and Wellington was looking very beautiful bathed in summer sunshine. The city is built around a lovely natural harbour and the surrounding hills form a necklace about the commercial centre. The suburbs are dotted throughout the hills and the nearest comparison I can find with Wellington is a Cornish fishing village, on a larger scale.

When the time came to fly out of Wellington I gazed intently out of the aircraft window wanting to soak up every last detail of the area below. It was a magnificent sight, the view spanning the Cook Straits to the South Island, which was easily within my line of vision. I had no idea, then, as to whether I would ever see it again and I tried desperately to commit it all to memory. I seemed to be losing my last ties with Graeme as I winged my way across the Tasman Sea to Sydney, my next port of call.

Mercifully I found a tape waiting for me at the home of Mike and Gail, with whom I stayed while there. Mike and Gail had had a flat in the same block of flats as my mother in Bromley and had become friends just before I left for the Solomons. The reason had been that one day my mother mentioned to me that she had been talking to the Australian couple upstairs and it had turned out that Mike knew the Solomons, having been a Purser on board a cruise ship which called there from time to time. Back in 1976, before I left for the Pacific, it seemed an incredible stroke of luck that there was someone living upstairs from my mother who actually knew Honiara! I had gone up immediately to pick Mike's brains for information and in the course of doing so had struck up a rather belated friendship with them both. Anyway, now was my chance to renew that friendship.

Mike was at the airport to meet me and it was great to see his smiling face, full of welcome. He drove me the quite considerable distance to the suburb of Menai, where they lived at that time, and he was now the manager of a nearby ANZ Bank. Nine months earlier their first son, Keiran, had been born and they were now living not so much the life of the 'carefree young Antipodeans doing the London scene' as the 'young married couple with a new baby'. Keiran had proved a handful and I don't think either of them had had a proper night's sleep since he had been born. However, they were as cheerful as ever and full of enthusiasm for my finally making it to Oz. What they had not bargained for was to have me arrive with only one topic of conversation – Graeme. I was totally lovesick and completely one-track minded. I must have been a crashing bore but they were charming enough not to let on if this was what they thought. They could see my predicament but clearly felt that I should be putting all thoughts of Graeme temporarily to one side while I explored the wonders of Sydney. I really couldn't drum up the enthusiasm needed although one day they put me on a train into town, armed with a list of what I should see when I got there, and expected a full account of my doings when I returned!

There was no doubt about it, Sydney was a really spectacular city and one with which I fell in love immediately. The weather was idyllic and the buildings shimmered in the sun, seeming to be all white. I went on a harbour cruise, which gave me a good idea of the beauty of the city and enabled me to see the obvious tourist attractions of the Opera House and Sydney Harbour Bridge. But I wasn't in the right frame of mind to be doing all these wonderful things on my own. I wanted Graeme to be there to share in it all with me. The fact that he wasn't only served to make me want to return to Mike and Gail so that I could resort to my favourite pastime of talking about Graeme. Poor things, they had to listen to tales of the man in my life *ad infinitum*; while they were preparing meals, while they were feeding the baby, while we were doing the dishes later and then they knew that it would start all over again at breakfast time the next morning! But they never once gave me the impression that they had heard enough. They listened patiently to everything I said, whether they had heard it all already, or not. I was happier to be with them, talking, than getting around and about. My one trip into the city had given me a good idea of the place and lovely though I thought it was I was simply not in the mood to sightsee while Mike was at work and Gail was busy with the baby. After a few days I was collected by a friend of Beverly's (the girl I stayed with in Tel Aviv) who drove me to her family's home in Yass, nearby to Canberra. It was fascinating to see the Australian countryside, or bush I suppose I should call it, and it was a marvellous opportunity to see a little more of the country than if I had flown the short distance to Canberra. Wendy's parents owned a farm in Yass and so, this too, was a good chance to see something so typically Australian. The following day Wendy drove me the remaining few miles into the Australian capital city of Canberra.

In Canberra I stayed with Nancy who had previously been secretary to the Australian High Commissioner in Honiara (she had taken over from Beverly) but was now back with the Ministry of Foreign Affairs in Canberra. She was not about to take any nonsense from me about not sightseeing and set about to educate me on the wonders of the capital. Not only did we see the parliamentary and governmental buildings, she took me to the lovely shopping arcades and out into the surrounding bush too. We saw lots of kangaroos and koalas and I certainly wasn't able to leave Nancy saying that I hadn't done much. Mike and Gail were pleased to hear it when I returned to them in Sydney and took heart from Nancy's success and decided to drive me round the Sydney area during the course of my last weekend with them before I left Australia. I had been away from Honiara for three weeks when the time finally came for me to bid them a fond farewell. They had been tremendous friends to me and, looking back, I have no idea how they coped with me then, particularly since they had got a new baby to look after. Their parting shot to me was, "Come back soon, and for heaven's sake bring Graeme with you!" I finally did so, but not for another six years.

For now it was time to fly to Kathmandu and this I did on the twenty-forth of February 1980. This was the journey I had planned, a year earlier, before I had met Graeme. So much had happened to me during the course of the past year that when the time finally came for me to go to Nepal to join the overland tour it no longer seemed such a good idea. I was missing Graeme so much that all I could concentrate on was getting to the next stopping point in order to collect another letter or tape from him. It hardly seemed to be the right frame of mind for undertaking a fairly arduous journey which was to take me to twelve countries over a period of three months. But it was prepaid, which proved a fairly powerful incentive to get at least as far as Kathmandu!

Chapter Eleven

The Long Way Home

My friend and travel agent, Neville Hill, who I had failed to recognise in Bangkok, had booked me on the overland trip so he was still doing business with me, fortunately. The Travel Order read, "ONE SEAT ON INDO-RUSSIA TOUR IRW5, KATHMANDU/LONDON, DEPARTING KATHMANDU ON 26 FEBRUARY 1980". I had been requested to report to a Mr Jon Rowe at the Hotel Blue Star in Kathmandu who was the tour leader. This I duly did on my arrival and Jon introduced me to the few other members of the group who had begun to arrive. I was glad that there were to be a couple of days in the city before our departure since this afforded me the opportunity to see something of the region before leaving. It was very different to anything I had seen before but the smells were certainly reminiscent of Egypt. Just one whiff told me that I was back in a Middle Eastern/Asian town. It was full of character and there were the usual street vendors plying their wares to the many tourists who were there either to enjoy the spectacular Himalayan scenery, or to go on climbing expeditions in the mountains. The faces of the people brought back memories of the Gurkhas I had worked with in Malaysia, naturally enough since this was the Gurkha's homeland. I wandered around, soaking up the atmosphere and feeling glad that I had now got the chance to see such a spectacular part of the world for myself. I joined up with one or two of the group, who were wandering around like me, and we stopped for a meal in town. I had already realised that I was going to be a fish out of water so far as the other group members were concerned. For a start they were travelling away from home, all being either Australian or New Zealanders, while I was just catching a bus home! The other factor was that I was much older than the majority of them, the only exceptions being one or two retired people who were doing it by way of celebrating the end of their working days. So, age-wise, I didn't fit in anywhere at all. I could see that this was going to be difficult because the young ones had a completely different lifestyle to mine and I did not feel that I could yet identify with the retired folk. I was piggy-in-the-middle and felt very conscious of this throughout the journey.

By the time we met up with Haggis, the driver, we were all assembled and ready to roll. We waved goodbye to the lovely old buildings of Kathmandu and set off westwards to Pokhara. That night we stopped at a small roadside eatery for dinner where only local food of a strongly spiced nature was available, and once we had eaten we ventured off to see a cultural show which included the 'dance of the Yeti'. Within a short time I realised that I was about to be violently sick and had to run out to a stinking ladies loo. We had only been out of Kathmandu a day and I now began what was to turn out to be a tummy upset which I never actually threw off during the entire trip. It was a nightmare to have diarrhoea and sickness whilst travelling on a bus. If my account of the journey home sounds superficial and scanty it can be attributed to the fact that I saw only the minimum since most of the time I was clutching my stomach and wondering if I dared ask Haggis to stop, yet again. Various remedies were tried, to clear up the stomach infection, but nothing seemed to work. I lost a lot of weight, which in itself pleased me, but at no time did I feel well enough to do what was required of me – to sit on a bus for three months.

The whole trip was being done on the cheap, although because of the length of time involved it was not actually a cheap holiday. This meant that the accommodation we had along the way was of the most basic imaginable. We always shared a room, sometimes with several others, and on occasions the entire complement of bus travellers were in one room, sleeping rough on the floor. We were travelling in some very remote areas, too, which in itself meant that classier accommodation would not, in any event, have been available. Of course it had its fascinating side to it, seeing the places from the eyes of the people living there, but for one such as me who likes the creature comforts of a bed to sleep in and a shower to enjoy, preferably a hot one, I was doomed to find it all difficult, to say the least. Not that I had commenced the journey with any idea that it would be comfortable, but some of the conditions surpassed even my vivid imagination. And the blessed stomach upset plagued me all along the way, making it even more difficult to eat the local food and drink the local water, particularly in view of the conditions we encountered when we arrived in most of our destinations.

From Nepal we travelled to India where the places we visited were Varanasi, Agra, Fatephur Sikri, Jaipur, Amber, Delhi, Jammu, Srinagar, back to Jammu, and finally to Amritsar. My insides gave me the very worst of trouble through India, and consequently the memory has been kaleidoscoped into a jumble of pictures, mostly of the lavatorial nature. From the central Himalayas the river Ganges flows for about one thousand miles to its mouth at the head of the Bay of Bengal, and to see this Holy River, at Varanasi, was our first stop. It is everything to the people living on its banks. They bathe in it, believing it will wash away sins and cure disease, and their dead are carried along it to the place of the funeral pyres on the banks and their ashes are then scattered on the water. It is a main artery. It is the source of their very existence. We saw many a sight along its shores, and not far away there were the more touristy sights of snake charmers, yoga demonstrators, monkey trainers, and dancing bears. Two of the most lasting memories I have of India, though, are the Taj Mahal by day and also by moonlight, the latter being perhaps the most stunning. By complete contrast the other lasting memory is of a hotel dining-room in Jaipur which had been preserved exactly as it was during the time of the British Raj. I imagine that this was by design, although perhaps it was just simply the way it was. The room was so evocative of a bygone age that I felt I was stepping into the past. The people of that earlier time would have gone, as we did, on a tour of the Royal Palace at Jaipur and rode an elephant to Amber.

Nothing had prepared me for the beauty of Kashmir though. Our time on a houseboat in Srinagar was another of the lasting memories of that stage of our journey. The only problem was that, in March, Srinagar is cold. Most of the journey was taking place in areas which were hot, and this was more or less our only sojourn in cold conditions so we all felt the change in temperature. We had been told that it was essential to travel light and none of us had the quantity of clothing needed to keep ourselves warm. But it is the beauty of the place which remains in my mind, far more than the cold. While I was there I wished, for the hundredth time, that Graeme could have been there too and enjoyed it with me. At least I had been able to collect several more tapes and letters from him at the various stops we had had, and these I had listened to and read until I knew them backwards, but, as always, they did not make up for his absence in my life. I had spoken about him a little to my new companions, but they could not understand why on earth I was not with him instead of doing this crazy journey, and so it was difficult to keep them interested in talk of him.

In Srinagar we all got our wallets out. The wares were far too tempting to pass them by. I made two purchases, one most worthwhile and the other total rubbish. The good buy was a lovely hand-woven Kashmiri rug which, since I could not keep it with me on the bus, I sent back to the Solomon Islands for Graeme to keep. As I did not know whether I would see Graeme again, how come I was sending Kashmiri rugs to him? Well, I didn't stop to work this one out myself, but if I had I think I would simply have sent it to him as a gift which, perhaps, one day we could share together. The rubbishy purchase was a fur coat sold to me as a mink. (This was in the days when people bought fur coats). The coats all looked so magnificent together that it was easy to be fooled into believing one was making a wonderful purchase, but once back in London and looking at it in the cold light of day, it was clear that the fur was anything but mink! But the spectacular scenery of Srinagar, a watery city in the mountains, and staying on the enchanting houseboats, is a memory that will remain with me always.

We came back down from the mountains and on the way to Amritsar, to see the Sikh Golden Temple, we passed by the gory sight of vultures disposing of their prey on the road. So thick was this flock of birds that the bus could not pass by, but we never knew what they were eating since by the time we arrived the carcass was unrecognisable. It did little for the state of my stomach. We would normally have proceeded from Amritsar through Afghanistan but there was fighting there at the time and this made it unsafe for our journey. We therefore travelled down to Lahore and on through Pakistan to Multan, Sukkur, Quetta and Nokkundi. If anything our conditions were now becoming more and more basic and the lack of conveniences of any kind became the norm. However, there was much of beauty to see on the way, particularly the Sikh Temple and Tomb of Raja Ranjit Singh, the founder of the Sikh Dynasty, in

Lahore. The Shalamar Gardens, also in Lahore, were very beautiful and these, we discovered, had been inspired by the same Shah Jahan of Taj Mahal fame. From these architectural splendours we progressed southwards, through the Baluchistan desert, where even getting diesel for the bus became more and more difficult. At Sibi we had the curious experience of coming across a signpost which, amongst other things, told us that it was only 5,979 miles to London. My stomach took another heave at this information wondering how on earth I was going to survive through the Baluchi desert without even a bush to hide behind. On the twentieth of March we reached the Bolan Pass, and at this stage there was to be no accommodation of any kind whatsoever. We passed a slow camel caravan on their way out of the desert as we proceeded in for a full night's driving to Iran.

Iran was another trouble spot, having ousted the Shah the year before, and the effects of the revolution were all about us. It had been touch and go whether the bus would be able to leave Nepal on account of the various troubles in the region, but having got this far we were left with little option but to continue. We entered south eastern Iran at Zahedan where we were all ready for a good meal, hot shower and a comfortable bed to sleep in. None of this was available and we had to make do with one huge room into which all twenty-five of us, men and women together, were just given a rug on the floor. Things did not improve much, either, until we got to Isfahan, via Kerman, two days later and there we were able to eat and sleep in a greater degree of comfort.

Isfahan was the only stop of note throughout the whole of Iran. The political situation was far too delicate (fifty-two American Embassy personnel were being held hostage in Tehran at that time), and it was decided that we must make as much haste as possible through the country. We had time to admire the beautiful mosques in Isfahan, particularly the lovely Shah Abass Mosque, and we also got our wallets out again when we visited the main Bazaar. I had wandered off on my own while in the Bazaar, preferring to browse through the lovely souvenirs by myself, and did, in fact, get a nice painting on ivory. It was not without incident, though, since it had been assumed by the shopkeeper that as I was alone I must be looking for a good time – of the fast-and-loose variety. When I enquired whether he had any other paintings to show me, he told me yes, he had, but that they were stored downstairs and he must, therefore, bolt the shop door before showing me to his basement. Before I could blink an eye I was locked inside the emporium with this creepy shopkeeper. A loud thud signalled the finality of the bolting of the door and immediately a trap door opened in the floor and I was being ushered towards it. I had visions of the white slave traffic and thought that nobody would ever hear of my whereabouts ever again. I was scared. He was bigger than me and was ogling me with popping eyes. He thought I was after a good time, in his understanding of the meaning of a good time, and this incensed me to the point of rising anger which in turn helped conquer my fear. I kicked up an unholy fuss, refusing to descend the steps to the cellar, and after some pushing and shoving the man finally decided that I was not worth the bother of any more fuss. Once the door had been unbolted I grabbed my purchase and ran.

We skirted Tehran and headed to Zanjan and then Maku on the Turkish border and I, for one, was not at all sorry to be leaving Iran behind. As soon as we crossed the mountains to enter Turkey my spirits lifted. It was now evident that we were no longer in such an under-developed or deprived part of the world and from east to west I loved everything about being in Turkey. I had not expected to have this reaction, believing that I would find it little different from the areas we had already passed through, but this was not at all the case and I found the country both beautiful and enchanting. We passed Mount Ararat, reputed to be the final resting place of Noah's Ark, and on one of our earlier stops in eastern Turkey climbed to the summit of a minaret in order to get a better view of the mountain. The stairs were very narrow, steep and unsafe, in fact almost non-existent in places, and to this day I have no idea how I managed to get to the top. Probably because I had no choice, being in the middle of a large group I simply had to follow my leader until I reached the top lest I frustrated those behind me who would never have been able to pass by me. The view from the top was spectacular but I was relieved to finally get down safely, a feat which I had doubted would be possible whilst climbing up. Our route through Turkey took us from Erzurum, to Urgup in the Goreme Valley, and on to Konya, Alanya, Antalya, Pammukkale, Bodrum, Kusadasi (Ephesus), Cannakkale (ancient Troy), and finally to Istanbul.

While in Urgup I bought a lovely onyx lampstand from the factory where it was made. It was yet another purchase which I posted, this time to myself in London, and was yet another disappointment when I opened it and found it smashed to pieces. One small section remained undamaged and Graeme later managed to fashion a small lampstand out of it, but in spite of his good efforts it has always been unstable. There was lots to see during the Urgup stop, and of particular interest were the Troglodyte dwellings in the so-called 'Fairy Chimneys'. These were natural caves formed by lava eruptions from three million years ago and had a beauty about them which man could never have imitated. The pottery factory was another point of interest, although I felt that the potter was playing his audience to the lowest common denominator, and I didn't particularly enjoy his coarse sense of humour myself. Turkish dancing was part of the floor show that evening and this reminded me very much of the Russian Cossacks – leather boots and high kicks from a crouched position.

We had done a lot while in Urgup, but now it was time to proceed on through the Goreme Valley to Sive, where we saw a very well preserved Roman Amphitheatre. From central Turkey we headed south-westwards towards the Mediterranean Sea and from Alanya went on a most enjoyable boat trip. On our return we headed into town to watch the local craftsmen making jewellery and ornaments out of onyx. I had a pair of cuff links made for Graeme, and I remember the looks of astonishment on the faces of the young Antipodeans when they saw them. Their faces said it all – "What on earth do you want with a pair of them?" As I said, we enjoyed different lifestyles!

The bus proceeded on daily, rarely giving us more than a glance at the sights around us. One day stalagmites and stalactites in a magnificent cave, the next watching a film being made at the fifteenth century Crusader castle at Bodrum, along with a quick look at King Mausolus' Mausoleum. This was built in 375 BC and was one of the Wonders of the Ancient World. It is from King Mausolus of Caria (died 353 BC) that the word 'mausoleum' is derived. The region is rich in Wonders of the Ancient World, and in nearby Seljuk we saw the Temple of Artemis (the goddess Diana, daughter of Zeus, sister of Apollo) along with the Tomb of St John, one of the apostles who spread the word of Christ two thousand years earlier. I found myself quite taken with two storks nesting high on a crumbling ruin – I would have liked to change places with them if Graeme could have been up there with me! They symbolised what I was missing most, and although I had by now collected lots of tapes and letters from him I was still feeling lost and alone without him. And my stomach was still no better in spite of thinking that by now I must have tried every remedy known to man. I was beginning to feel at the end of my tether after having spent one and a half months on the bus with this condition and my strength and will to continue were beginning to ebb. I was wishing that the journey was being done in reverse, with Scandinavia and Russia coming first rather than last, as these countries were places I had especially wanted to visit. The other advantage of such a route would be that it would take me *nearer* to Graeme, not further and further away from him. Jet travel makes the world seem a small place, given the distances which can be covered in such a comparatively short space of time, but this slow trundling bus was making me realise just how very big it really is.

While at Kusadasi we saw the wonderful ruins of the ancient Greek city of Ephesus. Also there we saw the church built over the site of the Virgin Mary's last home before her death. It reminded me of all the churches in Israel which have been built over the various holy sites in that country. On we moved, day by day, and at Cannakkale we saw the remains of Troy and a model of the Trojan Horse. For some reason it was much bigger than I had expected but as a hiding place for so many armed Greek soldiers it didn't seem to have afforded much space. By the time we had travelled north-westerly to the Aegean Sea we reached the Dardanelles, the sight of so many lost ANZAC lives during the bitter fighting between the allies and the Turks in the First World War. We stopped to ponder how any of them managed to survive the appalling conditions of landing at such a beachhead. We now made our way to Istanbul, where my first stop was to the main post office to see what mail there might be for me. Graeme's letter was there, together with one from my mother. Since my mother had decided that it might be difficult to time mail accurately during my journey home she had written only infrequently. I was, therefore, curious to know why she was writing now and opened her letter before Graeme's. Her first words told me that she had some dreadful news to convey and I found a small corner of the post office to sit down. She wrote to tell me that her sister, Barbie, had died three weeks earlier, quite suddenly and unexpectedly. She was about to commence further chemotherapy treatment, but contracted pneumonia and went downhill very rapidly indeed. There had been no way of contacting me earlier to enable me to get home before she died, and so she was writing now to tell me that Barbie's funeral had taken place.

It was all so final. Barbie was not only dead, but buried too. There was no chance whatsoever to say goodbye. I was devastated. She was not only my godmother, but also a very good friend and I had loved her deeply over the years since my childhood. I felt totally knocked over by this astonishing news and resorted to floods of tears. The tears came and would not stop. I knew that there wasn't any possible chance of my continuing with the overland journey. I had been struggling with it all along not only on account of my troublesome stomach, but also because I needed to be with Graeme. Now there was this terrible tragedy of Barbie's death to think about. How devastated my mother would have been. The two sisters could not possibly have been closer friends. I stayed at the post office long enough to ring my mother to tell her how desperately sad I was at the news and suggested that I come home. She said that since there was now little I could do, either for her or for Barbie, why didn't I give the matter some more thought and decide in a few days time?

I took her advice and proceeded on to Greece but from Istanbul to Athens the journey passed in a blur. I cried too much in Istanbul to be interested in seeing anything very much, other than the Blue Mosque which was quite spectacular. In Greece we saw Mount Olympus, home of the Greek Gods, and in Meteora found ancient monasteries which had been built atop strange outcrops of rocks, thus making it almost impossible to have any kind of contact with the outside world. How they had been built in the first place left one wondering, but how the monks had been able to survive in such completely outlandish conditions was also a wonder. There was one which allowed visitors to enter, via specially erected gangplanks, and it was quite an experience to see a little of the harsh conditions and to stare in amazement at all the skulls piled high, presumably of past occupants. At Delphi we saw the original stadium where in ancient times the Greeks had begun the Olympic Games. The original starting blocks were quite clearly visible, along with the area used for chariot races. In Delphi we also saw the Temple of Apollo, where the Oracle of Delphi prophesied. But once in Athens I headed straight for a telephone booth to ring Graeme. I had pretty much decided to abandon the rest of the trip but I wanted to know whether he thought I should too. I told him of Barbie's death, and how badly it had affected me, and of how I was still suffering bouts of diarrhoea, and how terribly badly I was missing him. He didn't want to make the decision for me, but I think, like me, he felt that I should go home. It was a tragedy to be missing the time in Athens and from Greece to Bulgaria, Romania and Russia from where the bus would go through Scandinavia before taking the ferry over to the United Kingdom. But that journey would take another month, and having now spent two months on the bus already I knew that I could take no more of shared rooms, cold showers (but only if I was lucky) and the weariness which had come about through journeying on and on, never really sleeping well and never feeling clean. My heart and my stomach won over my brain in the conflict which took place within me in coming to the decision, as I did, to fly home immediately. At 4.05 p.m. on the twentieth April 1980 I flew from Athens to London.

When I arrived I felt like an alien from another planet, not at all like a British woman arriving home. There were lots of factors which contributed to this feeling; not only had I been living in the Pacific for nearly two years since last being in London but I had also spent such a long time on the bus, mostly in very deprived parts of the world, living in deprived conditions myself. I was incredibly tired, very dirty indeed, to the point that I couldn't believe I would ever feel clean again. I was travelling in very old and disreputable clothes which were considerably worse for the wear that they had had over the past two months and which were also hanging off me on account of the amount of weight I had lost. Added to this generally dejected picture was the fact that although I knew my mother's address, I didn't actually know where she lived, as she had moved, yet again, to the third block of flats since leaving the Chislehurst house six years earlier. So here I stood, a bedraggled sight, at Heathrow Airport clutching a motley collection of bags along with several souvenirs acquired along the way. I gazed around me, watching the smart travellers and uniformed flight crews, all purposefully going about their business and I felt at a loss to know what I should be doing next. It was culture shock, of course, although at the time I had never heard the expression. In recent years much research has been done into the effects of travel and living outside one's own culture, and how, strangely, it can affect one equally badly on returning to one's native soil. This phenomenon had not affected me the last time I left the

Pacific, but being on a bus in such appallingly basic conditions for two months had completely disorientated me.

Once I had pulled myself together I got a coach to Victoria from where I caught a train to Bromley, and from there I flopped into a taxi which took me to my mother's new address. She hardly recognised me when she opened the door, so different did I look. This slim bedraggled person, with her hair in a completely unkempt condition was a stranger to her. These were all fleeting impressions, though, and we were soon sitting talking about Barbie and the shock her death had been to the family. Everyone was still stunned by the suddenness of her death, and although her funeral had taken place it was proving difficult to come to terms with her absence. My mother had lost her best friend and was incredibly sad at her passing. She showed me round her little flat and then I unpacked my few things and headed for the bathroom. What a glorious feeling it was to soak in a big warm bath. My feet were covered in hard, cracked skin, bleeding in places and I knew that it would take a chiropodist to put them right, but the soak did them good and I almost felt like a new person once I had dried and dressed. My mother told me that my crates had arrived from the Solomon Islands, having left there in early January, and I went down to the garage to see how they had fared during the long sea journey from the Pacific. They were fine, but as I closed the garage door I wondered just where they would be heading next.

I had only been home about three and a half weeks, during which time I had paid urgent visits to both the hairdresser and the chiropodist, and also the doctor for a remedy for my stomach, and I was, by now, feeling much more my old self, when I received a telephone call from Graeme. He had lots of news to tell me but first he told me of the tragic death of Robert, his houseboy. Poor Robert had been knocked over on the road by a cyclist, while he was walking to church, and had died of his injuries. Olivet was in shock, as was Graeme too, having had to take charge in this terribly unfortunate situation. Funerals must take place quickly in the tropics, and it had proved difficult to make all the necessary arrangements on a Sunday in the speedy way which had been required.

But that was not the main reason he was ringing. He had just received telephoned advice from Wellington of an urgent transfer from the Solomons. His Ministry had given him three weeks to be out of Honiara and on his way to Tehran where he was to be appointed as chargé d'affaires a.i.. This basically means that you are required to be head of post, temporarily, until either the political situation becomes clearer or a permanent Ambassador can be appointed. So, he was to head the New Zealand Embassy in Tehran, for a timespan which was not expected to be for long since it was hinged on the fact that New Zealand was downgrading its Embassy during the American hostage crisis. Nobody could believe that this situation would last for much longer and he was therefore urged to travel light. He was ringing me now to ask whether I would go there with him. Although it didn't take me a split second to know that the answer would, of course, be yes, I also knew at the back of my mind that it was the last place on earth I would have chosen to go to, again, in 1980. It was pretty clear that Graeme had been asked to go there because, so far as the Ministry was concerned, he was at this time a single officer and could therefore be posted unaccompanied. Just such an officer was what was needed. It must, therefore, have come as rather a surprise to the powers-that-be in Wellington to receive a request from Graeme, soon after his call to me, to take his 'fiancée' with him!

Chapter Twelve

Scrabble By Candlelight

It had all happened so unexpectedly. One moment I was wondering if I would ever see Graeme again and the next I was eagerly awaiting his arrival in England. It was an excuse for another 'shop till I dropped', but this time I was buying with a view to obtaining a wardrobe which would be sufficiently modest to accommodate the demands of living in post-Revolution-Islamic-Fundamentalist Iran. Six weeks after my arrival at Heathrow from my overland trip, in that bedraggled and disorientated state, I was once again standing there. However, this time I was indistinguishable from those smart travellers and aircrew going about their business. I was wearing the nicest of my new outfits, which included a navy blue velvet jacket which was a particular favourite, and was nervously scanning the arrivals door for Graeme.

I had arrived earlier than was strictly necessary, and so it seemed like an age before I finally spotted him wheeling his trolley of bags through the doorway. We were both nervous, for a moment or two, but it was a fleeting moment and soon we were hugging and kissing each other, all thoughts of those around us quite forgotten. We finally decided that Heathrow was not the best place to celebrate our reunion and headed for a Green Line bus to Bromley where I had booked us into a hotel for twenty-four hours. In spite of his jet lag, having flown direct from Wellington (which is a thirty-six hour journey door to door) Graeme seemed to be firing on all cylinders and at no time gave the impression of being exhausted. There was so much to catch up on. We had not been together for four months, although our tapes, letters, and telephone calls had ensured that we kept closely in touch, but even so there seemed to be a lot to talk about. It was late that night, on 6th June 1980, that we finally fell into an exhausted but contented sleep.

And late the next day before we surfaced for breakfast, or, more likely, lunch. That idyllic twenty-four hours passed all too quickly and soon it was time to take Graeme to my mother's flat and introduce her to her future son-in-law. There was an immediate rapport between the two of them and their relationship has never looked back over the years. My mother welcomed Graeme into her small flat and he felt completely at home in her company. Of course, they had both heard a lot about the other, from me, and indeed my mother had already seen Graeme, live as it were, through slow-scan television transmissions of a radio amateur who lived in Wimbledon. Before Graeme packed up his belongings in Honiara he had exchanged television transmissions with this friend. They had arranged a time and date to be in contact again, in our presence, in order for us all to see each other and hear one another's voices, albeit briefly, just a few weeks earlier. So the scene had already been set, and Graeme seemed to be part of the family instantly. We all had a wonderfully happy week together. I took him around and about the pretty Kentish countryside and we enjoyed meals together in places ranging from The Leather Bottle Inn in Cobham through to Quaglinos in London one evening, where we celebrated our engagement and I enjoyed watching the sparkle of the sapphire and diamonds in the beautiful ring Graeme had bought me.

Graeme had to deal with some administrative matters at the New Zealand High Commission in London which was going to be responsible, amongst other things, for paying him. It was a chance for me to be introduced to a few staff members too, and we spent a pleasant morning at the High Commission while Graeme made all necessary arrangements before taking up his new appointment. I had been giving much thought as to whether I should renew contact with my father, with whom I had not been in touch since he left my mother six years earlier. I had deliberated long and hard. I wasn't sure about what to do. My father had successfully wrecked every relationship I had ever had and I was scared that he might end up doing so yet again. At the same time I was completely certain of Graeme, and his love for me, and this certainty had led me to contact my father and arrange to introduce him to Graeme over lunch on the day we had been to the High Commission in London. It was an emotional reunion, and at the end of the short time we had with my father I felt that I had done the right thing.

The week had been a very full one and there had been no time to introduce Graeme to anyone other than my parents. They had both liked him enormously and embraced him as a prospective family member with open hearts. But the spectre of separation was ever-present with Graeme's departure at the end of one short week. It seemed like no time at all before we were both back at Heathrow once more, but this time with the comforting glow of certainty that our separation would not be for long. Graeme wanted to ensure that all would be in order for my arrival later, but the delay was really on account of my having to wait an inordinate length of time for a visa from the Iranian Embassy in London. In the event it was five weeks before I was able to return to Heathrow for my own flight to Tehran. Both my parents were there to see me off on what was, in the midst of the American hostage crisis in Tehran, undoubtedly an adventure. Although I was, like Graeme, travelling light, I did have three suitcases of clothes with me, but little else besides. It was clear that we would need to be in a position to evacuate quickly, should the need arise, and there was little point in having too much with us. My only piece of hand baggage was my pride and joy – a portable electric typewriter, which Graeme had bought for me at Selfridges during a shopping spree in London.

It is hard to believe that, such a short time ago, this was really a wonderful present. I had only used electric typewriters at work but at home had used a manual Olivetti. I felt like a traitor to my little manual machine, which had served me well over many years and was still in excellent condition. But this was progress and I could not deny that it was a joy to have the added facility of an electric typewriter. As I type this on our computer that self-same electric typewriter sits sullenly on my desk, ever reproachful that its motor has barely run for several years! It shouldn't complain though, for it had a very useful and eventful life, travelling the world and being plugged into some strange sockets over an eleven-year working life. So, there I was, waving goodbye to my parents at Heathrow and carrying this new acquisition. It was heavy, though, in spite of being a portable machine, and I was thankful to eventually reach the departure gate where I could rest my arm before boarding the plane. On the flight to Tehran I found myself sitting next to a mullah. He was returning to his country after many years in exile and held forth, during the entire flight, on the wonderful events which had recently taken place in his country. I was branded an 'infidel' and told I was 'unclean', all in a perfectly civil manner, and the whole experience was quite extraordinary. The nearer I got to Tehran the more I wondered just what was in store for me there.

Soon we were at Mehrabad Airport, and upon disembarking from the aircraft my travelling companion offered to carry the heavy typewriter for me. What a strange mixture this mullah was. On the one hand singing the praises of the Revolution and telling me I was 'unclean' and the next offering to help me with a heavy load to carry. Perhaps it was his time in exile in Paris that caused him to behave in such an eminently civil fashion? Who knows, but I didn't stop to question his offer, I simply accepted it gratefully. Before I knew it, though, I had lost sight of him since men and women were being channelled through separate immigration formalities. He had marched steadfastly ahead, carrying my typewriter, and I had tried to keep up with him until I was rudely told I could go no further but must join the long line of women waiting to pass through the various stages of officialdom. I had lost him and I wondered how on earth I was going to be reunited with my typewriter. So agitated was I on this score that I must have appeared thoroughly distracted when I finally met up with Graeme in the main concourse of the airport. "I'm trying to find a mullah who has got my typewriter," were my first words to poor Graeme.

"Well, there can't be too many mullahs around carrying typewriters," replied Graeme. We both stood and stared around us. The place was absolutely lousy with mullahs and they were all carrying something. It was like a Boy Scouts Day Out – mullahs were everywhere and they all looked exactly alike with their distinctive form of head-dress and their bearded faces. I was near to tears at the thought of never finding my present from Graeme when, out of the mêlée, my mullah appeared, totally unruffled and smilingly handing over my typewriter.

That crisis over, we now had to be reunited with my suitcases. I had not realised that there would be any kind of problem until the moment came when they were being searched. Since I was not travelling on a New Zealand diplomatic passport, simply my own ordinary British one, I was subjected to the kind of intrusive examination which, mercifully, I have mostly been spared over the years of travelling with Graeme. However, this was a very thorough search and the upshot was that they wanted exorbitant payment of duty for "this large quantity of new clothing". At this moment, Sarkis, the Embassy driver and general 'Mr Fixit' stepped in with the words "*Not new clothing* – they have very good dry cleaners in Britain!" This was my first lesson that it wasn't a question of what you knew, but who you knew, and Sarkis proved to be worth his weight in gold in the ensuing months in Tehran. So, after what seemed like (and actually was) a very long haul, we finally drove away from Mehrabad Airport, which is situated about five miles to the west of Tehran city. It was a bleak landscape, full of promise of what might have been, but more like a deserted building site with half-completed skyscrapers standing next to idle cranes. Everywhere there were signs reading "Death to the Americans", "Down with the Great Satan", both in Persian (Farsi) and English. Everything looked white, dusty and hot, and somehow deserted, although with a population of four and a half million it was also teeming with life. The standard of driving was simply appalling and horns were honking and cars were careering everywhere. No notice seemed to be taken of traffic lights, and Sarkis was constantly muttering under his breath with frustration as he drove Graeme and me to the New Zealand Residence in Tehran, located at that time at Shirkouh Alley, number three.

After the experiences of the day the Residence seemed like a haven of cool peace. Graeme introduced me to the house staff – a cook called Fateh, and a houseboy called Yasin, both Pakistanis. He then showed me round the house. The ground floor was geared towards official entertaining and consisted of a very long and narrow lounge, which stretched the full depth of the house, and a dining-room. The rest of the ground floor contained the kitchen, pantry, laundry and store rooms. Upstairs was much cosier and far more private. There was a large master-bedroom with a nice little sitting-room next door, along with an en suite bathroom. There were several more bedrooms, but they had fallen into a state of disrepair and were neither well furnished nor attractive. None of this mattered too much because we lived in our small quarters upstairs, which were well appointed and led out onto an upstairs balcony which was most attractive and overlooked a lovely garden and swimming pool. I was too happy, now that I was finally at home with Graeme, to mind about any of it, and certainly spectres of being virtually under house arrest were far from my mind as we fell into each other's arms that day, the seventeenth of July 1980, which heralded the beginning of our life together.

For the next five months we lived happily in Tehran. It certainly had its difficulties, but the main thing for us then was that we were together. But the country was going through a major upheaval, and the Muslim-Fundamentalist movement was taking a grip on the place and it meant that I was not free to come and go as I pleased. I could not have driven there, even if I had wanted to, and how Graeme ever managed to get about on those crazy roads always amazed me. Nor could I have wandered about, on my own, and so I was confined to the house during the course of Graeme's working day. This meant that it was difficult to get to know people, since we were only getting out and about to official functions, and even these had trailed off considerably in the months since the Revolution. There were few English-speaking western women about, in any event, since the Americans were either hostages, or had escaped; the British had evacuated (although were around in small numbers at some stage of my time there); the Canadians had all gone too; the Australian Embassy was staffed entirely by men, and so, really, that only left me and another New Zealand Embassy wife (who was lucky enough to have a job at the Chancery). For the first time in my life I had nothing to do. There were no household duties to perform; I never discovered a library, although I think that this was simply because I did not know how to go about looking for one; and I had not managed to meet any other women in the same situation as myself. It was just as well that Graeme was all I needed and wanted in my life at that time. However, I had to find a way of getting through the working hours of each day, and although I found that to begin with I was simply sorting out my things and getting to know the house, it wasn't long before I turned to the typewriter to help me pass the lonely hours.

My first idea was to type out my letters to Graeme, written during the overland journey. I thought that I might, at a later stage in my life, be glad of a permanent record of what had happened. Perhaps one day I might write a book! If I did, I would be glad to know what I had written then. I started to type the first letter. My writing was awful and I could hardly read it in places, and somehow, so much had happened since writing, I could not muster up the interest in going back on the events of earlier that year. I gave up the project as a waste of time and threw the letters away. That project put aside, I then read the only book I was able to get my hands on, found lying around the Residence and about the life of Sigmund Freud. But I had to find something more worthwhile to do and Graeme suggested I spend some time helping out at the office. This seemed a good idea, and although there was no paid employment available I did manage to help out on a voluntary basis in some small way. I did a little typing, some filing, and spent quite a long time reorganising the reference library, and was pleased with the results of my efforts. Being at the Chancery also provided some company and a change of scene from the Residence.

At other times I got back to my electric typewriter and wrote endless letters. This was enjoyable while it lasted, but it didn't last long. On the twenty-second of September 1980 the Iran/Iraq war started when Iraqi planes bombed Mehrabad Airport. As a consequence, the airport was immediately closed to commercial traffic. This meant that we could not get mail out of the country, nor could we receive any. Not only was this utterly frustrating and upsetting, for all the obvious reasons, but it also meant that a halt was placed on Graeme's impending divorce. He was unable to communicate with his solicitor in Wellington, and so the legal proceedings wound down just when we needed them to be speeded up. So, there we were, with all these letters to post and no means of getting them out of the country. It was a lot more upsetting than the bombs which dropped on Tehran.

Two month's after arriving in Tehran I discovered that I was pregnant. The whole episode of discovery was quite extraordinary. The only doctor we knew was not a gynaecologist but simply the Iranian doctor-husband of a delightful Swiss lady we had met at a party. We knew of no other means of getting me checked out and so rang Hedy one day to ask if we could have an appointment with her husband. That arranged, he said that he thought, in all probability, that I was pregnant. He arranged for the necessary test to be performed, and a day or two later Graeme returned from work carrying a large bunch of white lilies (which always remind me of death) along with a laboratory form stating that the test had been positive. I simply could not believe it. I had thought that I was entirely too old to be likely to get pregnant, and although we had both wanted to start a family and knew that time was not on our side, it still came as a complete shock to me. Even stranger that Graeme was telling *me*, rather than the other way around! Within days of receiving this information, the bombing of Tehran began, and with it the closing of the airport. Now that the need for a divorce was even more urgent we were placed in the invidious position of not being able to communicate with anyone.

At thirty-five I also thought that I should be having some medical attention through my pregnancy but the only time I saw a doctor was when I saw Hedy's husband. Luckily I had a simply marvellous pregnancy. It was the almost complete lack of symptoms which had led to the rather late diagnosis in the first place and I felt on top of the world. My skin had never been better, by hair grew thick and fast, and my nails hardly ever broke. But before I had the pregnancy test, I had become inexplicably exhausted. Suddenly, at a function, I became totally weary without having the faintest idea why. This phenomenon had passed and it was several weeks later before I had the explanation. But, other than that, I was in top form and never once looked back through the entire nine months. It was merciful really, since life in Tehran in those days was difficult enough without any added complications.

We were always hearing of people who had been hauled in by the authorities, never to be heard of again. Those who were not fortunate enough to escape often ended up in Evin prison, and who knows what fate awaited them there. We found ourselves harbouring a New Zealand journalist who was 'wanted for questioning'. Although we knew we were taking a risk by having him hide with us, we hardly felt that we could desert him to the whims of the local revolutionary guards. He did manage to escape, but we were glad that there was only one other episode of this kind.

When the war started in September, life changed even more dramatically. Hitherto there had been a semblance of normality amongst the diplomatic community, but now everything changed. There was a curfew imposed, along with a blackout from dusk until dawn. Neither situation was conducive to the continued attendance at National Day receptions! The crazy driving continued, nonetheless, in spite of the blackout, and now to the mayhem on the roads could be added the sight of cars driving around with blue cellophane paper over their lights. It all seemed so pointless, really, since sophisticated weaponry is hardly dependant upon visual sightings of targets, not even back in 1980. These new developments changed the course of our social life quite considerably. While it had been neither particularly busy nor particularly lively, hitherto, it now became practically non-existent. We got out the Scrabble board, night after night, and played by candlelight. This simple enjoyment is my lasting impression of Tehran in those days. I didn't know then, as I know now, that time to play Scrabble would become a luxury in the years to come, whereas now it was a necessity. We became very good at the game, and very competitive in our approach to it, but there were few times when one would thrash the other, rather more it would be a pretty close run thing.

The other way we passed our evenings was by playing bridge with a Canadian friend, Tony, and his Iranian girlfriend Shirin. They would either come over to our place, have dinner with us and then play bridge until the small hours, followed by spending what was left of the night in one of our indifferent spare bedrooms, or we would do the same at their house. It was the only way to get round the curfew, if not the blackout, but it provided an excellent excuse to get to know them much better by spending more time with them than would probably otherwise have been the case. The other attraction to coming to play bridge with us, for Shirin anyway, was our adorable little kitten, Billy. He had been acquired by way of 'company' for me and had proved to be the sweetest of little ginger Toms.

Billy had not been happy, though, when we first brought him to the Residence. He had cried all night, pacing the sitting-room floor, and I had been up to him a dozen times trying to calm him down. Finally we decided that we must give him a little freedom to explore and decided to let him out onto the balcony outside the sitting-room. He ventured forth, very gingerly at first, and then with increasing confidence began to explore what must have seemed to him a large expanse of new territory. When he got to the end of the balcony with one swift jump he was up on the railings, from where it was just a step onto a drooping branch from a nearby tree. He was so small, and so light, but even so the branch swung furiously up and down with his weight. Within moments he was on more secure branches further up the tree and, before any of us knew it, was firmly stuck there. This was the point at which I could do no more for Billy and ran to get

Graeme to see if he could get up to rescue the little kitten. Graeme had not had the same instant rapport with Billy, especially since he had been crying all night, and he wasn't best pleased to be faced with this situation now. However, he overcame these considerations and proceeded to climb up to where Billy was securely nestled within the branches. Poor Billy had another unfortunate episode some months later, after I had left, when Graeme brushed him away from where he was trying to claw away at his trousers, and inadvertently knocked him against the table. Billy's leg was broken in the process and he ended up walking around with his limb in plaster for several weeks.

Our quiet life was enlivened, once or twice, when in October I had my thirty-sixth birthday (for which Tony and Shirin stayed over and we had a pleasant birthday dinner, followed by bridge), and this was followed shortly by a farewell party for Graeme's secretary, Helen. Wellington had decided (a colloquialism, for the Ministry of Foreign Affairs had decided!) that Tehran was no longer safe for single female officers and had asked Graeme to make arrangements for Helen's evacuation. Since no flights were leaving from Mehrabad she had little choice but to depart by coach, via Turkey, following much the same route I had taken several months earlier on my overland trip. We sent her off in style with a party, before taking her to catch her transport out. We glanced up at the Iraqi warplanes overhead and hoped that she would make it safely out of the country. Her main worry, though, was having to leave behind two huge dogs who were her dearest friends. Not long after this there was a panic at the Australian Embassy and it rather looked as though they would evacuate too. For a day or two Graeme wondered if this would have repercussions on us (since it was unlikely that any distinction would be made by the Iranians between Australia and New Zealand), and I have to admit that I was secretly hoping that events would lead to our evacuation. In the event the Australians did not leave, so neither did we.

By November I was four months pregnant, and beginning to show it, and the time had now come to get some looser clothes. The choice was abysmal and I only purchased two hideous sack-like dresses which, in the event, turned out to be the mainstay of my maternity wardrobe. The weather was also getting very cold at nights and we could see that before long we would be gripped in a bitter Iranian winter. By the end of November, however, we were more engrossed in how to give due celebration on the occasion of Graeme's fortieth birthday. The blackout and the curfew were still in force, but we decided to risk all and have a party nonetheless. The futility of the security measures had already become apparent and we did not feel too guilty about deciding to hold a party. We had invited almost thirty people to help make Graeme's day special, and everything worked out beautifully. We obviously could not manage to offer beds to that number of people, but, as I say, by this time both the curfew and the blackout were hardly being observed. We made some concessions to the authorities, nonetheless, and endeavoured not to draw attention to ourselves by ensuring that we did not break the blackout. It all helped towards making for a cosy and intimate atmosphere and, if anything, enhanced the mood of the evening. There had been so little entertaining done in the past couple of months that people were very much in the mood to enjoy themselves, and this they did that evening. It was a happy and memorable occasion. Fateh, the cook, had practised his skills at birthday-cake making the month before, on me, and so on this day managed to produce a very creditable effort.

We were beginning to wonder if we stood a chance of getting out on Christmas leave. The airport was still closed, we were still deprived of mail in or out, and it was beginning to look as though we would have to think about leaving the country overland. There were few options open to us since departing via Turkey was no longer possible on account of the harsh winter conditions. Taking a train to Moscow seemed to be the only option open to us and Graeme started to make enquiries about the feasibility of this means of travel. It would take five days, from Tehran to Moscow, at that time of the year but once there we would be able to fly to London. Bearing in mind my pregnancy, which by the time of our departure would be five months, we were uncertain of the wisdom of such a means of travel. However, since it was that or nothing, we were left with little choice but to apply for our visas to travel to Moscow. It began to look as though, after all, I would finally make it to Russia. I was very excited at the prospect of travelling there, especially having got so near to making it earlier in the year, and I was firmly of the opinion that we should make the journey.

In the event I was pipped at the post by the airport opening up for a limited number of flights out. I was hugely disappointed, and to this day I have still not managed to make that longed-for trip to Russia.

No doubt it was for the best, all the same, since a five day train journey, mid-winter, would have been difficult to say the least. Seats on the first flight out, an unscheduled Iran Air 747 Jumbo, were as precious as gold and incredibly hard to come by. There was such a huge backlog of people wishing to get out of the country and it was definitely a question of *who* you knew not *what* you knew (as so often had proved the case in Tehran in those days) in order to secure a seat on the first plane out. Graeme had been lucky to do a deal with an Iran Air employee regarding a tourist visa for New Zealand in exchange for two seats on the plane! However irregular this may appear to be, it was simply a question of just the right person wanting a visa at just the right moment in time. We received tickets for seats on that flight and we cancelled our train tickets, but it was all being done at the last moment, simply hours before leaving. In the event my final departure from Tehran passed in a whirl of packing and last minute organisation, along with a tearful farewell to little Billy.

We had decided that I could not return, after Christmas leave, with Graeme. It was heartbreaking to realise this, but it was also clear that Tehran would not be the place to have my first baby at my advanced time of life. There was little available in the shops and at times one could go into a supermarket and find the shelves almost completely bare. The most basic requirements were more often than not unavailable and, as time passed, these deficiencies became more and more apparent. Little seemed to be freely obtainable other than cigarettes, caviar, and chicken. That didn't auger well for life with a new baby! I couldn't bear the idea of yet more separation from Graeme, but could also see the futility of trying to cope in ever more difficult circumstances. But first we had Christmas in England to look forward to, and this would present us with the opportunity to introduce Graeme to a number of friends and family members. So, on a wintry December day in 1980 we proceeded to Mehrabad airport to catch our plane to London.

It took us five hours to get through the various stages of security and Customs formalities, during which time there was simply nothing available other than caviar and thick black coffee. It was an appalling experience. Everyone was suspect. Everyone was assumed to have a devious or ulterior motive in trying to leave the country. Everyone had their jewellery examined, and if for one moment they thought that it had been purchased in Iran, it was immediately confiscated. I nearly lost items of sentimental value which had belonged to my mother and grandmother. They would stop at nothing to take gold and jewellery away if they thought that they possibly could. Even my camera was suspect and they wanted to be sure it was not being used illegally. One of the guards wanted to take a photograph of me with it, and when I refused, saying, "No, I'll take a photograph of you to remind me of this occasion," his reaction was so violent that I thought I would be clapped in irons. Finally, we got on board the Iran Air flight to London. If we thought that the five hours we spent at Tehran airport had been hard to cope with it was nothing compared with the five hours we spent stuck in Istanbul for a refuelling stop en route. It turned out that the engines had become jammed in reverse on landing and the mechanics had been unable to rectify the problem very quickly. During the five-hour wait we had not been permitted to disembark, nor had we been given any food or drink. We were told there was simply none on board. We were beginning to wish we had gone on that train to Moscow after all.

Many hours later than expected we finally arrived at Heathrow, in the middle of the night. I have never before seen the place so deserted, it seemed as though the only person who was waiting there was my father who had come to collect us and take us back to his house for the night.

Chapter Thirteen

Lady In Waiting

We were really exhausted when we met up with my father, in the small hours of the morning of the ninth of December, and no doubt he was too from the incredibly long delay in our arrival. He drove us the relatively short distance to his house in Worplesdon and we were relieved that the travelling was over and we could collapse into bed. I had not been looking forward to meeting my stepmother for the first time (she had first entered my life, in such an unhappy way, back in 1957), and I was not sorry that she had decided not to wait up for us. The following morning would be time enough to face her. When the time did come we found her behaviour extraordinary. She was bad-tempered and thoroughly unwelcoming. We had breakfast virtually thrown at us, and I was thankful that our arrangement had only been to stay overnight and leave after breakfast to go to Bromley.

My mother's welcome was reassuring after that unpleasant experience. Soon we set our minds to the happy prospect of being in touch with all the people we wanted to see while Graeme was on leave. He had a champagne reception all along the way. Everyone seemed so pleased to meet him and everyone liked him so much. My father had lent me his Ford Escort, which had been mine before I left for Tehran, but which on my departure he had bought from me as a second car. This was kind of him and meant that we could get around and about much more easily. Our first call was on my godparents, Cyril and Marjorie. It nearly went horribly wrong, though, because we had been told to arrive no sooner than half past midday. In the event, having been unsure of how long the journey would take and whether we would find their house near Colgate without difficulty, we arrived early. The main reason being that, as with all pregnant women, I was in urgent need of a loo stop. Rather than trying to scramble through bushes, we had decided to ring the doorbell half an hour before time. Oh dear, poor Marjorie wasn't ready for us, and it seemed as though our visit would be getting off to a shaky start. However, Cyril popped the champagne cork, poured champagne cocktails all round, and very soon we were over the difficulty and thoroughly enjoying our visit.

Great-aunt Ness (my maternal grandmother's sister) was high on the list of people to visit. Although temperamentally very different from my grandmother, she was dear to me and always reminded me so strongly of my grandmother. She was now in a nursing home in Tenterden and seemed pleased when we told her that our baby was due on her birthday. My friend Vicky was working at the Royal Naval College in Greenwich at this time, and Graeme and I had a lovely evening with her there. She was able to introduce Graeme to the splendours of the Painted Hall and the wonderful ambience emanating from those beautiful old buildings.

After spending Christmas day with my mother, we went over to Worplesdon to be with my father on Boxing Day. We found him alone, his wife having left him only a matter of days after we had first met her. While this was obviously a complete shock to us, we were personally rather thankful that she was not there. Nevertheless, my father was extremely upset at this turn of events and I could not help but feel sorry for him. His Christmas had not been a happy one and we tried our best to make Boxing Day memorable. We went along with his wishes to play games and wear silly hats, and my heart went out to him in his distress at losing his wife. But I was not sorry for what had happened and believed that it could lead, in time, to a better relationship with him than would otherwise have been possible. On New Year's Eve he joined Graeme, my mother and me at Trafalgar Square where we had decided to show Graeme one of our traditional British customs. We had all had dinner at the Savoy Hotel beforehand, and so were well fortified to cope with the rather 'over the top' merriment displayed by some of my country-folk. In the New Year we fitted in as many more visits as we could, including seeing my friends from HMS *Raleigh* days, the Carpenters. Nigel took us over to HMS *Dryad* where it was interesting to see the original D-Day map for the Normandy invasion. Our last visitors to come to Bromley were my father's brother Roy, his wife Joy, and Roy's son William. After that there was precious little time left before Graeme had to return to Tehran. Before he went we called in at a supermarket to stock his cases with cereal, sugar, marmalade and a host of other food items which he would otherwise have had to manage without. His departure, in January 1981, coincided with the American hostages' fourteenth month of captivity. Their fate was now my fate. When they were free I would get my man back.

After Graeme's departure, monitoring the news became a way of life to me. The hostages were always on the brink of release, according to press reports, and I found the whole business totally absorbing. I was learning so much more about the wretched affair than I had been able to learn whilst in Tehran, where it had been extremely difficult to get accurate information. None of the hostages' nearest or dearest could possibly be wishing for their release any more than I was. The tension mounted with every new hope through that month, only to be dashed once again when hope evaporated into disappointment. The days after Graeme's departure passed so slowly, always waiting for news and never hearing what I wanted to hear. When, on the twentieth of January 1981, the hostages were finally released, after 444 days in captivity, my hopes that Graeme, too, would soon be out of Iran soared. The arrangement had been that he would go there, for a duration not expected to be longer than six months at the outside, and that he would have to go with very few possessions to help pass the time. Surely, now, it would not be long before relations would be normalised and an Ambassador appointed?

I could not expect that this would happen overnight, of course, but in my wildest dreams I did not believe that Graeme would be left languishing in Tehran for a further seven months. In the event he spent almost as long there as the hostages themselves. If I had known, it would have helped me come to terms with the situation, but living daily in hope of hearing something was utterly soul-destroying. Hope turned to despair, despair turned to resentment, resentment turned to anger at the way Graeme was being treated and, finally, that anger turned on Graeme.

However slowly time was passing now, nothing could alter the fact that my pregnancy was advancing towards its conclusion. I had desperately hoped that we could have been married at Christmas time, while Graeme was in England, but it had long since been apparent that this would not be possible. I had little choice but to try to accept that I was going to have to go this last bit alone. I decided it was time, however belatedly, that I saw a doctor and register at antenatal classes. There were no complications and all I had to do now was wait. During the course of one of my regular check-ups I was asked at which hospital I was planning to have the baby. It struck me as a strange question, since I had not thought that I had any choice in the matter and that I would simply be admitted to the local maternity hospital at Stone Park. However, it transpired that I was not going to be permitted to have my baby on the National Health. I had left England four and a half years earlier, and during my time in the Solomon Islands I had not kept up my National Health contributions. I was now disqualified. After paying into the scheme for so many years, throughout my working life since the age of eighteen, I could not come to terms with the fact that I was now being treated worse than a foreign immigrant. Nor could we afford the thousands of pounds it would cost to have the baby at a private hospital.

My father was equally astonished when he heard this and set about trying to find a solution. As an ex-Army officer he was still entitled to use the medical facilities at military hospitals and thought that I, as his daughter (and an ex-WRNS officer) should at least be entitled to the same opportunities. He made enquiries at the military hospital in Aldershot and got a positive response. It was kind of them and I appreciated their generosity of spirit, particularly since this was so lacking at the local medical centre in Bromley. However, it was a totally impractical arrangement and meant that I had to continue being monitored in Bromley, but that the doctors and midwives I was beginning to know would not, in the event, have anything to do with the delivery. Although I explained all this on the telephone to Graeme, there was little he could do to help me from Tehran. So now, not only were my hopes of Graeme's release turning to despair, but also I had this ghastly situation to contend with which conjured up visions of trying to drive myself over to Aldershot whilst in labour.

While I was going through my own personal turmoil, Graeme was continuing to struggle with the frustrations and difficulties in Tehran, none of which ever got any easier. In fact, in spite of the hostages' release (or perhaps even because of it), life became even less secure for the foreigners still there. Tony and Shirin had become anxious to leave, but the main difficulty was for Shirin since exit permits for Iranians were hard to come by. Tony did not want to leave until he was confident that she was safely out of the country. By the time her permit finally came through, and she flew out to freedom, Tony's position had worsened. He was being tied ever tighter by bureaucratic red tape, all of it designed to put him in an increasingly difficult situation.

Finally the time came when he knew that there was only one way out for him and that that was to escape. He turned to Graeme for help, not in the planning or implementation of his departure, but to lie low, undetected, at the Residence for a few days until the scent had died down. This he did, followed by a most daring escape which would not have shamed the pages of a James Bond novel. When he finally made it to the Gulf, he headed straight to the airport to catch a plane to Athens, where he would be reunited with Shirin. As he was sitting back in his seat, thanking his lucky stars that he had got this far, safely, he heard the announcement that the plane was about to depart for Tehran. He turned to jelly. How could he possibly have been so stupid as to get a plane going via Tehran? Of course, he had misheard, and it was in fact going via Dhahran in Saudi Arabia. When he tells the story of his exploits in escaping Tehran, he always says that nothing at all compared with the moment when he thought he was heading straight back there!

Communications with Iran were still difficult, and besides, Tony had much to do to get his life back together again and so was not in touch with Graeme until quite some time later. For this reason Graeme did not know, at that time, whether Tony had made it safely out of the country, or not. Meanwhile, the pieces of our lives were coming together again. I now knew that I was going to have to get over to Aldershot to have the baby; Graeme had also booked himself on a flight out of Tehran on the 6th of April (there was only one flight a week from Tehran to London and the baby was due on the ninth) in order to be in England for the birth; and Tony and Shirin were now reunited in Athens, where they had a holiday before flying on to London.

Shortly before everyone was due to arrive, including the baby, I developed a painful abscess which was going to give me awful problems during the baby's birth. I went to a new doctor, my normal one being off duty, for the abscess to be lanced. He gave me what turned out to be my final antenatal check-up and asked me where the baby was going to be born. I briefly explained the situation and watched his face change from mere social enquiry to total disbelief. I have rarely seen such a radical transformation in a doctor's demeanour. He was outraged, on my behalf, that I had been treated so shabbily and that I was going to have to travel such a distance to have my baby. There was little time to lose but he had quite decided that he would, if necessary, take on the Health Minister to achieve his aim, which was that no matter what I would definitely have my baby locally. Whilst it was nice to know that I had someone fighting my corner for me (I had felt very alone and powerless to change things throughout my final months of pregnancy), this unexpected turn of events was, nevertheless, very unsettling. The problem was that I had already been down the path the doctor was now travelling (although I had stopped short of approaching the Health Minister), and I was not at all convinced that he would be successful. The baby could arrive at any moment now and then what would I do? Should I go to Aldershot, or Stone Park? I felt in a state of turmoil and waited for days by the telephone until I heard what the outcome would be.

The telephone rang. It was Tony to say that he and Shirin were now in London and were looking forward to seeing the three of us. How strange that sounded. The three of us! Somehow it made the baby seem real, not just a lump in my tummy. I was thankful to speak to a friend, someone who could and would help me in what might turn out to be a very fraught situation. I explained to Tony what had happened and that I might have to drive over to Aldershot. He told me that if it came to that he would drive me. With those words a heavy load was lifted from my shoulders. The telephone rang again. This time it was the doctor to say that he had made all necessary arrangements and that the baby was to be born at Stone Park. Phew! It was all beginning to seem unreal again. I contacted my father and asked him to cancel my admission to the military hospital, which he did with all due apologies. Then on the 6th of April Graeme arrived, as planned, on the flight from Tehran. Tony drove my car over to Heathrow, with me giving directions in the front and Shirin sitting in the back. It was a very happy reunion with two good friends from what, at that time, seemed like another life ago. They had so much news to tell me, especially Tony who had risked his life getting out of Iran, and we were off to collect Graeme to complete the foursome.

While I stood and waited for Graeme to emerge from the Customs hall at Heathrow, Tony and Shirin made themselves scarce elsewhere. After I had greeted Graeme I suggested that we walk over to the lift which would take us to where the car was parked. He pressed the button and as the lift doors opened, so out stepped Tony and Shirin! His face was a picture of complete astonishment and surprise. The last he had seen of Tony was as he left the shelter of the Residence in Tehran and he had received no news of him since. He had known of Shirin's safe departure, but he had not known that they were both in London now. It was truly all a surprise to him and he was quite speechless for several moments. Tony and Shirin had so recently been reunited with one another that they did not need to be told that this was not the moment for the four of us to get together, and after fond farewells and promises to come and see the new baby, they melted into the crowd.

We collected the car from the parking building, and Graeme drove us back to Bromley. We didn't go to bed that night. There was so much to talk about and so little time left to sort out our lives. My first question was whether Graeme had anything new to report about leaving Tehran. He had heard nothing from Wellington on that score. My second question concerned his divorce. His decree absolute was due within three months, so that was good news but we were still not in a position to either get married or even make arrangements to do so, not knowing where we would be in three months' time. It was all so unsatisfactory. By the morning we still hadn't covered all that needed to be said.

The following day we went into town to buy a pram. I had already fashioned a small crib out of a cardboard box, and bought a blow-up baby bath along with nappies and some baby clothes, but I had kept the purchases to a minimum since I was aware that not only was there precious little space in my mother's flat but also we would be moving soon. The trouble was I didn't know where or when. I couldn't end up in a position where I had a mass of baby equipment to transport halfway round the world. I had not, therefore, bought a cot, nor a highchair nor a proper baby bath. Not even a pram! I had been overcautious in my purchasing and this latter omission needed to be rectified.

At nine month's pregnant and without sleep the night before the crowded town seemed too much to contend with and once we had bought a carrycot-cum-buggy we returned to the flat and dismantled my cardboard-box handiwork. I had spent ages padding it and making it so pretty with soft and frilly fabric that I was really sad to see it all coming to pieces. It had been the only labour of love that I had been able to perform under the circumstances. I certainly hadn't been able to spend the past nine months lovingly preparing a complete room for the baby and this could well be the reason why I still felt the whole thing was unreal.

When I had first registered with the antenatal clinic in Bromley I had discussed with them the difficulty I would have to ensure that Graeme was around for the birth of the baby. Since there was only one flight per week from Tehran to London it was clear that if we left the matter to nature it would be highly unlikely that he would be there for the event. The doctors had agreed to induce the birth, on the due date, if nothing had happened up until then. On the matter of the due date we had fiercely disagreed. They were telling me that the baby was due on the ninth of April and I knew that this could not possibly be so. I had not arrived in Tehran until the seventeenth of July and on the basis of a forty-week gestation period this brought us to the twenty-forth of April at the earliest. The ninth was much too soon. No matter how often I queried the date I always got the same answer. They got out their little circular dial, twiddled it round, and every time came up with the ninth. They were immovable on the matter, and since I was dependant upon their help I had no choice but to accept what they said.

If induction was to take place they wanted me in hospital on the night of the seventh and so, within twenty-four hours of Graeme's arrival and without sleep since the night of the fifth, I reported in to Stone Park Maternity Hospital. Graeme was told that nothing would be happening for several hours and that it would be best if he went and got some sleep. He returned on the morning of the eighth to find me in a pretty unhappy state, having, for the second night running, gone without sleep. Contractions were not getting us very far and little progress was made during the course of the eighth. Hushed comments were reaching my ears along the lines of the baby not being ready to come. I was the last person to be surprised at this news (and indeed, when the baby was examined later it was discovered that her back was covered in a downy sort of hair which is, apparently, a sure sign of prematurity). Labour continued slowly through another night and once more Graeme was advised to return home for some sleep. By the time he returned, very early on the ninth, they had decided to try a forceps delivery. The baby had become a 'face presentation' and was showing signs of distress. After three nights without sleep, so was I, and nothing at all seemed real anymore. I simply wanted the whole thing to be over. I was told that I would be moved to the theatre for a Caesarean section to be performed, under general anaesthetic. This latter point amazed me, since I had already opted for an epidural and this was in place. Why the general anaesthetic? A further delay ensued while the anaesthetist was called in, but finally the operation took place and our seven-pound-twelve-ounce daughter, Nina, arrived in the world at 8.21 on the morning of the ninth of April 1981.

Sometime later that morning I roused from the anaesthetic to see Graeme standing nearby, holding our baby. My first question was to enquire if she was all right. I had to be reassured several times that she was completely perfect and very beautiful. I fell back to sleep. The next several days passed in a whirl of pain and sleeplessness. I had no idea that there would be so much pain and I could barely move, much less get out of bed, without being in agony. Once the anaesthetic had worn off, sleep was yet again a commodity which escaped me. The day after Nina was born I was visited by someone from the Health Department who had come especially to tell me that there had been a dreadful mistake made. I should not have been admitted to Stone Park and would have to pay the costs not only for the delivery, but also the far greater costs of having had a Caesarean section, along with the ten-day stay in hospital as a consequence of this operation. I was utterly dumbfounded. I was only there because my friendly neighbourhood doctor had rung to tell me he had made all the necessary arrangements. Now we were being faced with a bill running into several thousands of pounds. I should never have listened to him; I should have gone to Aldershot after all.

Everything seemed to be one huge nightmare. Friends and family came to visit Nina and me and found me always in tears. Not only was I faced with the realisation that I had a new little person to look after, but I was now going to have to embark on a fierce battle to resolve the injustice of being told we had this huge amount of money to pay. The friendly neighbourhood doctor was called in to fight this battle for me. It was all down to him now. He had started it and he must finish it. In the end he resolved the matter to both his and our satisfaction, but it was a hideous worry hanging over our heads at a time when we should have been a happy little family. The other thing which had done nothing whatsoever for my morale was that my father had visited, with his wife in tow. She was back now, and although this was what he wanted and he was happy again, she was the last person I wanted to see at that awful time.

Graeme's leave was ticking away furiously, and instead of spending it together with our new baby, Nina and I spent most of it in hospital. There was little time left, after we were discharged, to enjoy ourselves. I was in a tremendous amount of pain still and the nightly feeds were very difficult since getting out of bed was the most painful of all. I devised a method, which suited me best, of sliding out onto all fours. I found that getting up off the floor and putting the strain on my arms and legs was far preferable to trying the 'sit up' position. For the few days that Graeme was with me back at my mother's flat he did an enormous amount to help, and I was going to miss not only him, but all the help he gave me too, very much indeed once he had gone. Just before he left, when Nina was only two weeks old, we took her to St Nicholas' Church in Chislehurst, where she was christened.

Then we were on our own. I hadn't even been able to go to Heathrow to see Graeme off but had only managed to drive him to the Green Line bus stop in Bromley, and I had had to wave goodbye to him from there. I wished, so desperately, that Nina and I could be leaving with him too, but now that I had had a Caesarean this meant it was completely out of the question. I would not have been allowed to fly for at least six weeks, and perhaps by then he would be out of Tehran anyway. In the event it was just as well I didn't go since I got a post-operative infection in the wound and it did not heal up for three months. Nina and I soldiered on, with help from my mother, and we lived a very quiet little life for the next three months. My mother's flat was on the third floor and the three flights of stairs were hard to manage with the carrycot, and so I found that we were venturing out very little. By now most of the family and lots of friends had come to visit us and all were thoroughly taken with our beautiful little girl. She had blonde hair and lovely cornflower blue eyes and was as pretty as a picture. The two of us gradually got to know one another and understand what we were supposed to be doing, but I, for one, was certainly on a steep learning curve.

As the days without Graeme turned to weeks and the weeks turned to months I began to wonder what on earth it was all about. Wasn't this supposed to be the most wonderful experience? Wasn't it all supposed to be cosy-togetherness, free of worry and anxiety about the future? It was quite bad enough that we were not yet married, but to be separated as well began to frustrate me beyond words. I started to believe that Graeme was not doing enough to extract himself from Tehran. He had already been there long beyond the original expectation, and the American hostages (who had been the reason for his going there in the first place) had now been released for several months. The weariness from lack of sleep, the pain from a wound which would not heal, the sadness and the worry all began to get me down. My spirits plummeted day by day and finally I started to feel angry with Graeme. Why did he not get in touch with Wellington? He had already fulfilled his part of the bargain and it was time for him to be released. We spoke quite often on the telephone and our conversations became less and less productive and less and less happy.

One day he rang with news. It should have made me happy, but it didn't. I burst into tears. He was not at liberty to speak freely on the telephone and so gave me the cryptic message that he had been posted to 'the place where your cousin Brian is living'. I immediately knew that he meant Bahrain. How could the Ministry do this to him? Another Islamic country; another Middle Eastern posting; all the restrictions on our lifestyle that this would impose. I was so unhappy at the prospect of going there. It was made worse, too, because it was not to be until early 1982. There was to be a six-month secondment to the Department of Trade back in Wellington before going to Bahrain. This would mean travelling halfway round the world, setting up home in New Zealand for a few months, followed by another pack up and starting all over again at the beginning of the next year.

Graeme was mystified by my reaction. He had thought that I would be pleased. He had finally been given a date for departure from Tehran, (on the sixth of July — he always seemed to be returning to me on the sixth!) thirteen months after having gone there. This had been the news I had waited for for so long and now that I had it I was in tears. There was little point in Graeme paying for an expensive telephone call just to listen to my sobs, and we decided to speak again after I had calmed down. The days until his arrival to collect us passed more quickly now, but I was despondent and made little in the way of preparations. There was little to do, really, since I had been living out of a suitcase ever since I had packed up in Honiara one and a half years earlier.

Chapter Fourteen

Setting Up Home

For the two and a quarter years that Graeme and I had been a couple we had had to face constant separation. In Honiara Graeme had been away twice; the second time for almost all my final two months in the Solomons. Then there had been my long journey back to England. After having had to wait several weeks for a visa to travel to Tehran, I only managed to be there with him for five months. This had been followed by the past seven months with my mother in England. It had been those past seven months, when Graeme was doing the extra time in Tehran that had not originally been envisaged, which had been my 'bridge too far'. Out of a possible twenty-seven month period we had managed to be together for approximately twelve. Since April 1979 Graeme had been my whole life; he was never out of my thoughts and I was always praying for the day when he would return to me. By the time that he did I was at a very low ebb indeed. I was still feeling angry at the events which had surrounded my pregnancy and Nina's birth and all the extra problems which had been put in my path. Under different circumstances we could have been married earlier, not faced separation, and I could have left Nina's birth to nature to arrange. I felt certain that all those problems had arisen as a result of having the baby induced, simply to try to ensure that Graeme was with me when she was born. As it turned out, neither of us had witnessed her arrival.

Now that Graeme was coming back, and further separation looked unlikely, I was in a very unhappy frame of mind. Of one thing I was quite certain, however, and that was that New Zealand was the last place where there would be a chance to mend the wounds and put the wrongs right. The three of us had been through too much to now be part of a much wider family, all of whom would be needing his time and attention. He had felt unable to tell his family about me until just a couple of weeks before Nina was born, by which time we had shared our lives for two whole years. It had been deeply hurtful to me to be cast in this light, particularly since he, as a married man, had been so completely welcomed into my family in spirit from the beginning, and in flesh for the past thirteen months. Now he was proposing to take me to New Zealand to meet his family who had had to be sheltered from news of me. Not only that, but his first family lived in Wellington, and this would mean constant and ongoing contact with Diana (his soon-to-be ex-wife) if he was to see his children as much as he wanted to. I wasn't ready for him to swoop in from Tehran, pluck up the mother and baby, and fly us halfway round the world. I needed time to heal.

He wanted me to go with him. He implored me to see sense. He said that we were a family now and should remain so. I said that I couldn't face what was to come, by going to New Zealand. I had already had so precious little time alone with him; the time we'd had together had constantly been punctuated with separation. At the very least I needed to be with just the three of us and I was now being told to make do with a day or two before leaving for Wellington. That day or two was spent in an agony of decision-making, doing nothing but talk. Again we had no sleep. Again Graeme said the same old things, and so did I. Eventually he won and Nina and I flew to New Zealand with him. But I was still not happy and I knew, in my heart, that this was not what we needed, right now, to get our lives together again.

At that time the Ministry paid for temporary accommodation back in Wellington, for a couple of weeks, while returning officers either moved back into their own homes, or, as in our case, found one. It just gave people some breathing space while they sorted out their affairs. It wasn't long, but it was welcome all the same. Travelling that long journey, with a baby, had been exhausting in spite of breaking it for one night in Los Angeles. Our biological clocks were now twelve hours out of kilter, none more so than Nina's. We had allowed her to remain on British time throughout our travels, but now we were in Wellington she slept all day and wanted lots of attention at night. It did nothing for our ability to cope with the change and, it seemed, she was quite content with the arrangement and was as bright as a button throughout the night for the following couple of weeks.

There was lots to attend to and we couldn't let exhaustion stand in our way. Although Graeme was technically on leave at this stage, he did, nevertheless, have to attend to some administrative matters and was often out of the apartment during the first day or two in Wellington. We had been there little more than twenty-four hours when, during one of Graeme's absences, Diana rang me. She was requesting a meeting with me to 'ascertain whether I would be a suitable person to have anything to do with her children'. I froze. Every fibre of my being resented this approach. Never have I had to muster so much strength to be civil, but somehow I managed to convey the message that on any matter concerning the children, she would need to speak to Graeme directly. Her next ploy, the following morning, was to send a telegram addressed to Graeme in which she informed him that unless he was around to remove his remaining items from her (their) house, they would be deposited in the street for his collection.

I had barely arrived and it had begun, just as I had feared it would. I was shaking with exhaustion and rage when Graeme returned. On our fifth day in Wellington, Graeme decided that we must leave to visit his family in Wanganui. On our way out of town we looked at one house, which was for sale in Johnsonville (in the northern suburbs of Wellington) and bought it then and there, just like that. Of course, the formalities would take time, but the decision was made with no further searching, no further deliberation, no further thought. I felt I was being rushed again. We had our apartment for two weeks, fully paid for by the Government, and we should have benefited from this arrangement and taken more time in looking for a house. But the need to get to Wanganui was, apparently, more urgent. I was not ready to go, in any sense, and particularly since we were still having our nights disturbed by a wakeful baby and our days disturbed by Diana. However, that was how it was and off we went on the three-hour journey north to Wanganui. July is mid-winter in New Zealand, and because the winters are not generally severe there, few houses have the central heating which is so common in Europe. My overriding recollection of that visit was that I have never been so cold in all my life.

Once back in Wellington after our visit north it was time for Graeme to commence his secondment to the Department of Trade. We had been away during the time we could have benefited from the free accommodation and now we had to pay for it. Our house would not be available to us until the twentieth of August, and so the Capital Hill Apartments were our home for the first five and a half weeks in Wellington. During that time Graeme's children visited us each weekend which, as I had expected, meant that Graeme was seeing Diana twice over the weekends. Her previous relationship had broken down and she was now on her own with the children. She seemed deeply resentful of the fact that Graeme had made a new life for himself, with a new baby to boot. But on the twenty-second of July their divorce was finalised and we would therefore be free to marry.

Now that the legalities were dealt with, we were far too busy with a prospective move to be able to give any thought to our own wedding plans. It had all come about too late already, so there was little to be gained by rushing it. Instead we sat and watched the fairy-tale magic of Prince Charles and Lady Diana Spencer's wedding on television in our apartment. It made me very homesick. I knew that there would be far greater coverage of it all back in Britain and it was only the wedding ceremony itself which was being received in New Zealand. This homesickness was another big problem. In Wellington the only person I knew was Eileen (of the 'snake in Honiara' fame), but she was working so could not come and have a natter during the time that Graeme was at the office. With a growing baby to look after, my time was fully taken up, but I was very lonely all the same.

By the end of August we had moved into the house in Johnsonville and were busy trying to furnish it, albeit sparsely since we knew that we would only be there four months. Graeme had nothing but his clothes and radio equipment to unpack, having left his house and all his household effects to Diana, and so, until my crates arrived from England, we had to borrow a transit box from the Ministry. Although this provided us with the basic essentials, it was a very depressing and motley collection of items. Graeme's only other possessions were a caravan (which we sold) and his car. The car was an American left-hand drive Ford Fairlane which I found very scary to drive in a country I did not know. It was far too big for New Zealand roads and I felt nervous, as the driver, being on the near side of the road. However, at least it enabled me to get to the local shops, and there was plenty of space to strap Nina's carrycot into the back. Gradually the house took shape, and while it was nothing very special it was really all we needed at that time. The children continued to visit us every weekend, and so, it seemed, we were just too busy what with one thing and another to give any more thought to our wedding. There were lots of DIY jobs for Graeme to attend to, particularly since much of the furniture we had bought was of the self-assembly variety. We had little time for anything, in fact, since the whole business of moving overseas and setting up home for only four months meant that no sooner had we got unpacked, than we were having to turn our attention to packing up once more.

In the end my crates arrived on the fifth of October. We had previously decided to get married on the sixth (that having proved to be such an auspicious date so far), and so the timing could not have been worse. Normally I would simply have taken delivery of them and left them in the garage. But this was not to be. The Ministry of Agriculture official, who accompanied their arrival, was most concerned about a 'grass skirt' I had listed on the inventory. He would not leave until he had seen the offending item, and so, on the eve of my wedding, I had to unpack every single crate until I came across the Solomon Islands grass skirt. When he saw it, he couldn't have been less interested in it, only commenting, "That's no problem." Sadly I threw the grass skirt away. I knew that I could never return to New Zealand again with it in my possession without having to repeat that nightmare. The official left me in a very unhappy frame of mind. I was getting married tomorrow, my future in-laws were arriving tonight and I would have liked to finish all the cleaning of the house in readiness for their visit. But no, this grass skirt had to be seen to be harmless to the economic infrastructure of New Zealand. There was chaos in the garage now, and endless chores not yet finished. Not for the first time I asked myself if this was really what it was all about.

When Graeme's family arrived that evening I had not had time to change. A most inauspicious day was topped off by Graeme, as it happened. When he was getting the dinner out of the oven, ready to serve it up, he lost his grip on the casserole dish and spilt the entire contents of the meal onto the floor of the oven. It had the potential of being hilariously funny, but humour somehow escaped us after the events of the day. The next morning I tried to feel calm enough to get ready for the wedding, but I wasn't calm at all and was more in a frame of mind to cancel the whole thing. Graeme tried his jollying-me-along tactics, but I was finding it difficult to concentrate on any one aspect of getting ready. Should I be making up my face, or should I be making up some more bottles for the babysitter to give to Nina? I was in a flurry and wishing it was all not happening at all. Finally Graeme was ready to go, leaving the younger of his two elder sisters, Helen, with me.

Eileen, who was to be the only friend of the bride at our wedding, came to collect Helen and me. Having had no-smoking rules imposed upon us while in the company of Graeme's family, I was in a highly nervous frame of mind and asked her to let me have a cigarette in the car. She too wasn't very happy about this request, but having been an avid smoker herself in Honiara, she finally relented. It calmed my nerves a little as we drove into downtown Wellington. We were getting married at Wareham House in Armour Avenue which specialised in wedding services and receptions. By October the weather in Wellington should be turning towards spring, but it was a cold and wet day on the sixth of October 1981 and I felt ridiculous in my turquoise chiffon dress (part of my wardrobe-for-Iran shopping spree). The only items I had been able to afford for the occasion were a matching hat and a bouquet of pink roses and both these accessories seemed equally ridiculous on this blustery cold day. The Vicar who was marrying us came to escort me in under the shelter of a big black umbrella and at the entrance Graeme was there to greet me.

Already waiting inside were Graeme's parents, his eldest sister Beth, her husband Bill, and Brett and Carl, Graeme's two eldest sons. Helen and Eileen slipped in before us and then finally the service was ready to begin. Graeme's father was the official photographer, but it transpired that his film had only five exposures left before it was finished and all those five photographs were horizontal head shots only. Once the service was over we dashed out to our car and retrieved my little camera and a few more photos were taken until that too, ran out of film. With all this unexpected kerfuffle over the photographs, it wasn't until it was too late to take a picture with my camera that we realised we hadn't got a group photograph. Graeme returned to the car to get his Polaroid camera, and the final pictures were taken with that, by his sons. It was a higgledy-piggledy group with nobody standing in the right place. I tried in vain to stand next to my new husband, but in the event his mother stood by me, forcing Graeme into the back row. It was such an inappropriate grouping that I threw the picture away, which was a pity really since it was the only full-length photograph which showed what I was wearing. Having been unable to attend the wedding, my family would have been glad to see some nice pictures. As it was, they had to make do with a few amateurish snaps.

Once the ceremony and cake-cutting were over, Graeme's brother-in-law said a few words and then read the telegrams from my friends and family in England. We adjourned to the next room for the reception, and once again I wished that I could have a cigarette. It never seemed to worry Graeme on those occasions when we couldn't smoke in his parents' company. Although, having said that, he had been the one responsible for our failed attempt at giving up in Tehran. Once I knew I was pregnant we had decided that we would both give up the habit and had succeeded rather well until the first bombs fell on Tehran. I had walked into his office just as news of the Iran/Iraq war was coming through, and found that he still had some cigarettes in his drawer. He clearly needed one at that moment and offered me one too. It was the end of our success in quitting the habit.

When the last sandwich had been eaten and the last glass of champagne drunk, it was time to leave. The arrangement had been that Graeme's parents and Helen would return to our Johnsonville house to look after Nina for five days while Graeme and I went away on honeymoon. Without that offer we would not have been able to get away alone. We drove to Palmerston North that evening, where we spent the first night of our honeymoon, and then drove on up to Rotorua the following day. The city of Rotorua stands on the shores of a beautiful lake, by the same name, and is about one hundred and fifty miles southeast of Auckland.

This is the celebrated 'thermal' (hot springs) region of New Zealand and is an important cultural centre for the Maoris (the indigenous people of that country who settled there eight hundred years ago). There are many attractions by way of geysers, which send scalding jets of boiling water high into the air to descend in a shower of drops amid a veil of steam. Boiling pools and steaming earth vents abound in this weird area, while the overpowering smell of sulphur fills the air. The surrounding countryside is very beautiful. Mountains, of which Mount Tarawera at 3,642 feet is the highest, tower over surrounding hills covered with evergreen forest. Lovely lakes are set in the hills, adding to the variety of natural beauty. The Blue and Green Lakes, named after the colour of their water, the steaming cliffs alongside Lake Rotomahana, the many Maori legends, and historic sites are all part of Rotorua's charm. We went to the Huka Falls, a spectacular waterfall in the area, and would have loved to have gone into the Huka Falls Lodge too. This is reputed to be one of the best hotels in the world and, as such, I doubt if we could have afforded so much as a glass of juice there. As it was, we were staying at the Four Canoes Inn, which, while pleasant, was a far cry from the Huka Falls Lodge. After doing all the touristy things, during the ensuing five days, we returned to Wellington where we found that our little girl had mastered the art of holding her foot! Two days later she hit the next milestone – sitting up unaided. At six months old she was doing so well, accomplishing all the landmarks I had been told to look for, and was a bright and beautiful baby who captured the hearts of all who met her.

Once we were back in the swing of things in Wellington we continued living much as we had before but now we were able to return the transit box to the Ministry. It had been nearly two years, now, since my things were packed up in Honiara, and once more the crates were full of surprises. Things I had forgotten I had emerged from dark corners of the boxes and others filled me with amazement that I had bothered to pack them in the first place. Anyway, for a short while, we were able to enjoy having a few personal possessions about us. It wasn't for long, though, because before Christmas we had to get our things crated up again for shipment to Bahrain. Christmas was spent at Wanganui and then on the ninth of January we were back at the Capital Hill Apartments once more, only this time awaiting our departure from the country, rather than our arrival. I, for one, was thankful to be leaving and I believed that now, at long last, we could concentrate on building up our lives as a family.

We took a week's holiday in Singapore, on our way to the Middle East, and it was wonderful to be back there again where so many memories came flooding back to me – like inadvertently entering the wrong house in the small hours of the morning when I had been staying with Janet. Singapore had changed beyond recognition since I had last been there in 1964. The intervening eighteen years had brought about the creation of a thoroughly modern city, based on a thriving economy, and there was now little sign of the old Singapore I had known. I found it quite disconcerting to recognise so little, although old familiar memories came back to me when we ventured down some of the side streets. We had a meal at Raffles, that lovely old colonial hotel, and it was one of the few places which had not changed since I was last there. We had a wonderful week together, and Nina was introduced to the joys of swimming. She loved the warmth and wetness and cried every time we said no, she'd been in the water long enough now, it was time to come out. The upshot of her insistence to be so long bouncing around on the water was a sunburnt bottom and I had some explaining to do to Jessie (the housegirl in Bahrain) to account for why I was arriving with a baby with a burnt bottom!

The week's holiday had done us good, and although we had been away for the few days of our honeymoon, this was our first break with Nina as well. In the early hours of the morning of Friday the twenty-second of January 1982 we landed at Bahrain airport. A small delegation from the Consulate-General was there to greet us and after the formalities were complete we headed for the New Zealand Residence. All was very quiet and we almost felt that we should be whispering lest we disturb someone. The office staff who met us stayed for a cup of coffee, which we managed to make after fumbling our way around the kitchen. Nina distinguished herself by spilling the entire contents of the sugar bowl onto the carpet in the lounge, and then we headed for bed. One thing we had not expected, however, was to be too cold to be able to sleep. We had only thought of Bahrain in terms of being very hot and humid and although we knew there was a cooler season during the northern hemisphere winter, we did not expect this. There was one thin blanket on the bed and it was not nearly enough to keep us warm. We tossed and turned and kept staring at the huge envelopes of 'handover notes' which had been left in 'his' and 'hers' piles in the bedroom by our predecessors. We had started the night determined not to look at them until we had recovered from the flight and our very late night, but when sleep would not come we decided to open them all the same. Really, it would have been better to leave them, as we had originally planned, because several surprises, not all of them pleasant, awaited us within.

The following morning we had to wake up the house staff in order to get things going. We were in a strange house, and although we had managed to make coffee in the middle of the night, we didn't know where anything was, how things worked, nor even the layout of the house. The staff had imagined we would be having a lie-in after such a few hours sleep, but since there had been no sleep we were keen to get on with the day. Both staff members were Indian – Jessie, the housegirl had been there from the beginning when New Zealand first set up a Mission in Bahrain four or five years earlier, but Fernandez, the cook, had joined more recently. Jessie was very excited that we had a baby for her to lavish her time and attention on and immediately took our little blonde nine-month-old bundle of joy to her heart. She asked if she could take Nina round the local compound, called Yateem Gardens, for a walk in her buggy to show her off to all and sundry. This she did and for the next three and a half years the two of them became a familiar sight with plenty of friends along the way to wave and talk to.

For our part, now that it was daylight, we took stock of the house and what was there. Since it was a Friday (the Islamic holy day) Graeme did not have to commence work immediately and he was therefore free to accompany me. The ground floor consisted of a very long and narrow lounge-cum-dining-room which was for official purposes in the main. Rather strangely, butting up against the dining-room end was the downstairs loo and next to that the kitchen. Also on the ground floor was a small family sitting-room with its own little bathroom. The entrance hallway was huge and ran almost the entire length of the house, forming an enormous amount of wasted space since it could not be used for any other purpose. Stairs led up to the first floor where there was the master bedroom with en suite dressing room and bathroom, also an official guest bedroom with its own bathroom plus two other bedrooms, both very depressingly furnished, which had a shared bathroom between them. The smaller of these two rooms became Nina's, and I could see that a lot of attention would be needed to make it a welcoming room for a growing little girl. There was, again, a huge area of wasted space in the form of a large upstairs landing and then another flight of stairs led to the roof. This was a large flat area which would normally be too hot to usefully enjoy. It housed the central air-conditioning plant, a washing line and the flag pole, but had the weather been less overpowering, it had the potential for being an attractive addition to the house.

By the time we reached the roof the day was warming up and it astonished us that what had been such a freezing cold night could be turning into a warm and pleasant day. We surveyed our new surroundings and saw that we were in an attractive residential area with lots of expensive villas nearby. Nearly all had their own swimming pools, lots had tennis courts too, and all were surrounded by high protective walls. The sound of the muezzin calling the faithful to prayer from the minaret of the many mosques in the region wafted to our ears on the still air and we knew we were back in the Middle East.

The grounds of the Residence were small but quite attractive. However, there was little besides the very thick, coarse grass which is the only variety readily grown in the region, along with dozens of date palms. These palms were an absolute menace since the ripened fruit was always dropping on the surrounding pathway which ran on all sides of the house, causing one to either slip or trample them underfoot unknowingly, and then bring the mushy result into the house and onto the carpet. There was the usual wall surrounding the garden, with two wrought iron gates, one leading to the open-air car porch from where one would enter the back door which was at the side of the house, and the other leading to a blank wall! If one entered the latter way, it would then be necessary to walk halfway round the outside of the house to reach the front door, which was situated at the back! Butting onto the car porch was a small building in which the two house staff had their rooms, bathrooms and a small, shared kitchen. By the main gate leading to this area was a police sentry box in which the Bahraini guards did a round-the-clock vigil to ensure our safety. This only left the swimming pool to be inspected. It was an above-the-ground construction and consequently not in the least attractive, looking more like a huge and ugly bathtub in the back area of the garden. However, we immediately saw the advantage of this arrangement in terms of Nina's safety, since the steps leading up to it could be raised or lowered according to whether the pool was in use or not. We had now surveyed our new home and it all looked pleasant enough.

We returned inside to take a closer look at what was there, and did a mental stocktake as to what we would have to do without until our crates arrived. We had the use of the office transit box in the meantime and several things had also been lent to us by the Wellington-based staff. However, as we had discovered the night before, we were certainly short of a thing or two, particularly warm bedding. The rooms downstairs were furnished well enough, although there was a preponderance of blue for me (being a 'pink' person) but the upstairs rooms had had little money spent on them for quite some time, if at all. They would clearly be requiring my urgent attention, but little did I know that I was going to have to literally drop everything in order to get what was needed before the promised money would no longer be available. This turned out to be a very time-consuming task, choosing materials, finding furniture and generally trying to get things done quickly whilst at the same time not knowing my way around the shops.

Now it was time to unpack the few suitcases we had brought with us the night before, and the most pressing need was to set everything up for Nina as best we could with what little we had. Fortunately in Bahrain it was not difficult to find things for babies and children. I have never seen so many shops and stores selling exclusively to the youngest members of the population. This made the task a whole lot easier, but I remember that it took me about a year to discover where to buy elastic! Once we had got our basic essentials in place we began to feel utterly exhausted. The adrenalin was pumping through our veins and this had kept us going, but now that phase one was completed weariness took over. We had been invited to spend that first night with a group from the office but in the event only Graeme, out of a strong sense of duty, went. By the time he left I was feeling like a complete zombie and would never have got through the evening. I collapsed into bed and didn't even dream about the contents of those daunting handover notes, directions, invitations and general information regarding what was going to happen in the ensuing first weeks and months in Bahrain.

Chapter Fifteen

Learning The Diplomatic Ropes

Bahrain is an Arab island state located off the eastern coast of Saudi Arabia, near Qatar in the Arabian Gulf. It is small, just 266 square miles in area, and is ruled by a hereditary ruler, the Emir, Shaikh Isa bin Sulman Al Khalifa. Bahrain's history can be traced back for five thousand years, and mythology has it that it was the Garden of Eden (although the dry desert landscape belies this). In recent times it was under British protection (from 1820), but in 1971 the country became independent. The Port of Manama is also the capital, while other main urban areas include Muharraq, Isa Town, Hamad Town and Awali. The climate is very hot, with one hundred per cent humidity most of the year round. Dates, fruit, rice and vegetables are grown reasonably successfully, while traditional industries include fishing and pearling. Oil, accidentally discovered by a New Zealander called Holmes in 1931 (while he was prospecting for water), is the mainstay of the economy. Industrial ventures include an oil refinery, ship repair dock, and a large aluminium smelter processing alumina from Australia. Offshore banking has become a significant service industry. Bahrain is also a major transit point for commercial air traffic handling the routes between Asia and Europe, while deep water anchorage just off the port provides ample berthing space for the massive oil-tankers which ply the Arabian Gulf.

It was in this strange new environment that we commenced our working and family lives. While Graeme began to get to grips with his new job, I was being telephoned by several people who were keen to show me the ropes too. As soon as our first working week began, little more than twenty-four hours after landing, we both found that our time was planned for us with engagements here, there, and what seemed like everywhere. The wife of the Australian Consul-General rang to tell me that the Emir's wife, Shaikha Hassa, would be holding her regular Majilis (open house, for conversation and refreshments) on the Tuesday following our arrival the previous Friday. I was not mentally prepared for such an important occasion so soon, and indeed had had no warning that I would be expected to attend such a function. I really didn't know what to expect, nor what I should wear. Anne told me to stop fussing and that everything would be fine, but it would have been much better if she had warned me of all the various 'dos' and 'don'ts' for such an occasion. Soon I found myself in Shaikha Hassa's palace (yes, she had her own palace across the road from the Emir's) and being guided up to an elaborately attired and striking-looking Arab lady seated in the centre of one wall of an enormous rectangular room.

All around her were seated ladies in chairs, which stretched in a long line round the perimeter of the room. Many were in full purdah, with the older generation wearing the face mask as well. As each new woman entered the room they went first to pay their respects to Shaikha Hassa and then to shake the hand of every person in the room. Anne guided me to do likewise, and it was some several minutes before we returned to the point at which we had arrived. Being a newcomer, it was indicated that I should sit next to the Emir's wife, and this I did. I felt exceedingly uncomfortable and at a loss to know what to talk about, particularly since Shaikha Hassa had only a limited command of English. After struggling with a conversation for about half an hour I found myself increasingly looking at the simply magnificent carpet which stretched the length and breadth of this huge room. I had never seen anything so beautiful before and all my natural instincts took over when I said to her how lovely I thought it to be. As soon as I had spoken a long-forgotten piece of Arab folklore returned to my mind. Never, ever, admire anything belonging to an Arab. If you do, by custom they must give it to you! Oh, my goodness, that had been the very last thing on my mind, and even supposing, for one moment, that I had been given it I would never have had a house large enough to accommodate it! Well, I thought, I've really done it now. What an awful start to an association which was to stretch over the next three and a half years. I was quite mortified at my stupidity, and barely knew how to get through the remaining time before the arrival of the incense which was the indication that it was time to leave. I had got to do some swotting up on Arab customs, that was for sure, but why had there been nothing of this kind in all the massive amount of handover notes which had awaited us on our arrival? Surely local customs would have been the most important things to be told to newcomers. Things like never cross your legs lest, inadvertently, you point the sole of your shoe towards another person; never eat or drink with your left hand; if you do not want any more coffee to be poured into your tiny, handleless cup, then you must shake it, otherwise it will continue to be filled *ad infinitum*; and many other customs besides. To her credit, Shaikha Hassa seemed to have forgotten the episode by the time I returned to her Majilis a month later, but I never was able to look at that carpet again without being reminded of how badly I fluffed my first visit to her palace.

Once back at the house I knew that a visit to the supermarket was going to have to be fitted in between all the other things to attend to, and the Trade Commissioner's wife offered to take me to the shops. After the quiet little supermarkets of Johnsonville, I was not prepared for the five-star emporiums which were available in Bahrain. There was nothing which could not be found, and the range of items available represented the best of what could be imported from around the world. The best of European and American goods and the best from the Orient too. There was so much to choose from that it almost made it difficult to decide and it was with several trolley loads of foodstuffs that the two of us finally escaped from that first shopping trip. I was glad that Graeme helped me do the shopping for the few times after that, before we bought a car, when I could then do the supermarketing independently of others. At least we could decide together which of the tempting wares available we would purchase. It was expensive, though, and it was probably just as well that I had not got to grips with the actual pounds sterling value of what my shopping sprees cost because if I had, I think we would have starved.

A week after we arrived we had to turn our attention to the fact that we were to be hosting our National Day function the following week. Waitangi Day invitations had gone out a week or two before we arrived and a couple of hundred people were expected to attend. Although the preparation of the food and drink were not going to fall to me, thankfully, it did, however, involve clearing the whole of the ground floor of furniture. So now, just when I was hoping to be able to unpack the unaccompanied air-freight cases and begin to feel more at home, the upstairs area became a furniture depository with every last chair and table from the ground floor being stored upstairs. It was absolute chaos and not conducive to trying to unpack and get organised. I would have to wait a while longer for that.

Quite a while longer, as it happened, because once the Waitangi Day function was out of the way a week later we were to be hosting a wedding, this time for a hundred or more guests. It was hardly worth bringing all the heavy furniture downstairs again, only to have to carry it up once more so soon afterwards. So, there it remained, constantly getting in my way for well over the first three weeks in the country. The National Day reception would have been enough for now; the wedding was certainly carrying things too far particularly since the bride and groom were unknown to us before our arrival in Bahrain. One of the junior staff at the office had decided that the Residence was just the place for her wedding reception and had rung Graeme in Wellington shortly before we left. It is difficult to say no, to a stranger, when you know that shortly that person will be working for you. I had not been too pleased when he put the telephone down and told me what he had just agreed to. However, we were stuck with it now and had no choice but to go with the flow. On the day of the wedding the telephone hardly stopped ringing with requests from the guests to bring their babies along with a view to Jessie looking after them. It was another situation which was difficult to handle satisfactorily, particularly since we already had our own baby who would need to be looked after by Jessie.

In the event we had several babies upstairs, including Nina, who, at nine months old, was crawling everywhere and had to be watched constantly to avoid her getting into some sort of danger. The stairs were the biggest concern since they were far too wide to be able to find a suitable baby gate to stop her falling down. If the wedding had really been more than I had wanted, all these babies as well was entirely too much and when, during the course of the reception, I went up and found that Jessie was unable to look after Nina adequately, I decided that there was nothing for it but to give her a hand. The relief on her face when I arrived told its own story, and for the remainder of the time I stayed with her helping to keep some semblance of order amongst these demanding charges. It was a bad start, and one from which I never really recovered. There was too much which was new for me then. I was still getting to grips with coping with my own baby; had been married only three months myself; had been in the country barely three weeks and had been plunged, headlong, into the duties of Head of Mission's wife. I was very overstretched to cope with it all at once, and had felt all along that it would have been easier had I at least been given the chance to get unpacked without all this furniture in my way. By the time the last guest had gone and the house was quiet once more I was pretty much ready to bar the way to anyone entering the place again.

Those difficult first weeks were made more so by the knowledge that I was about to lose Fernandez. Our neighbour (and landlord) had persuaded him to go and work next door and this he had decided to do. I now had to recruit a new cook. My choice of replacement turned out to be a complete disaster and I think we were lucky not to have all gone down with food poisoning, although his lack of hygiene was highlighted when Nina succumbed, and closer inspection revealed that things were not at all as they should be in the kitchen. By the time this unsatisfactory situation had come to light, Jessie had departed on long-leave back to India. She had gone for a stipulated six weeks but while there had lost her passport and the length of time she was away was doubled on account of the wait involved while she obtained a new one.

During her three-month absence my mother came to stay with us in order that we had someone to look after Nina while we were out attending official functions. This meant that she was with us when Nina had her first birthday and so, in a foreign land, we were able to make this a family celebration by also inviting my cousin Brian (who was working at the British Bank of the Middle East in Bahrain), together with his wife Karima and Karima's daughter Fawzia. Nina delighted us all by taking her first steps, unaided, at her birthday party in April. The family theme continued through May when Graeme's sons, Brett and Carl, came to stay with us during their school holidays. Many times I wished that Jessie was there to help combine the needs and demands of a baby with those of teenagers, but at least she had returned by June which enabled me to go to Rome with Graeme when he attended the Middle East Heads of Mission meeting there. It was the first time for both of us to be in the Italian capital, and although it was only a short visit it was a very welcome break from the difficult few months we had encountered since our arrival in Bahrain.

Once back from Rome we felt we had turned the first page and were glad to be looking forward to a more settled and better managed life in the Middle East. We had, by now, recruited our third cook — a delightful young Indian whose name we shortened to Venu. He was inexperienced, but hardworking, and conscientious in his duties, and we were happy that he remained with us for the following three years. Things also looked up once we had received our crates from New Zealand and had got the house looking more like a home. Nina was developing rapidly and, having got the hang of walking, was now right into dancing. Not only did she amuse us at meal times by jigging about in time to the background music we would play, but on one occasion, when we were having a meal at the Holiday Inn, she ran away from us and climbed the steps to the stage where a band was playing, and turned herself into the star attraction by doing a very creditable 'dance' in time to their music.

She was a thriving and happy little girl, enjoying her daily routine of walks in Yateem Gardens with Jessie, playtime with me, and a nap in the afternoons. We had redecorated her bedroom and it was now bright and cheerful, and we had also made some headway in doing many other things around and about the Residence to generally improve the facilities. It had been a very busy and demanding period in our lives, constantly out at functions and hosting parties at home too, trying to get to grips with a new life and a new way of doing things, but by the end of July, five months after arriving, we were beginning to see the results of our efforts in that we felt we had, at last, made some headway towards belonging in the country which was now home. This task had, of course, been helped along by the Bahrainis themselves. Although their culture is so different from our own, they have a very tolerant approach towards foreigners and 'non believers' and made it easy for the two cultures to meet in a harmonious and mutually satisfactory fashion.

It was time for our first leave, which was supposed to be six monthly since Bahrain was designated as a hardship posting in those days, and Graeme and I took a fortnight away in Kenya, leaving Nina in the capable hands of Jessie and Venu. We were definitely ready for a break from the interminable heat and humidity and the general demands of diplomatic life and it was wonderful to be free of functions and duties for two glorious weeks. We went first to the Amboseli National Park and then on to the Masai Mara Game Reserve, where we did the true safari trek leaving early in the mornings to watch the wild animals in their natural habitat and then again before dusk. It is truly a beautiful country and we thoroughly enjoyed the wonderful opportunity of being in such a different environment. We slept in what amounted to little more than tented accommodation and enjoyed meals out in the open while watching elephants, zebras, and giraffes casually wandering by.

One day we went on a game walk, which took several hours, but which afforded us a far better opportunity to watch the animals which were thus not disturbed by the arrival of a vehicle in their midst. This walk took us through a Masai village, and it was fascinating to see how these proud but primitive people lived. Our tour took us finally to Mombassa where we enjoyed a few days of relaxation in the sun and swimming in the hotel pool. During our time in Mombassa there was an attempted *coup d'état* in the country, which made it impossible to return to Nairobi to catch our plane back to Bahrain. It was a very uncomfortable moment, and our thoughts rushed to Nina and just how we could get back to her when all movement in the country was prohibited. By the time we eventually boarded our plane to return I had developed a kidney stone and the flight was passed in a nightmare of pain. When we eventually landed in Dhahran en route for Bahrain I was taken off in a wheelchair to receive medical attention. Somehow, or other, we managed to find ourselves on the wrong side of Immigration, and the whole of the time we were there, when I was supposed to be seeing a doctor, Graeme was frantically trying to explain our position to the Saudi authorities who were on the point of arresting us as illegal immigrants. The relief to finally be back in Bahrain, where I was taken immediately to hospital, was enough to make us thankful to be home once more.

Over the past several years I had been kept in touch with Don's whereabouts and doings by my cousin Brian, who had become a close friend of his, and one day Brian told me that Don's daughter, Fanny was living and working in Kuwait. She was now in her early twenties and married to an Argentinean who was also working in Kuwait. Fanny had, apparently, indicated that she wanted to see me again (we had, after all, been good friends when she was a little girl of eight), and I was also happy at the prospect of seeing her once more. In

October Graeme was planning a cross-accreditation visit to Kuwait, and it was decided that I would go with him and while there we would visit Fanny and Charlie. Once in Kuwait, and while getting ready at the hotel to go and visit Fanny, I suddenly found that I was extremely nervous. I was nearly thirteen years older than when she had last seen me (in that car park in Cambridge) and I found myself worrying that she would not realise that I was no longer the young twenty-something woman I had been. Having just had my thirty-eighth birthday, I was increasingly conscious of the advancing years bringing me firmly to the doorstep of middle age. I need not have worried, though, for it was a very happy evening and it felt as though I had seen Fanny only yesterday. The following day we arranged to meet, just the two of us for lunch, and during that time our friendship returned to one of mutual affection. She told me she desperately wanted a baby but had so far been unlucky in her attempts to get pregnant, and I laughed that we too had been trying for ages to have a second child. We decided that we would both be lucky soon and thought how funny it would be if we ended up having babies at the same time.

Christmas was rapidly approaching and we arranged to spend it with my mother in Bromley but before leaving for England we took Nina to see Father Christmas at the Diplomat Hotel. She took one look at this apparition in red and burst into inconsolable tears. She wasn't able to forgive him for frightening her so until she opened the nice little bag of presents he gave her! On the two successive evenings before our departure I found myself in the curious position of being invited to a royal wedding, but without Graeme. His involvement was minimal in that he attended a short function at the Emir's palace to mark the event, but it was the women who really celebrated. All the diplomats' wives were invited to join in the festivities and this we did. It involved the need to purchase, at huge cost, two long formal ball gowns for the occasion. So expensive were they that I have been unable to replace them with anything more modern since and they are still 'in service' to this day. The elaborately gold-embossed and gold-lace-decorated invitation read:

> The Shaikha Moza, mother of the Emir,
> and Shaikha Hassa, wife of Emir, both
> wish to invite you to attend the wedding of
> their "sons" Khlood and Mohammed at

7.30 p.m. on Monday 20 December at the
house of Ibrahim bin Hamad Al Khalifa.

Although the function commenced at an early hour it would be
midnight before dinner would be served (a normal hour to eat in the
Middle East) and I could see that I would be in for a couple of very
late nights before leaving for England. However, it was fascinating to
be present at an Arab wedding celebration, which seemed to consist
mainly of dancing. But it was the magnificent dresses worn by the
Bahraini 'royal' ladies which were, in themselves, a treat to the eye.
Elaborately embroidered in gold thread, with jewels both sewn to the
delicate silks and worn in profusion as well (on the head, arms, neck
and hands), their colourful gowns were a spectacular sight indeed.
Nothing, however, matched the diamond 'belt' worn by Shaikha
Hassa. It must have been two inches deep and spanned her waist in
solid diamonds. It caught the light and dazzled the eye at every turn
of her body.

The diplomatic wives were really spectators at a family celebration
which stretched into the night and would be repeated, in much the
same vein, the following evening too. The invitation for the second
night read much as the first, but with the curious addition of 'Please
do not bring children'! So involved had I been with these two nights
of wedding celebrations that it was difficult to step back into the
humdrum reality of our lives. Being back in my mother's small flat,
just a few hours afterwards, was the most unreal experience of the
two! No sooner had we unpacked our cases than Christmas Eve was
upon us and we excitedly prepared Nina's Christmas stocking. At
twenty months old she was certainly well able to enjoy its contents the
following morning and we enjoyed a happy Christmas day with
Barbie's husband and two children, Paul and Sheila. My mother's
sister, Joan, also joined us and it was a tight fit to get the eight of us
round her small dining-room table. However, it was lovely to be back
in England again, amongst family and friends, and it was another
opportunity for Graeme (and now Nina too) to get to know people
there. We had a lovely reunion with the girls (and their husbands)
from the Gloucester Road flat days, which Janet and Alan hosted in
their London flat. The New Year was spent with my father and his
wife, who also had her family visiting then too, and although I tried
very hard to enjoy it all it was very much a duty occasion to enable

my father to see something of his granddaughter. After a very eventful four weeks in London we returned to Bahrain two days after the anniversary of our arrival there the previous year. One week later, when she was still only one and three-quarter years old, Nina started at play school.

She had been enrolled at a kindergarten run by an English lady, Una, in her home in Yateem Gardens, and on Nina's first day she took with her a large box of nappies under her arm, just in case! She was so excited at the prospect of joining this happy little group of children that she didn't even pause to say goodbye to her mother. It was left to me to shed a tear! From that day to this Nina has never looked back so far as her schooling is concerned, and I am convinced that her successful academic track record is, in no small part, due to the lovely atmosphere of her first learning experience. We have a lot to thank Una for – not only, as will be seen, for giving Nina such a lovely start. I was also glad to have a little more time to devote to the functions I had to attend and all the other hundred and one things which seemed to need my attention.

Now that we were back into the swing of events we found that there was a repetitive nature to it all. Our own National Day function had rolled round once more and a host of other events which we had first attended so soon after we had arrived. In February Nina took possession of a Wendy house given to her by neighbours across the road who were returning to England. Their small son had used it as a 'police station', and so we painted the black house a bright red, furnished it with little tables and chairs, and generally had great fun making it into a delightful little house for Nina and her friends to play in. We added perspex windows, chintz curtains, and plenty of stickers and pictures on the walls. Not only were we delighted with the finished result, but Nina's reaction, spoken in an incredulous voice, "Ma 'Ouse?", was a joy to behold and made all our efforts thoroughly worthwhile. Over the remaining years in Bahrain she had hours of pleasure from the little house and it seemed to become part of the family.

In March we were delighted that Tony (our friend who escaped from Tehran) was able to pass through Bahrain and stay with us for a couple of days and were only sorry that Shirin's job in New York had prevented her from joining us too. It was lovely to catch up with Tony again, albeit briefly, and we were able to give him the exciting news that we were expecting our second child on the 5th of November that year. Our patience had been rewarded at last, and in spite of everything, I had been quite unable to believe the news when Mr Hutchings, the gynaecologist, rang to tell me that the pregnancy test had been positive. I had embarked on another perfect pregnancy during which time I felt extremely well and, once more, blossomed. I was glad that I found I had developed a craze for something (it helped to make it all seem real), and while I discovered that I needed gallons of tomato juice all the time I also found that I couldn't abide the taste of alcohol. I wonder if that was my little son dictating my tastes? Although he is still too young to be drinking alcohol, on the odd occasions we have offered him a sip of wine or shandy he has totally refused, saying that he intends never to drink alcohol! Our busy life continued as usual and all the same events continued to roll around, and one such was Nina's second birthday. We made "Ma 'Ouse" the focus of the party and much fun was had by the crowd of little friends Nina entertained on her special day.

At the end of April the then New Zealand Minister of Health, Aussie Malcolm, and his wife Astrid paid an official visit to Bahrain. It was a busy time, with much crowded into the ten-day Gulf tour, and it was left to me to entertain Mrs Malcolm throughout. It all went very smoothly and this ministerial visit afforded me an opportunity which would not otherwise have come my way. The Minister was scheduled to have an audience with the Emir at his palace, and because he had his wife with him he was extended the courtesy of bringing her too (men and women live largely separate official lives in Muslim countries), and because Mrs Malcolm was invited so was I. The Emir's reception room was laid out in much the same way as Shaikha Hassa's had been, with everyone seated round the perimeter of the room, but since it was such a small gathering it meant that we all sat in close proximity with the Emir. The Ruler proved to be the most charming of hosts and quickly put everyone at ease. It was a fascinating glimpse into a world which would not, normally, be open to me.

In May it was time for Graeme's children to visit again, and this time three of them came to stay. Only Brett was unable to come due to other holiday commitments. It was a busy time, with four children to look after, and another on the way, but it passed soon enough and by June it was time for another break away from our small island home. We had booked into a self-catering apartment within a hotel in Cyprus which had looked ideal for our purposes when viewed in the brochure. However, on our arrival there, it transpired that the kitchen facilities had been removed the week before, and we were disappointed that this impinged on our ability to be independent. We managed well enough, though, with simple things, and in the main managed to feed Nina by boiling eggs in the kettle and preparing other simple dishes as best we could! We had not, however, realised that Cyprus would be as hot as the Middle East, and although we enjoyed our holiday, and hired a car so that we could see much of the island, it was far too hot for comfort. I was, by now, six months pregnant and was eagerly awaiting the results to come through from an amniocentesis which had been performed in London at the end of May. I had made arrangements for the documentation to be sent to me in Cyprus, and in the middle of our holiday we got the wonderful news that all was well and that I was expecting a boy. I would be thirty-nine when he was born and so we knew that we had been really lucky, and we toasted his safe arrival with a long glass of tomato juice!

The heat of Cyprus curtailed our movements to some extent, but we enjoyed a trip into the Trudos Mountains where it was considerably cooler and where Nina had her first ice cream cone, suitably draped in numerous napkins to protect her from the dripping which inevitably occurred owing to the length of time it took her to get through it. At two and a quarter Nina was a bundle of fun and energy and was always leading us on a race to catch up with her. She also took to swimming and in particular enjoyed jumping off the side of the pool into the water where she would play happily for hours. The only blot on the holiday was that I picked up a particularly unpleasant skin rash from a filthy loo I had been forced to use at one of our lunch stops. While it was treatable, I was warned that the ointment was potentially dangerous to my unborn child, and so I had to be extremely cautious in using it, thereby lengthening the time it took to clear up.

Finally the holiday drew to a close and it was time to fly back to Bahrain. There was a lengthy delay at Larnaca airport, while we waited for our Gulf Air plane to arrive, and during this unexpected sojourn I spotted the familiar face of Pene, the school friend who had rescued me from my father's fury all those years ago. *I couldn't believe it*! She still looked just as she had when I had last seen her the night my father went to his club and became reunited with his new wife. I had lost touch with her since then as she had become too embroiled with the final tragic break-up of the family. But here she was now, and it was lovely to see her again. She was living in Kuwait (and also knew that Fanny was there), and so, now, another friend from the past had re-entered my life. We would meet again, but for now it was time to return to Bahrain.

Chapter Sixteen

2·0 Children

To return to Bahrain in the middle of July, when most people are escaping for the long hot summer, was just too much given my increasing size, and so Nina and I were barely there a week before we flew to London to spend August with my mother. Little did we know that we would be hitting the hottest summer in England for three hundred years, and in fact it would have been cooler to be in the air-conditioned house in Bahrain! Nina felt it too and not only was she too hot, but she was also missing her friends, her routine, her toys and, of course, her father. She behaved very badly indeed and I had a severe case of 'the terrible twos' on my hands. What had set out to be a good idea ended up as a big mistake, and although it was lovely to be in England with my mother and to have the opportunity of seeing some more of my friends, I began to wish that I had stayed in Bahrain.

By the summer of 1983 my friend Vicky had met her George (as predicted by the Ouija board at Greenwich) and I was so very happy for her and glad that this visit afforded me the chance to meet him. But it was time to pack the suitcases again, for my pregnancy was reaching the end of the seventh month and I would soon be into the 'no go' zone for flying. Nina's behaviour on the flight back to Bahrain was so bad that a message was delivered to me, from the Captain, saying that in the interest of safety and comfort of passengers, would I please control my child! She needed to be back in a proper routine and needed the structured atmosphere of Una's play school, and it was with a certain amount of relief that I returned her there at the beginning of September.

The silly season for parties had begun again and with everyone's return from the long summer break we were quickly back into our busy schedule of events. One particularly enjoyable occasion was to be invited to attend a performance of a play by Derek Nimmo's travelling players. We saw all the plays his company performed during our time in Bahrain and they were always of a high standard and unfailingly good entertainment. On this occasion we were invited backstage afterwards to meet Derek Nimmo and the cast. This included David Jason who, at that time, I had never heard of, and it is hard to reconcile my image of him on that occasion with the household name we know him to be today. But my mind was more on the imminent arrival of our son, and I had been busy making all the preparations which I had been unable to make for Nina. Lots of her possessions would be put back into service for him, but there were many things besides which needed to be prepared. I was having regular checks at the International Hospital to monitor my pregnancy, and it continued in a most satisfactory fashion although I knew that this time I would definitely be having a Caesarean section. (To my lasting regret I never received a satisfactory explanation as to *why* this had to be the case, nor why by general anaesthetic). In the early hours of the morning of the twenty-sixth of October 1983 I went into labour naturally, and once my waters had broken we knew it was time for Graeme to get me to the hospital.

As I lay shaking on the hospital trolley, under the full glare of the operating lights, I got into conversation with the anaesthetist. We were waiting for Mr Hutchings to arrive and indeed I would not be put under general anaesthesia until the knife was poised (in order to protect the baby), and it was good to talk rather than think about what was in store. It turned out that she was a Rhodesian (Zimbabwean) and I asked my inevitable question, "I suppose you don't know Jacquie Stokes of Umtali, do you?" Well, I nearly fell off the trolley when she replied that yes, indeed she did. So now, just moments before my son was born, I was able to receive up-to-date information about my friend Jacquie from all those years ago at St James's Secretarial College in London in the early sixties. It was just the diversion I needed and it helped pass the time as we waited.

I remember nothing more until I roused back in the maternity ward to be told that I had a beautiful baby boy, who had arrived in the world at 6.35 that morning. Marc weighed in at seven pounds four and a half ounces and once again Graeme got to hold him first, but soon he was in my arms and I could see that I had a lovely son. He was indistinguishable from Nina as a baby with the exception that he had a mass of black hair and eyes of the darkest blue (which by two years of age had turned to brown). With this colouring my Bahraini boy closely resembled his Arab crib-mates and he certainly did not stand out as being different when he was in the nursery with the other newborn babies.

There was no trauma associated with his birth, no problems to contend with, no shock in having had an elective Caesarean section, and although the pain was just as acute at least I had not gone several nights without sleep. I recovered much more quickly and was only in hospital with Marc for eight days before the two of us were allowed home. Now we were all a family together. Graeme was there to help me and so was Jessie, and there was no prospect of separation to cloud our happiness. However, Nina was none too sure that having a brother was all that it had been cracked up to be and was highly disappointed that he wasn't ready yet to kick a football around with her. Her first request, when introduced to him at the hospital, had been, "Can we put him on the floor?" At two and a half she needed lots of attention and found it hard to have to take second place when Marc was being fed or changed. However, he was here to stay and all we could do was to pray that she would come round to seeing that, in time, there would be lots of advantages in having a brother to play with.

Everything went well for the first few weeks, although Marc did develop bronchitis at an early stage. We would have liked to make plans to spend Christmas in England but felt that it would be easier to cope with the early months of Marc's life in our own house. It meant that we would be unable to take the leave which was due to us by then, but all in all it was probably better to be in our own home. Things were not destined to be smooth sailing and on the night of Boxing Day, when Graeme was attending one of the interminable men-only functions, I was at home alone with the two children. I had fed Marc and then took him to the bathroom to change his nappy and, to my utter horror, discovered a lump in his groin. Although I had no idea what this could be, it was clearly abnormal, and I felt sick with fear as to what it could mean. It was late at night but I knew that I must get him to a hospital to be looked at. However, I could hardly leave Nina alone in the house. I ran to see if Jessie was in her room and was relieved to find her in, but then I realised that I also needed someone to hold Marc while I drove the car to the hospital. She couldn't do that if she remained with Nina, so I asked the guard at the gate to come inside to watch over her. He was fairly astonished at this request, when his duties required him outside, but although I couldn't speak to him in Arabic, my frantic gesturing seemed to do the trick. Having made these somewhat unsatisfactory arrangements for Nina, the three of us set off for the hospital.

It turned out that Marc had developed an inguinal hernia and would need to be operated on. However, his bronchitis would prevent this being possible. It was now essential to nurse him through this before surgery could be performed. Once he was in hospital I felt much better that at least something would eventually be done to repair the hernia. He looked so tiny on the big hospital trolley as he was wheeled in for his operation. Graeme and I had stayed with him until he entered the theatre and were there to see him as he emerged afterwards. His recovery was good, but keeping his wound clean was difficult given that he was a tiny baby wearing nappies in the part which had to be kept clean and dry. He was barely out of hospital before Graeme had to leave on a tour of the Gulf with the New Zealand Minister of Energy, Bill Birch, who was accompanied by his wife. During Graeme's absence Marc developed projectile vomiting, which was a huge cause for concern since he was now unable to retain his feeds. I returned with him to the hospital and we embarked on a period of investigation and trying different feeds to see if he was, perhaps, allergic to what he was being given in his bottle. I wished that Graeme could have been there to help us through this latest set-back, but by the time he returned to Bahrain, with the Minister and his wife, Marc had been re-admitted to hospital in a fairly serious condition. He was badly dehydrated and had to be put on a drip. The medical staff were becoming increasingly concerned for his welfare, but were unable to get to the bottom of the problem on account of lack of suitable laboratory facilities. We were losing him and his condition worsened by the hour.

There could have been no worse time to be involved in a full-scale Ministerial visit. There were endless functions to be attended and, indeed, a couple of hundred had been invited to a reception at the Residence in the Minister's honour. I wanted to spend all my time with Marc, but not only was there Nina who needed my attention, but also the Minister's wife. It was only the beginning, though, and as it

Nina's 2nd birthday party, with Jessie and "Ma 'Ouse" in the background — April 1983

The children with my godparents, Cyril and Marjorie (en route to Spain) — July 1984

Visiting my father, his brother Roy and their wives — August 1985

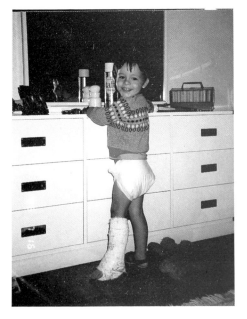

Marc smiling in spite of a broken leg — July 1986

Nina at Gala Day, Tonga Side School — August 1986

A good team of domestic staff and drivers, which didn't last long, and in fact crumbled the day after this photo was taken! A pregnant O'u is on the far left — August 1987

During my trip to England my mother takes me around Broadstairs where we see her father's old office at 28 High Street — August 1990

Marc and Nina watch as their mother enters the carriage taking their parents to the Credentials Ceremony at Noordeinde Palace — March 1991

Nina at ten years old, also outside the Bad Oeynhausen house, like her mother before her — April 1991

WRNS OCT 3/70 Reunion at Royal Naval College Greenwich — September 1991 (me front right, Graeme back 2nd right, Caroline back centre, and Vicky to the right of Caroline)

*Another reunion with the girls from the Gloucester Road flat
— December 1992*

Gail and Mike with their children, Sydney — August 1993

The Sungei Ujong Club dance floor, 30 years on — August 1993

That's My Last Chance — at the 'back' front door of former
New Zealand Residence, Bahrain, just before demolition began
— August 1993

Nina on her first day at Sevenoaks School with the girls in her dormitory — September 1994

Marc on his first day at Sevenoaks School with some boys in his dormitory — September 1994

turned out there were weeks and months of worry ahead for us. Once Bill Birch had left Bahrain, we flew to London to take Marc to the Queen Elizabeth Hospital in Hackney, having taken Nina to Una to be cared for by her while we were away.

We arrived in London, late at night, and the following morning Marc was taken to undergo investigations as to the cause of his problem. Half an hour later he was returned to the ward and we were told that he had gastro-oesophageal reflux and this was the cause of his projectile vomiting. There was hope, though, since the remedy is relatively simple and involves keeping the baby in an upright position at all times and thickening the feeds with cornflour. He was immediately treated in this fashion and remained in hospital for eight days, during which time he kept down his feeds and started to regain some of the weight which he had lost. He was on the mend and we were overjoyed. We had been so busy with Marc that there had been little time to see anybody or do anything while we were in London, but we did have one visit from the immediate family and on another occasion managed to have dinner with Vicky and George, who had, by now, been married. Vicky had asked me to be her Matron of Honour, and it was with much regret that I had been unable to do so.

On the twenty-fifth of January 1984 we flew back to Bahrain, once again almost on the same day as we had arrived there two years earlier. We were sitting in the Gulf Air plane, rushing down the runway at high speed prior to taking off, when Marc started projectile vomiting all over again. This continued throughout the flight back to Bahrain. We were returning with a baby with all the same symptoms as the baby we had had to evacuate from Bahrain on medical grounds. We were flying away from the hospital which could help him and right back to the one which could not. I wanted a parachute! I wanted to stop the plane! I wanted to go back to London! None of these options were open to me as I headed inexorably back to the Middle East. As we landed in Bahrain, we seriously wondered if we should get the next flight back to London, but finally decided to return him to hospital locally. This turned out to be a thoroughly unsatisfactory decision because not only did his renewed illness turn out to be a case of having picked up gastro-enteritis while at the hospital in London but Marc managed to contract several more conditions (such as conjunctivitis, a cough, a cold, and nappy rash) while in the hospital in Bahrain. When we finally decided to discharge him on the second of February, in a much worse condition than he had been when we returned to Bahrain, we wished that we had simply nursed him back to health at home. At least we could do this now, but it was a slow process and although he made steady progress, it was many months before he regained lost ground.

Four days after Marc returned from his final hospitalisation we were due to host our National Day function for the third time and by then we had both gone down with flu ourselves. We were feeling exhausted and ill as we stood in line to receive the four hundred guests on that occasion, but at least the sheer numbers involved had meant that we held the reception at a hotel rather than trying to squash people into our home. My presence on this occasion was interpreted as meaning that everything was fine and I would now be able to return to full-time attendance at functions. This was far from the case and I felt resentful of every party which took me away from nursing Marc back to health.

In April 1984 Nina had her third birthday and the occasion marked the transition from Una's play school to a proper infant school. She wore a pretty little brown and white checked uniform, went off to school with a lunch box instead of a box of nappies, and once more thrived in the happy atmosphere of Nadeen School. At the end of April Graeme had to go to the Oman for a three-day visit and I decided to go with him. I had not been well since Marc's birth and it seemed like a good chance to get a short break. Having last seen Muscat in 1974, it was interesting to see the developments which had taken place in the past ten years. Shortly after our return three of Graeme's children arrived from New Zealand for their annual May visit (this time it was Carl who was unable to come) and forty-eight hours after they landed our Minister of Foreign Affairs, Warren Cooper and his wife Lorraine, paid an official four-day visit to Bahrain. An article appeared in the Gulf Daily News which read "Bahrain and New Zealand are to increase their diplomatic representation to ambassadorial level, it was announced in Manama last night. The agreement was signed by Foreign Minister Shaikh Mohammed bin Mubarak Al Khalifa and his New Zealand counterpart, Mr Warren Cooper. The New Zealand minister arrived in Bahrain after a two-day visit to Saudi Arabia. He is due to leave today for Qatar. Talks centred on economic and trade relations between the two countries as well as the situation in the Gulf and the

Middle East. Mr Cooper, who is also New Zealand's overseas trade minister, was received by H.H. The Emir, Shaikh Isa bin Sulman Al Khalifa. In recent years, New Zealand's trade with Bahrain has been boosted considerably – lamb exports have nearly doubled to two hundred thousand tons and dairy produce exports have soared from fourteen thousand tons in 1980 and 1981 to forty-four thousand tons." The article was accompanied by a photograph of the Emir receiving Mr Cooper, but on this occasion Mrs Cooper and I were not included.

We were busy with a schedule of events drawn up for her, one of which was to attend a function at the Red Crescent Society (the equivalent of the Red Cross) and although the occasion was marked on Lorraine's programme, together with a notation that a short speech would be required, she had not noticed that this would be necessary. To rectify this oversight we drove into a layby while I briefed her as best I could about the work of the Society and what aspects might be worthwhile mentioning, and once she had collected her thoughts we continued with our journey. In the event her impromptu speech was very well received and her visit was a happy and successful one. However, we saw little of the five children at home, and it was not until after Marc's christening, two days after the Minister left, that things quietened down sufficiently to do anything as a family.

By the end of June, Graeme and I were really exhausted. We had gone a year without leave, in this so-called 'hardship' post, during which time we had had a very sick baby to nurse back to health. Marc was now making excellent progress and Nina would shortly break up from Nadeen School for the long summer holiday. We decided to recharge our batteries by taking a five-day break alone in Hong Kong, this time leaving both children with Jessie and Venu. For Graeme it was the first time there, for me the third. Twenty years had passed since my first unhappy visit but I still found the place exotic and exciting and we thoroughly enjoyed our few days away. It was such a contrast to Bahrain (although in June the climate is just as hot and sticky in both places) and the lush green mountainous landscape was a feast to the eye after the flat desert vista we had become used to. The hustle and bustle and bright lights all provided us with an environment quite different from the Middle East, and although the time passed far too quickly we were glad to have those few days together.

Three weeks after our return Graeme went to Gudaibiya Palace to present his credentials to the Emir of Bahrain as the first New Zealand Ambassador to that country. The announcement had been made during Mr Cooper's visit in May and we were glad that the reality had now come about. The wish to upgrade had been talked about before we had even arrived in Bahrain and so, two and a half years later, it was a relief that the procrastination was finally over. Nice though it was for Graeme to have this new title, in fact it made little real difference and business carried on just as before both at work and in our social lives. Three days after the credentials ceremony we flew off on our long-overdue leave, this time to Spain. We travelled via Gatwick (where we collected my mother who was to join us for our holiday) and during the few transit hours while waiting for our flight to Malaga we went to see my godparents, Cyril and Marjorie, at their lovely home in Colgate. We barely had time to introduce them to Marc before we returned to Gatwick to catch our flight to Spain, but I was glad that we had, nevertheless, taken the time to do so.

The Spanish holiday was, no doubt, as all Spanish holidays tend to be – lots of sun, swimming and lazing about. We had hired a villa at Torreblanca which proved to be ideal. Set back in the hills, overlooking the sea, it was built in the typical Spanish style with many attractive archways and newly whitewashed. It had its own pool, which provided the children with plenty of enjoyment, and in the main we spent our time being as quiet and lazy as anyone with two small children can be. There was a double swing in the garden which both children thoroughly enjoyed, and a barbecue which provided us with a pleasant way to eat in the cooler evenings. We had hired a car, which enabled us to get about on several trips and in particular gave us the chance to drive as near to Gibraltar as we were permitted. My mother and I would have loved to go back and see it all again, in spite of its unhappy associations, but the border was closed and so we were only able to view The Rock from the barrier dividing it from Spain. We should have thought to go over to Tangiers, from which direction it would have been possible to enter Gibraltar, but regrettably we did not think about doing so. It was so frustrating to have got so near and yet to be so far. We discovered that many of our neighbours in Bahrain were also holidaying in villas nearby, and on one occasion, we were invited to a party given by Ali and Shirley Yateem (whose family owned the Yateem Gardens compound where Nina and Jessie went for their regular walks). It was a pleasant occasion and nice to see friends out of their usual environment, but in the main we kept to ourselves and tried to forget about our official life.

The time passed far too quickly and it was with the feeling that we could easily have done with longer in Spain that we headed off back to the Middle East. On the way Marc became very ill once again, and this time his sickness was accompanied by a high fever. He was hospitalised in Redhill, between flights, where they managed to reduce his fever sufficiently to continue the journey. All our old fears for his welfare returned to haunt us, but mercifully, this time, he made a fairly speedy recovery. Time continued to pass far too quickly once we were back in the 'silly season' in Bahrain, and just before Marc's first birthday Graeme and I went off to Rome for the Heads of Mission Meeting. Another wonderful opportunity to enjoy that beautiful city and another chance to catch up with our colleagues from the Middle Eastern region. Back in Bahrain I had the dubious pleasure of celebrating my fortieth birthday alone while Graeme attended a dinner given by the British Ambassador for the Duke of Gloucester. What a splendid birthday treat it would have been had it not been a men-only function! Ten days later Marc celebrated his first birthday and his party was quite different from Nina's since we now knew lots of little children to invite, and although they were mostly Nina's friends, he was still excited by all the attention they gave him.

By the end of 1984 we had spent almost three years in Bahrain. It was a two-year posting and this meant that we were not only overdue in terms of our stay there, but we were also overdue for leave back in New Zealand. Normally this would not apply on a regular two-year tour of duty, but we were now falling behind the leave conditions which applied to our colleagues in 'temperate' four-year postings who would expect to return to New Zealand after two years at post. So, somewhat belatedly, we were scheduled for home leave during the December of 1984. It was decided that Marc and I would go first in order that I try to find a house to buy (having now sold our Johnsonville home) so that we didn't have to spend our leave house-hunting. As I placed the last items in our suitcases I stood up in acute pain. Some movement I had made caused extreme discomfort in my coccyx and it was in this condition that I made the long flight to Wellington with Marc. We flew on a Qantas flight and I will always remember the sight of two stewards watching me carry Marc, his collapsed pushchair, his flightbag of baby provisions, and my hand baggage up the spiral staircase to the upper passenger deck. Even though they could not have known I was in so much pain, common courtesy might have prompted them to help a woman as laden as I was then. But no, they stood there watching me struggle up the stairs.

I had two weeks to achieve my aim of finding a house to buy before Graeme and Nina arrived. Having enlisted the help of an agent, the search began. I finally decided on a partly-built architect-designed property in Khandallah, a pleasant residential area not far from where we had been in Johnsonville. I naturally wanted Graeme to see the house before I bought it, but the agent put the hard word on me (taking me for the novice that I was) and said that if I did not sign the contract immediately I would lose it since there were several others displaying interest in the house. I couldn't risk this being true, and as Graeme and Nina were winging their way to New Zealand I sat up at the house and signed the contract to purchase. It was an awful feeling to be taking such a big decision on my own, but mercifully Graeme also liked what he saw when he arrived and considered that I had done the right thing.

However, the whole business turned into a nightmare as we found ourselves more and more embroiled in the processes involved in purchasing a house which was not yet completed. At first this seemed to be an advantage, since we were given the chance to chose our own colour-scheme and fittings, but endless complications and delays meant that I had to stay on in Wellington for three months while the house was finished. Every time I thought that a decision had been made and we would go for this wallpaper, or that light fitting, or this bathroom suite, we struck a problem of availability. The sagas grew more unbelievable by the day and finally we lost all patience with the builders and our solicitor even found himself having to take legal action to get them to incorporate things, such as a ceramic hob, which were clearly itemised on the contract of purchase.

We had little by way of leave as a result of all these hassles, and although I am sure we went to Wanganui for Christmas I have no recollection of any time spent other than being embroiled in huge battles over the house. One day we were up there to see how things were going and we noticed that they were erecting the chimney. To our horror we saw that this now covered the only window in what would be Marc's bedroom. The ensuing battle of the chimney was never really resolved (since the fireplace in the lounge below had already been constructed), and to this day Marc's bedroom has a chimney blocking the light and the view through the only window. The worry and frustration continued, unabated, and soon I was facing it without Graeme's support since he and Nina had to return to Bahrain at the end of January 1985. Mafia-like tactics were employed, and shortly before the house was handed over to me I was sitting alone in the courtyard when I was accosted by the builder's 'strong man' who used a threatening approach and I was half expecting to be beaten up. He left me in tears and when I finally flew out of Wellington, after the house was ours, I had serious doubts about whether I would ever be happy to live in it.

When Marc and I returned to Bahrain we discovered that Nina had developed chicken pox and Graeme had nursed her through this. As it transpired, he had contracted a mild dose of it too and came out in spots just in time for our National Day function (which had now rolled round again for the fourth time). There was nothing for it, but he had to attend his own National Day reception, spots or not! Shortly afterwards Fanny came to stay with us from Kuwait. While it was lovely to see her again, the circumstances were sad for she and Charlie had split up, and Fanny was about to make a new life for herself in Bahrain. I fondly imagined, as we went round to see the flat she had found for herself, that we would see lots of her and cement our friendship, but she withdrew into herself and we did not become part of that new phase in her life. Perhaps it was because we were always so busy, never having time for anything but the job and what was required of us. Maybe she felt we could not be her friends. I don't know, because I lost touch with her for ages and even when the sporadic Christmas cards started arriving again, her news was scanty. Her last card, received a few years ago now, told me that she had remarried, this time to a Lebanese.

In April I went to London to make some purchases for our next posting for by this time we knew that later that year we would be transferred to Tonga, in the South Pacific. My wardrobe would need to be seriously revised for this new location and I would no longer require the overly modest garments needed in the Gulf. I took this opportunity to shop for Graeme too, even to the extent of buying him the morning dress he was going to need so often in Tonga, along with the top hat. During my attempts to buy what was needed I had occasion to ring the High Commission in London to clarify what I should be purchasing. I was astonished to find that my friend Jan, from Honiara days, was now working there. I had no idea she had been employed by the New Zealand Foreign Service after she left the Solomons, and therefore I had not expected to come across her again in London. I was flabbergasted to be rung up, at a men's clothing shop, by Jan, who had established what was needed and was ringing me back from the High Commission to let me know! Once back in Bahrain our final visitor in May was my mother, who again came out during Jessie's leave in India to help me with the two children when we were tied up with our interminable functions. It was lovely for them to get to know her better and she enjoyed being with the family again.

Our final leave from Bahrain was due two months before our departure and we chose Switzerland as our destination. Two days before we left Nina became ill with a high fever and it looked as though our holiday would have to be cancelled. She rallied round, but, as the doctor had feared, she spent the two weeks in Switzerland far from well. We were, consequently, confined to our hotel rooms for much of the time, and although we went on one spectacular train trip through the Eiger and up to the top of the Jungfraujoch, Nina missed most of it on account of being asleep (the main manifestation of her illness now). Our holiday pictures are of Nina asleep in front of an ice cream sundae, Nina asleep on the bathroom floor, Nina asleep while Graeme read the story of Bambi for the hundredth time, and Nina asleep on the train journey up the mountain! Although we thought Switzerland was really beautiful and the mountainous scenery was so refreshing after Bahrain, a sick child in a hotel bedroom does not make for a very successful holiday. By the time we left Nina was better, but it was, by then, too late to do very much in the way of sightseeing. The view from the top of the Jungfraujoch had been so spectacular that we were happy for that to be our lasting memory of Switzerland.

Now it was time to return to Bahrain for the last time and to pack up our possessions and attend a host of farewell functions. The Bahrainis are very generous in their hospitality to those leaving their shores, and our experience of departure was no exception to this rule. We seemed to be going from one farewell straight to the next, and while we had very mixed feelings about leaving we knew that we were going to miss many aspects of life in Bahrain. We would need to travel a long way to find the same degree of friendliness and hospitality towards foreigners. Our three-and-a-half-year tour had ended on a very good note, too, on account of the forthcoming State Visit to New Zealand by H.H. Shaikh Isa bin Sulman Al Khalifa. The Emir was to be the first Arab Head of State to visit New Zealand, and our Government was delighted that he had accepted the invitation. Graeme had been heavily involved in the planning and organisation for this State Visit, but it was scheduled to take place after our departure from Bahrain. Since the new New Zealand Ambassador would not, at that time, be at post, it had been decided that Graeme would accompany the Emir. It was a happy note to leave on. But for me our final departure day dawned with much sadness as I realised I was leaving behind much which was dear to me.

Chapter Seventeen

The Friendly Islands

On the twenty-second of August 1985 we flew from Bahrain to London. Graeme's long service leave was overdue and we had decided to use that extra leave now by touring round England in a camper-van. We wanted to see as many of our friends and family as we could before departing to the other side of the world. We also took that opportunity to revisit several of my former homes, including my grandmother's house in Broadstairs and also Underhill House in Shorncliff where I had had my ghostly encounter so many years ago (thereby giving a whole new meaning to the expression 'returning to old haunts')! Sadly, Underhill House had been burnt down and the ruins were now being used for army training purposes. The last man to live there (an army chaplain) had committed suicide, apparently, and the whole sorry mess seemed to be a tragic end to such a lovely old house.

In the middle of this holiday Graeme had to return to New Zealand in order to accompany the Emir of Bahrain on his State Visit there. This was unfortunate, in the sense that it interrupted our holiday, but Graeme found the whole experience most worthwhile and thoroughly interesting. While Graeme was away the children and I stayed with my mother, and this break afforded me the opportunity to attend the christening of Vicky's first child, a daughter, Suzie. I had been asked to be her godmother and so was delighted that I could be there for that special occasion.

Once Graeme had returned to the UK, we were able to continue with the camper-van holiday, but before his departure we had been to see my father who was by then living in Winchester. However, a few days before a planned visit to his mother (my American grandmother) she died, and so in the end neither Graeme nor the children ever met her. We didn't make it to her funeral either. Another event we missed was Brett's wedding. Graeme's eldest son was a student nurse at a hospital in Cambridge and at only nineteen had decided to marry a girl ten years older than himself. Graeme was none too happy about this decision and felt that Brett was far too young to marry. However, we went to Cambridge to see them and wish them luck.

We then continued northwards and our travels finally brought us to Ulster where we revisited old haunts of mine from Belfast days, and then finally over to Donegal to visit my ex-WRNS friend Anne and her artist husband. They had had a second child by this time and the four children all played happily together. We celebrated our fourth wedding anniversary with Anne and Ken and then bade them a fond farewell before travelling on to New York to meet up with Tony and Shirin. It was fun being back there but it was not really the right place for entertaining two small children, although they enjoyed going to the Bronx Zoo with Tony. It was a flying visit, literally, to say hello to our old bridge friends from Tehran and then we went on to Honolulu to relax for a few days before returning to New Zealand.

Once more we found ourselves at the Capital Hill apartments where we had stayed when we first went to New Zealand and it was odd to be back there again. Our time in Wellington went all too fast and for Graeme much of it was spent working. We caught up with the family in Wanganui, and Graeme's children too, although sadly by this time his daughter Karyn was in hospital suffering from anorexia nervosa. She was not allowed out of hospital for Marc's second birthday unfortunately, which he celebrated at a hotel with his other New Zealand relatives around him. But before long it was time to fly to Auckland to catch our flight to Tonga on the eighteenth of November. During the course of trying to cope with endless suitcases, two young children, and the whole business of getting everyone on the bus between the domestic and international terminal, Graeme ended up putting Marc in the luggage trolley along with the cases. At least we knew where he was that way, but in the course of unloading it all he came tumbling out, only to graze himself badly on the head. Oh dear, now we were going to arrive at post with yet another injured baby, just as we had when we went to Bahrain! His protestations at this turn of events had been loud, but he was still not talking. Although I was concerned at this fact, Graeme felt sure that he would do so when he was ready.

We were somewhat apprehensive about what we would find on our arrival but believed that we were sufficiently old Pacific 'hands' (for Graeme this was his fourth posting in the region) to cope with the local conditions. As we surveyed the scene from the plane on approaching the airfield we could see that Tongatapu (the main island and the location of the capital Nuku'alofa) was exceedingly flat and appeared to consist solely of coconut palms. On landing we were met by an official from the Protocol Department of the Ministry of Foreign Affairs and then driven up to our new Residence, a mile or two east of the town. It looked beautiful, set as it was on the only hill on the island, with a long driveway leading up from the coastal road from town. We found the single story house was, in fact, two houses joined by a central corridor – the official wing and the family wing. Both were huge, but the official wing was rather better placed than the family wing, which was understandable but unfortunate too. While it was all very grand, it was also very dark since the whole house was shaded by huge verandahs to provide outside sitting areas. We rang the doorbell to be let in, but nothing happened! We rang again, and then once more. Just as we began to think that we had better find an alternative means of entry we heard shuffling footsteps coming down the passageway inside. It was Liliani, the seventy-five year old Tongan cook-cum-housekeeper whose lack of mobility had prevented her from answering the doorbell earlier. Besides, she had been expecting us to enter through the back door. So, this was our new house staff. A nice enough old lady, but one who, it transpired, was totally unable to cope with even the simplest of demands.

The Protocol official had told us that Graeme would be presenting his Credentials to His Majesty King Taufa'ahau Tupou IV within forty-eight hours of our arrival. As soon as we had unpacked we decided that we had better not ask Liliani to iron all our formal clothes for the occasion since she did not seem up to the task. Having settled the two children with some toys to play with, we set off in search of an iron. The laundry area was in a separate wing, which included the gardener's bathroom and an enormous garage, along with a huge loft area which eventually became Graeme's radio room. For now we thought we had done well to have discovered the laundry, but once there were horrified at what we saw. Everything was absolutely filthy. The washing machine was caked in grime and congealed soap, and the ironing board was filthy and torn. As for the iron – well, it was encrusted with melted fibres from previously burnt items. It looked like being a hopeless task to prepare ourselves for our formal presentation at the Palace.

When the big day dawned we were introduced to the nanny who had been engaged by the High Commission to help with the children during our frequent absences at official functions, and she was presenting herself now just moments before we left for the Palace. While most Tongans can speak good English, this particular one could not speak any and so we had to leave our two year old and four year old in the hands of a young girl who was totally unable to communicate with them. It was dreadfully unsatisfactory, but we had no choice but to leave for the Palace and pray that they would be all right. They were tearful as we left, and who could blame them?

The Credentials ceremony at the Palace was all very formal and while Graeme presented the King with his official letter from the Governor General of New Zealand I was entertained in a side room nearby. Once the formal part of the ceremony was over I was escorted in to the King's presence and Graeme introduced me. Queen Salote's son was an imposing sight, a middle-aged man of huge girth, reputedly weighing in the region of twenty-one stone. The greater the weight of a Tongan the greater esteem is afforded him, and here we saw an imposing man. We then sat talking for an hour while being offered light refreshments. It was all very pleasant and also quite fascinating to see the degree of formality being engaged in such a faraway and primitive island Kingdom. Even while the ceremony was taking place, Graeme's morning dress and top hat seemed extraordinarily out of place. Nothing like this had ever happened in the Solomon Islands! At the completion of the audience Graeme and I stood, bowed and curtsied to the King and then proceeded to walk out backwards together. We reached the door at precisely the same moment and for a second we were both jammed in the frame together. Once freed and in the passageway, we were led to the verandah where Graeme took the salute and we listened to the King's Band playing the Tongan and New Zealand national anthems. It was all over and now we could go home to a champagne reception with the High Commission staff and their wives and find out if our children were all right.

The first thing we discovered on reaching the Residence was that Nina was not there. We learnt, through translations between Liliani and the nanny, that the latter had taken the two children to the beach, which they had enjoyed, and once there Nina had refused to leave. So the nanny left her to play alone there. Oh, no! Now we fled back down the driveway, praying that Nina would be all right and that no tragedy had befallen her whilst on her own. There were plenty of dangers down there for her since the beach was most unattractive and covered in sharp coral and masses of broken glass bottles. Mercifully, she was all right and was just sitting playing with shells. No harm had become her, so we heaved a huge sigh of relief and returned with her to the group waiting for us at the house. That was the nanny's first day and she was given her notice to leave the job at the end of the week! Now we only had Liliani to keep things running in this enormous house, and we already knew what her limitations were.

Our first eventful forty-eight hours were over and it was time to take stock of our new country of residence. The Tongan archipelago (referred to by the explorer Captain James Cook as The Friendly Islands) is situated in the South Pacific some one thousand two hundred miles due north of New Zealand, and midway between Fiji and Western Samoa. It comprises one hundred and sixty-nine small islands, the southern-most island of Tongatapu being the largest and the location of the capital, Nuku'alofa, and seat of government. Further north are the equally flat islands of the Ha'apai group; and further north again the more physically attractive islands of Vava'u. Two tiny islands far to the north, the Niu'as, complete the group. Submarine volcanoes are something of an exotic feature of this tiny island country (along with some of the deepest waters in the world, reaching depths of 35,702 feet) which is situated directly to the west of the International Date Line. It experiences the unique phenomenon, therefore, to be twenty-three and a half hours ahead of its nearest neighbours in Western Samoa.

Tonga is a feudal monarchy, ruled by a hereditary monarch and a small group of nobles. All other inhabitants (total population 95,300 in 1988) are known as commoners. Its Parliament nonetheless accommodates a certain number of seats to commoners elected under democratic process. Tonga has never been completely colonised, although it was under British protection between 1905 until independence in 1970. Demographic pressures have been significantly relieved by emigration to New Zealand. Its economy has traditionally been dependent on a narrow range of exports, notably copra, bananas, vanilla and fresh vegetables (particularly in recent times the export of significant quantities of pumpkins to Japan). It has benefited from substantial overseas development assistance, particularly from Australia, New Zealand, Japan, and the European Union, especially in relation to its infrastructure. It has been strongly influenced by early Christian missionary activity, from which has emerged the Church of Tonga – "the King's Church". Christian values, with a certain Tongan interpretation, are particularly influential in everyday life, and Sundays are strictly observed, it being an offence to engage in any form of work such as mowing the lawn, or playing a game of golf.

So it was just as well that they did not know what was going on behind the scenes at the New Zealand Residence, because Sundays there were a day of particularly hard work for many weeks and months to come. The house was huge (4,205 square feet) and we had no house staff besides Liliani, who was wanting to retire as soon as she could be replaced. But we also needed another staff member to cope with the cleaning and another to help with the children. The recruiting process started, but we found that in the main Tongans were neither interested in working, nor very keen to come out to the far end of town where our house was situated. There were nice living quarters available for them, but even this attraction did not seem to hold much sway. They preferred to stay talking all day in their villages. They failed to arrive for an appointment for interview, or if they did and were employed they soon left, mostly through pregnancy, and even when working put very little effort into what they were doing. Our social engagements during our first weeks, and building up to the Christmas period, were heavy and many of them were during the day time when the children needed my attention. Often we were out when it was time to bath and feed them and put them to bed. Initially I accompanied Graeme to all these functions, but as time passed and more and more girls were passing through in an attempt to find suitable employees, I was becoming tired and less able to cope with the cleaning of the house, the constant socialising and the ongoing needs of the children.

Throughout our early weeks we had constant power cuts. Not only did this mean that we were without electricity, but we would also be without water too since the supply was dependent upon an electric water pump. Also the weather changed considerably and not only was it appallingly hot, but the humidity levels reached ninety per cent and more. I frequently needed to go to the Deputy High Commissioner's house in order to bath the children (which in itself made me even hotter) and then return again immediately in order to shower myself before attending a function. At such moments Graeme was glad of the shower in his office since this was not affected in the same way as the water supply at the Residence. For our first two months on the island, throughout these difficulties, I was working hard in the Residence doing all the things which were beyond Liliani to manage.

As the weeks went by I seemed to be getting fewer opportunities to turn my attention to the unpacking of our sea freight – all eighty-seven large boxes of it. Throughout this pre-Christmas period we were serenaded by bands. They came up to the house with the intention of raising funds for overseas tours and would never take "No, not now" for an answer, even to the extent that on one occasion they woke the children up long after they had gone to bed. When the first band arrived we gave generously, but then the word got around that we had done so and we were inundated with others, some of which were no more than a few youths banging on empty tin cans! It was something to be wary of the next year. By the time Christmas was upon us we had discovered the extent of the filth in the house and some areas had clearly never been cleaned at all. The laundry wing was a case in point and the dirt that we cleaned out of there had to be seen to be believed. Graeme helped me whenever he could and together we spent all possible time available to us cleaning and sorting out the many store areas and rooms, which also involved washing all glassware, all crockery (both of which ran into several hundreds of pieces) along with much of the five hundred and fifteen items of silverware. The best official glassware had previously either not been washed at all, or had been so badly dealt with that much of it was beyond our ability to salvage. Approximately seventy-five per cent of all the official linen could not be used until it had been taken to the local laundry and put through stronger cleaning processes than were available to us. A particularly attractive and very large tablecloth had become quite useless through lack of proper cleaning and this was included in the consignment which went to the laundry. It never came back and we discovered much later that they had taken such a liking to it that they had cut it up for pillowcases for themselves!

All the mirrors in the house had been incorrectly cleaned by using a wet cloth and then leaving the mirror to dry naturally. They all bore the tell-tale stains which resulted from this treatment. The list of spoilt and damaged items was endless and Graeme and I continued on right through the Christmas break trying to make headway in rectifying as much as we could. But we still had not unpacked our sea freight and we had still not made any kind of start on the kitchen. The latter was in such an appalling state that we knew we would have to get the rest of the house clean before beginning what would be a huge job to put it right. Much of what was there had never been cleaned and would simply have to be thrown away; a lot more would require a man's strength to scrub away the filth. All the while that we still had Liliani we were unable to really make the sort of impression on the kitchen that was needed. She would have been very upset to see the High Commissioner in her kitchen doing something she had never done – cleaning the place! We were aware that much of it was a health hazard, but we could not run the risk of upsetting Liliani. On New Year's Eve, Graeme finally succumbed to the inevitable and went down with a bad stomach upset. This prevented him attending the King's midnight reception to see in the New Year, and so I ended up representing New Zealand alone.

It took us both two months to clean the house, with the exception of the kitchen, and we had become very aware that one maid could simply not keep up any kind of standard alone. It would require at least two, for to clean either the louvred windows, or the vast quantity of silverware alone would take far too long to attend to general cleaning requirements as well. We had tried all through these early weeks to engage new house staff, but in the case of the cook's job this looked to be entirely hopeless since there were no qualified cooks available for employment. We tried to recruit from Fiji, but even this line of action drew a blank. I was becoming more and more caught up in the task of getting the Residence in tip-top shape and less and less able to perform the duties which were really required of me.

In those days Nuku'alofa was a very rundown bedraggled looking place and shopping there was no pleasure. If one shop was out of something, then one could be sure that the other shops were out of it too. We were all dependent upon the next ship or plane coming in with supplies, and often, like Honiara, it might be weeks before we could get even basic requirements again. More than once I wished that I had brought more with me, but until you arrive in a place you can never be certain of what your needs will be. We discovered that there was no such thing as a plumber in town, nor a dry cleaner (what were we going to do about freshening up Graeme's morning dress, given the number of times he would be wearing it in that heat?), nor anywhere to get films developed at that time. It was primitive to a greater degree than I had encountered before. This fact also became obvious since building work was now under way to construct new housing for all High Commission staff sent up from Wellington. The Clerk of Works may have been a New Zealander, but the builders were Tongans and this soon transpired to be a distinct disadvantage.

For the first two weeks in Tonga the children had been enrolled into the local Mata'aho Kindergarten, and this had provided them with some activity and opportunity to get to know some other little children. In Nina's case this was only a temporary measure since she was due to commence school the following term. However, we had arrived in Tonga just as the southern hemisphere schools were about to commence their long summer holiday through December and January, and so she would have to wait another couple of months before she could start. It meant that she had finished school in the middle of June in Bahrain (when they started their long summer holiday) and would be unable to commence again until more than seven months later. This had been far too long a wait for a little girl who loved school and who had already been attending for two and a half years. But there was nothing we could do about it other than placing her in the Kindergarten for a couple of weeks before the end of term. Marc went along too, and for him it was his first such experience. While it occupied him to some extent, it was not entirely successful. The Tongan women looking after the children found him far too adventurous and could not keep him in one place long enough to get him involved in what they were trying to do with the children. He was always off somewhere else and they could not keep track of him. They asked me not to bring him back in the new year until he could talk more than the few distinguishable words he could say then and until he was ready to sit quietly and pay attention! It was a pity because both children were in need of full-time occupation, and besides, the short time they were there afforded me a greater degree of freedom to continue with trying to get the Residence in better shape.

None of us felt very settled. The domestic problems we encountered meant that we could not get ourselves sorted out properly, nor could I find the time to unpack our things. However, Marc, at two, coped with the whole unsettling business better than the rest of us put together. He thrived and became fat and brown like a true Tongan boy. He slept well and in the main ate well, although there were still inexplicable periods when he refused just about everything that was put in front of him. However, he developed a passion for bananas – a craving which was all too easy to satisfy in Tonga – and soon became potty trained when we let him run around for a couple of days with nothing on at all. It turned out to be a simple, if rather messy, way for him to learn what was required of him. For all his early problems he had turned into a happy, healthy, loving little boy who brought us great joy. Nina, on the other hand, had found that the long period without the stimulation of school, coupled with all the difficulties in the house which she was well able to comprehend, caused her to be very unsettled and, consequently, as difficult as she knew how to be. Also, unlike in Bahrain, where all her friends were within walking distance, we now found ourselves at the furthest limit of town with no children nearby to play with. One or two contacts had been formed through the Kindergarten, but it meant that elaborate arrangements had to be made in order for the children to play. By the middle of January, nearly two months after we arrived, I had finally managed to recruit both a replacement nanny called Amelia and a part-time maid to help with the cleaning. They both seemed, in the Tongan context, to be reasonably good and if they worked out and could cope with the volume of work, then maybe my problems in this area would be alleviated and we could all begin to settle.

The extra help meant that I was able to go with Graeme to the Pacific Heads of Mission meeting in Fiji, which was a welcome break from all that had been going on. While we were there we met some Americans who asked us how things were going for us in Tonga. It wasn't long before we got onto the matter of our need of a cook and they made the suggestion that we contact an excellent Tongan cook who was at that time working in Pago Pago. We had already heard a lot about this woman, how good she was and how nice too, but had never thought of suggesting that she come back to Tonga to work for us. However, with this prompting, we did just that, and much to our astonishment she accepted the offer immediately. It was then that the six-week saga began, in a slow way at first, building up to a crescendo by Nina's fifth birthday. At first we got messages that she couldn't come this week, but would come next week (we had already sent her the money for her air fare). Then we were told that the man she was working for in Pago Pago had been murdered and she was a key witness in the murder trial since she had found the dead body. This went on until Easter, but we were assured that she would be able to commence work on the first of April. On the basis of this information we let Liliani retire on that day with a little party for her in the office with a present and some nice words being said by Graeme. Well, of course, the lady in Pago Pago did not materialise, but we were then told that she would be coming in a few days time. The final deadline came and went and the plane from Pago Pago landed without her. Eventually we received a telephone message to say that she would not be returning to Tonga after all. She had decided to stay on and work for the widow of the murdered man (although she was, apparently, the prime suspect for having murdered her husband). We felt greatly frustrated at all the time and money which had been wasted pursuing this particular lead, especially since we had let Liliani go already. Now we had no cook at all. We did all that we could, under the circumstances, and promoted the part-time maid into the cook's job and recruited another part-time maid. This was far from satisfactory particularly since she was no better at the job than Liliani, only younger and more agile. A few days later I was at a lunch party and was told that the cook in Pago Pago had, in the end, returned to Tonga. She never came to work for us though!

During the six week wait for the cook situation to clarify itself Graeme was continuing to make his official calls round and about and this included going to the islands of Vava'u further to the north. Although it was an official visit we decided that the children and I would go up too, to give them the break which they were also ready for. We took Amelia with us so that she could look after the children when we were busy officially, and for her this was quite a thrill since she had never flown in a plane before. I was none too sure that Amelia deserved this treat since the week before I had been getting ready for an important wedding and had been interrupted by the police wishing to interview me concerning Amelia's movements. This turn of events had so upset me that I had quite overlooked completing my makeup and dressing and had gone to the wedding far from ready, although I had not realised this until it was far too late and I was already sitting in the church. Anyway, off we all went to Vava'u and we found it all much more attractive up there than our surroundings in Nuku'alofa. It was a most pleasant break away and the children in particular enjoyed the experience of flying up there in the little seven-seater aircraft.

We got back on Good Friday and were surprised that the plane was allowed to land since no aircraft were permitted to use the airport on a Sunday and we had imagined this would also apply to Good Friday, but apparently not, and anyway we were glad to get back to hear the latest news on the staff front. The day after Easter was Liliani's final day in the job and the next day we set to to start the clean-up in the kitchen. The job took four of us five days of solid work to complete, but we left the oven to Graeme to attend to at the weekend and this he did magnificently, although it was a long hard job to remove the years of grime in there. He completely dismantled the oven and in so doing was able to get it out of its place and scrub all sides of it, including the floor where it had been standing since the house had been built. At this point Marc came along to investigate his labours and, when Graeme's back was turned, began to play with something on the floor under the oven. Nina came into the room just as he was putting it in his mouth and asked if he was supposed to be doing that! To our horror we discovered that it was rat poison which Marc had been prevented from swallowing in the nick of time by Nina. On this particular Saturday, Graeme and I had had to take time off from our scrubbing to go to the airport to see the King and Queen off on their latest travels, and this had taken quite a sizeable chunk out of the day since the airport was an hour's drive from our house. We returned from the airport to continue cleaning up the kitchen for the rest of the weekend and were really pleased with the results. It was now a wholesome organised place in which we were to have welcomed our new cook from Pago Pago and for whose expected arrival we had made so much effort. Of course, in the middle of the job we had discovered that she would not be arriving.

It was from this newly-cleaned kitchen that we prepared some nice things for Nina's fifth birthday party and she had several little friends from school to come and help her celebrate. By this time Marc had reached the stage where his favourite word was "No", followed closely by "Mine", the latter being applied to anything and everything which he decided he wanted! No doubt some of Nina's birthday presents were among these items, and when he liked something he would always add, after "Mine", "Nish". Nish, or rather, nice, was another favourite word, but still his vocabulary was small and he had particular difficulty with 's' and 'th'. In fact, it was around this time that we began calling him Mr Birshing and Mr Firsty since he always seemed to be alternately either 'thirsty' followed very soon afterwards by 'bursting to go to the loo'. Both children shared a particular friend in Tonga, a little three year old French girl called Stephanie, with whose mother I had struck up a friendship through trying to help her improve her English. It was nice to have this diversion in an otherwise overly busy lifestyle which, as well as an endless stream of official functions, included being on the honorary board of the Red Cross. The Queen often attended the board meetings and was in the habit of selecting this person, or that, to organise a fund-raising activity of one kind or another. When my turn came it turned out to be a Red Cross Cookery book which proved far more difficult to co-ordinate and get printed than I had imagined when I first embarked on the project.

At least I had been spared trying to do too much in the way of official entertaining, not only because we lacked a proper cook, but also because when we arrived we discovered that there was no money left in the official entertainment fund. We had to fund what official functions we did hold out of our own pocket, at least initially. This included not only our huge National Day reception, but also the one hundred people who were expected to attend the ANZAC day function. For the latter event we were up at four o'clock in the morning. on the twenty-fifth of April, since it is customarily a dawn service, followed by refreshments. We knew that the Police Band would be arriving at that early hour to start tuning up for the occasion, and we also had the finishing touches to the food to attend to, although the bulk of the work had been done the day before. We felt that the children would probably not appreciate this early start and so on the night of the twenty-fourth we put them into the Dateline Hotel, along with Amelia, so that they could have a peaceful night undisturbed by the early start. At dawn the next day, when the guests started to arrive, one or two mentioned to me that they had seen Amelia wandering about the hotel late the night before with both children in tow. I wondered what on earth had been going on and asked her when we collected them later in the morning. It transpired that the bottom had fallen out of the cot which the hotel had provided for Marc, and he had, of course, been considerably disturbed by this. When Amelia and the children had been seen by some of our guests, she had been trying to get a replacement cot provided for Marc. I took a deep breath and once again reminded myself that this was, after all, Tonga.

Chapter Eighteen
The Pacific Turns Grey

In May Graeme's two younger children, Karyn and Nigel, arrived to spend their school holiday with us, and so it was exciting for them to be coming to a different location from their previous destination of Bahrain. During their visit we had to attend a semi-Royal wedding between the son of Baron Vaea and the daughter of the Governor of Ha'apai. The bride and groom did not look the picture of happiness. We were somewhat surprised by this, and also by the high profile being taken by a former New Zealand High Commissioner and his wife who returned to Tonga for the wedding. There is an unwritten understanding that it is simply not the done thing to return to a former posting and attend high-profile functions!

It wasn't until June of 1986 that I was able to take Marc back to the Mata'aho Kindergarten and even then Amelia had to be with him throughout the time he spent there. The supervision was minimal, and in spite of Amelia's presence, on one occasion Marc wandered off by himself, leaving the Kindergarten and walking some distance to Nina's school. Nina happened to see him, since she was playing outside at the time, and was able to rescue him from the dangers of the road (he was only two and a half at the time) and she told him to go back to the Kindergarten. I was astonished to learn about this from Nina later and had to speak firmly to Amelia to ensure that such a thing did not happen again. However, her limitations became clear not long afterwards when she was playing with the children in the garden. Graeme had just hung a swing for them from the huge old mango tree and as soon as it was finished we left to attend a function. On our return we discovered that Marc was not all right. He had fallen off the swing and hurt his leg. Amelia had put Nina on the swing with Marc on her lap, and Marc in turn was holding onto "Pooh Where" (the name he gave to his favourite teddy bear). It had only taken a moment for him to come off as soon as Amelia started pushing.

Marc was clearly distressed. We dashed him to the hospital where we thought his leg would be x-rayed. However, this was not done since we were assured by the doctor that he had not broken his leg. A nightmare ten days ensued, during which time Marc screamed all the time. He would not walk and he could not sleep, so nor could we. We took him to a private doctor who gave us the same story — the leg was not broken, only sprained. Two days after this accident we commenced the week long celebrations for the King's birthday (Halala week) which involved us being out morning noon and night. This week was made even more difficult by the loss of the cook who had sent in what transpired to be a bogus sick certificate. She had clearly decided that she would prefer to be in her village for the week-long celebrations. So now there was nobody at home to prepare food for the children during our perpetual absences, and on each day of the celebrations we returned to the sound of Marc's continued crying.

During the course of Halala week we had to be up at the crack of dawn one morning to attend a prayer breakfast at the Dateline Hotel. When we were shown to our table, erected on the outside open-air dancing area, we discovered that the bacon and eggs had been cooked the night before and were sitting on the plates staring at us in a glazed fashion, and this was repeated at all the many tables. When we realised that we were going to have to eat rock-hard glazed bacon and eggs, we didn't know whether to laugh or cry. If this was a hurdle to overcome, greater fortitude was needed later to get through the hours of speeches and prayers and singing. And then the rain came down. It was a deluge and the water began to accumulate in the overhead tarpaulin which had been erected over the VIP seating where we were. It was clear that the canopy would eventually come tumbling down but nobody wanted to be the first to take avoiding action. Eventually there was an undignified scramble as Ambassadors and High Commissioners fled to the drier verandahs behind us. By noon we escaped back to the Residence where we had time only to dry ourselves off before leaving for the next function.

In the middle of all this frenetic celebration we lost the remaining house staff who had become exhausted with us being out all the time and trying to cope with Marc who never stopped crying. So now we were alone with a distraught baby, a little girl, no maid, no nanny and no cook, and a list of further functions to attend. There was nothing for it but to ask Liliani if she would come out of retirement to help us. Kind old lady that she was, she readily agreed. I didn't have time to wonder if she would recognise her former kitchen or be able to find anything in it now, but somehow or other we got through that week, with her help. Even when the cook returned, she then disappeared again to a wedding in Fiji for which she had been granted three days leave to attend. Two weeks later she finally returned (as it transpired having had an abortion rather than attending a wedding) with the excuse that she had missed the plane back to Tonga. We had discovered that reliability was not the Tongan's strong suit long ago and so this latest demonstration of it was no real surprise to us.

After ten days of trying to believe that the doctors were right about Marc's leg we could believe it no longer. We took him to the hospital again and insisted that the leg be x-rayed. Sure enough, his leg *was* fractured. The poor child had had a broken leg for ten days with no more than a bandage on it. No wonder he had been unable to walk. Once his leg was put in a plaster cast, the screaming stopped and we went home. We had never been so tired in all our lives before. Not only had we had all the drama with Marc's leg, and all the attendant screaming and consequent lack of sleep, but we had been to more functions in a week than we had ever been to before, and all without the help of anyone but Liliani.

By the time we reached August we were relieved to be due for some leave and this we took in Sydney. It was simply wonderful to be in such a lovely place, surrounded by so much sophistication after our first traumatic nine months in such primitive conditions as existed in Tonga. However, the strain of the past months had taken its toll and we were all ill during that holiday. Added to which Marc was having a lot of pain teething and once again didn't stop crying. However, being in Sydney gave us the chance to fulfil my promise to Mike and Gail that I would be back one day to introduce them to Graeme. To see them again, after six long years, meant that there was a lot of news to catch up with. They had had another son in the meantime, and although the four children were of different ages they got on well, and we all thoroughly enjoyed our visit to their lovely home in Menai. On our way back to Tonga, while waiting for our connecting flight in Auckland, we bumped into a senior officer from Graeme's Ministry. He asked us how we were and whether we were looking forward to returning to Tonga and I couldn't look him in the eye when I decided I had better answer "Yes"!

On our return Amelia greeted us with the news that she would be leaving to have a baby. She wasn't the first staff member to leave for this reason but she was the first one who was really going to be missed. The children were so fond of her, as was I, in spite of the occasions when I had been frustrated by her stupidity. So now we would have to recruit a replacement and my heart sank at the prospect. At least the children were doing well now. Marc's leg had healed and the plaster cast had been removed two days before we went to Australia, and Nina was doing extremely well at school. The notation "outstanding" had appeared several times on her mid-year report and she appeared to be the teacher's pet.

Our life back in Tonga resumed and, for once, was relatively uneventful for a couple of months. I began to think that we had reached a plateau of relatively safe ground with nothing untoward happening. Just the endless round of functions of one kind or another. Everything was turned into an event in Tonga. The opening of this, the closing of that, the arrival of a foreign naval vessel or visiting dignitary. All required a Tongan 'feast' on tables set up outside, which needed many helpers just to fan away the flies. Then there would be the music and the dancing and singing. At first it was nice to watch but the occasions would always drag on far too long on account of the interminable prayers, sermons and preaching, all in Tongan which we couldn't understand, and so the boredom factor would always creep in. After dozens and dozens of such occasions, they began to pall badly since there was seldom any variation to the same old theme. Hairdressing was another problem with so many functions to attend and the one 'professional' in town turned out to be so hopeless as to be worse than nothing at all. Graeme cut my hair and, with a bit of help, I permed it myself, having picked up a home perming kit in Fiji during the first trip off the island for the Heads of Mission Meeting. The results were pretty awful but there was no way I was going back to the 'hairdresser'!

By now we had decided to spend our mid-tour Christmas leave in England. It had been over a year since we last went there, and after my frequent trips from Bahrain I was beginning to feel dreadfully homesick and in need of being with my family and friends. It was decided that I should go on alone earlier than Graeme could get away, and this I did on the 4th of November, almost a full year since arriving in Tonga. Two weeks later Graeme flew the seventy-two hour journey from the South Pacific to London with the two children. Marc had by now had his third birthday and Nina was five and a half, and so it was quite an undertaking to go such a long way alone with two young children. He survived it, intact, and joined me at my mother's flat for Christmas 1986.

Our routine in England on that occasion varied little from previous visits and our time was spent seeing as many people as we could manage. We saw Brett in Cambridge. He was cheerful but had already separated from his new wife. We took him out for a meal and caught up with his news. We saw several other friends and also went to London to meet up with my father at Harrods so that the children could visit Father Christmas at his Fairy Grotto. That was a magical outing for two children who had been in the wilds of Tonga for the past year. I was glad that my father had come alone and was pleased that he also spent the day at my mother's flat, later, to deliver presents for the children. It gave us a chance to talk more freely, without the constraints of my stepmother's presence. We also went down to Sevenoaks to look around the school and meet the Headmaster, Mr Barker. We were very impressed by what we saw and decided to register the children in the hope that, one day, the cogs would fall into place and it would be possible for the children to become boarders there. We were asked for the name of a guardian (which seemed strange at such an early stage) and could think of nobody other than my father. His name was, therefore, entered on the school records for future reference. I filled in the papers at the school, and consequently had no opportunity to take photocopies of the registration forms, but this didn't seem a problem since all the information given was of a fairly basic nature. We paid the registration fees and came away feeling very happy that we had taken this decision.

After a very pleasant Christmas spent with my mother we spent three days, between Christmas and New Year, with my father and his wife at a hotel in Christchurch in Hampshire. For me the whole visit was an ordeal to be borne in order for my father to spend some time with the children. They were not affected by the underlying tension which existed between me and my stepmother, so for them it was a pleasant break away before returning to celebrate the new year with their granny in Bromley. They saw their grandfather twice more after that for he came up to take Graeme and the children out for a day in Greenwich to see the Cutty Sark and the Thames Barrier. This was just prior to our departure from England, and I stayed behind to do the washing and packing before our long flight back to Tonga. The morning of the seventh of January 1987 dawned and my father came to Heathrow to see us off. When we met up with him we were in the middle of a major panic, having lost Nina. Eventually we had to put a message out over the Tannoy system in order to find her and so, soon after this was all over, we had to bid him farewell. He told us that he and his wife had split up again and that he was planning to find a small house to move into. We were fairly astonished, having seen them together so recently, but on reflection wondered if the underlying tension which had been in the air at Christchurch had had anything to do with it. It seemed that every time I saw my stepmother soon afterwards there would be a breakdown of their relationship. Once again my sympathy went to my father and once again I thought that it would be beneficial in terms of my association with him. As we waved goodbye I did not know that that would be the last time I would see him.

Our flight back was uneventful, except for the fact that Marc became locked in the lavatory on the plane and the steward had to remove the door in order to free him. The door could not be replaced, for some reason, and so the passengers were thereafter deprived of one of the lavatories. Quite a hardship when cooped up with hundreds of people on a long flight to New Zealand! When we reached Christchurch (the New Zealand city by the same name as the one where we had stayed with my father so recently), we were exhausted from our long flight from London. We were waiting in the transit lounge, and when we heard passengers called forward to board the British Airways flight to London we did not for one moment think that that meant us. How wrong could we be! The same aircraft which was to fly us on to Auckland had now taken on a different flight number and instead of being on its outward journey was now on its return flight to London! We, on the other hand, had assumed that the flight from London finished in Auckland, but once the lounge emptied of passengers we thought we had better check what was happening. Sure enough, we were now supposed to get onto the same plane which was beginning its return flight to London! Just knowing that made us feel even more tired. We finally disembarked at Auckland, where we spent a night before catching our flight to Tonga the next day. By this stage of the journey we were too tired to sleep well and so the overnight stop did little to refresh us for our onward connection to Tonga. When we did finally land, we were greeted by a torrential downpour, with no umbrella to shield us while walking from the tarmac to the VIP lounge, and humidity which was up in the high nineties again. We were like limp wet rags by the time we reached cover. Nobody had thought to arrange for the driver to come and collect us from the airport and so we spent the seventy-third hour of our journey waiting to be collected. There is no such thing as a taxi rank in the middle of a desert island, and so we had no choice but to wait, soaking wet, until the driver arrived, having been rung from the airport by Graeme.

When he met us he was brimming with bad news for us. The house staff had all decided to leave, or had already done so, during our absence. The reasons ranged from pregnancy (Amelia left to have her baby two weeks after our return); to wanting to go back to their village to be with relatives; to grandchildren who needed looking after. Not only were the present staff leaving, but Amelia's replacement, O'u, who had been recruited to take over from her when she left, had decided to go to Australia to marry an Australian. It seemed as though we would now be in an even worse situation than when we had arrived. Mercifully, in the end, only one of the girls left and O'u decided to replace Amelia after all. She proved to be the best of a fairly indifferent lot and she is the one who stands out in my mind as being the only Tongan girl (out of twenty-two who passed through the Residence during our two years there) who possessed the integrity and reliability which was needed in such a job.

We had three days to recover from our journey before the socialising started again. It was a frantically busy time and we were out every day, sometimes to several functions, for the next month. The British High Commissioner was leaving, and so was the Bank Manager, and there were a number of extra parties held in their honour. There were many other comings and goings, including a change of staff in the form of Graeme's First Secretary. For the latter's departure we gave a reception for one hundred guests within a week of being back. The Royal Family was travelling a lot, too, which meant extra round trips to the airport to see them off and welcome them on their return. All in all, we had not been so busy since Halala week the year before. This state of affairs continued and before long it was also time to host our annual National Day reception once more. Our cook, who had let us down so badly during Halala week, got drunk on the wine she was supposed to be serving to our guests. She behaved in a disgraceful fashion, in front of a couple of hundred people, and was so sick by the end of the event that she was unable to take any part in the clearing up afterwards.

When we got back from leave we found that our pot plants, scattered throughout the massive verandahs at our Residence, had all died. Considerable time and expense was involved in replacing them and, having done so, we got our new head gardener to be responsible for their ongoing welfare. He proposed to make light work of watering them and decided to use the spray backpack (used for weed killing) to keep them moist. What he did not think to do was to ensure that no traces of weed killer remained in the container. As a result of his actions all the new pot plants died, with the exception only of the huge rubber plant, which simply looked somewhat dejected. So much effort to get the plants looking nice had now gone completely to waste. At this time we also discovered that our beautiful Abyssinian cat, Tao, had gone missing. It transpired that he had been poisoned (a common occurrence since the local children would often take acid out of car batteries and then dip meat or fish in it before offering it to animals). His body was found at the bottom of our garden, near to the beach, and we had a little burial ceremony for him under the mango tree in the garden. We were so sad. Although he had been bequeathed by our predecessor and we had been none too please to have him foisted on us, we had, over the time he was with us become very fond of him. His death was an awful blow. So now our plants and our cat were dead – all having been poisoned. The gardener was not on the top of my list of favourite people, and so I was none too pleased that he was, apparently, romantically linked with my newly recruited housegirl. None of the others could stand this particular gardener and consequently gave the new housegirl a bad time with their repeated moaning about him. A week after joining us the new girl could take these comments no longer, and left.

I was cross when I had all this explained to me since finding staff was almost impossible in Tonga. I made my feelings known and to my complete astonishment found that they all walked out, then and there, because I had told them that their mean behaviour to the new girl had caused her to leave. Only O'u stayed. The rest simply left. I made it clear to them that if they persisted in this line of action there would be no job back at the Residence waiting for them once they had reflected on their actions, which in time they regretted. Unfortunately the timing was bad since the following day we were to be hosting a farewell dinner for the departing British High Commissioner and his wife. The Crown Prince was invited to this dinner and now I had no help in the house to produce the meal for fourteen guests. I rang my French friend and mercifully she agreed to come up to help me produce the meal which was required.

The humidity soared, and the kitchen was stiflingly hot as the two of us laboured all day to produce the meal. It was necessary to do it the day before since I was expected at functions that night and all the following day. It was a severe test of our friendship, in that heat, for we both had very different ideas of kitchen etiquette and did not make a good team. However, she was a brilliant cook and I could never have done what she did, and therefore had little choice but to accept that my kitchen was rapidly resembling a bomb scene from some war film. At the end of the day, having produced a lovely four-course meal, my friend left to wash her hair in readiness for the function we were both attending that night. O'u and I were left to do the washing up in the kitchen and to restore order to chaos. It took the two of us two and a half hours by which time there was no time for me to even shower for the function, much less wash my hair. I couldn't believe that I could be attending a dinner in such a state, but I had simply run out of time. When I returned at midnight, I then went into the dining-room to set the table for our dinner the following night. I was doing this until the small hours of the morning since there were napkins to iron into fancy patterns, along with ensuring that the table was fully ready to receive the Crown Prince. I collapsed into bed for a few short hours before commencing day-long engagements the next morning.

To cope with the serving of the meal that night we had had to bring in staff from the office, dress them in the uniforms of the house staff, and give them a quick run-down as to what would be required of them in order to heat the meal and serve it correctly at the table. Inevitably the whole evening was doomed to be interrupted by one disaster following hard on the heels of another, and it was at a considerably later time than expected before I got the word that the meal was ready to serve. With this advice I approached the Crown Prince with the invitation to come to the table. "Anne, I thought you would never ask," he said, at which moment he proceeded to light another cigarette, thereby delaying the start of the meal by a further ten minutes. By the time we eventually got to the table the meal was cold again and did not do justice to the efforts which had been put into preparing it the day before. Funnily enough, despite the disasters with the food, the dinner was the most successful we had given up to that time. However, we were out so much for the following week that it was not until much later that I was able to clear up from this function and be sufficiently organised to ask the housegirls at the British High Commission Residence to come up and help with all the washing and starching of the table linen. They were by then without a High Commissioner to work for and had time on their hands which enabled me to ask for their help. O'u and I had had more than enough difficulty finding the time to clear up from this function and so were thankful for their assistance.

The days after the dinner had been so busy. By day we were at functions and by night we were either at dinners or at the airport until one in the morning to welcome the King back from another overseas trip. The night after the airport duty we did not get to bed until half-past midnight after yet another dinner, by which time we were completely exhausted. Just before he went to sleep, that Saturday night, Graeme thought he heard a noise. He was too tired to investigate it and assumed that it was Marc turning over in his cot and knocking something in the process. When we woke the next morning we discovered we had been burgled.

That was another bit of bad timing too for that particular Sunday we were having lunch with the King, who was hosting a farewell function for the British High Commissioner (who else?!). I had hoped to have a peaceful morning in order to set my hair and generally prepare for the lunch in a calm way. However, none of that happened because firstly we were in a state of shock and also horrified to find that it had been perpetrated out of spite, not simply to acquire our possessions. Odd things had gone, such as Nina's new bicycle, which she had only just received a few weeks ago as a Christmas present; Nina's school bag; all the mops and brooms; one hundred and twenty dollars worth of Omo; some wine and chocolate from the fridge. All the newly-laundered uniforms, which I had laboriously prepared for our reception for one hundred the next day to welcome the new First Secretary, had all been dumped on the laundry room floor and trampled on to enforce the point. It was to be yet another occasion, within five days of the last, when we would have to bring staff in from the office to do the serving at the function. Also, for good measure, a puddle of urine was left on the family room floor. Only the stereo unit which was stolen fell into the category of what one would normally expect to lose in a burglary.

It took the police one hour to arrive after we informed them of what had happened. They took fingerprints and questioned us, but they did not listen to what we said because it was so clear that this was a deliberately spiteful burglary and therefore obvious who had perpetrated it. I even showed the police the clear impression of a face on the window where the burglar had peered into the house from the outside before breaking in. It was all there, the eye shadow, the pressed-in powdered nose, and clearest of all the lipstick from the mouth. The height of this impression on the window could have told them quite clearly that they needed to look for a woman of a certain height who might be able to 'help the police with their enquiries'. However, they did not want to pursue this line of questioning, nor to take our views into account. This approach was in stark contrast to the protection our diplomatic status had afforded us in Bahrain where we had been provided with round-the-clock guards. The approach had now become a 'them' and 'us' situation and they did not want to know that we knew exactly who had done this to us.

We went to the King's lunch, leaving dependable O'u alone at the house to look after the children that Sunday. She was dreadfully upset by what had happened to us and was as sure as we were about the culprit. However, for now we had to do our duty and attend the lunch party at the King's palace. It was yet another function I had to attend without having prepared myself suitably. The next day the reception for one hundred went ahead as planned (I had laundered all the uniforms again after I got back from the palace). The day after our reception we went to the airport again, this time to say goodbye to the departing British High Commissioner, and I couldn't help feeling thankful that this would now bring to an end all the extra work which had been involved in their departure.

However, the Bank Manager had not yet gone, and so we still had daily functions to attend, plus the usual round of Red Cross

Committee meetings and so forth. Three days later Marc developed yet another ear infection (he had had repeated bouts of otitis media throughout our time in Tonga), and in the middle of the night he was in such pain with this new infection that I had to drive him to the hospital. Graeme stayed behind to look after Nina, who had also woken up with Marc's crying, but at least I was able to get him onto antibiotics quickly. Our repeated trips to the airport continued, frequently to farewell or welcome the King and Queen, and then again very soon afterwards to welcome the new British High Commissioner and his wife.

Our conviction regarding the perpetrator of the burglary continued to be unheeded by the police, and we now discovered that the person concerned was wanting to go to New Zealand to visit her Tongan boyfriend down there. She was also involved with a New Zealander, who was already married, and she had persuaded him to pay her air-fare down ostensibly to move in with him. She had earlier persuaded this same man to pay for her air-fare to Fiji and for the abortion she had had there, telling him that it was his child she was carrying. In fact, the child had been that of the Tongan boyfriend. Anyway, she was determined to go to New Zealand and stopped at nothing to try to achieve her aim. However, she was listed as a prohibited immigrant in New Zealand (for past misdemeanours) and now that Tongans had to get a visa to visit New Zealand she was going to find it impossible to get the necessary stamp in her passport. She thought she could achieve her aim in Fiji, but our office there had already been warned by Graeme to look out for her, and so that application failed. She had no choice but to walk into Graeme's office in Nuku'alofa and request a visa to travel to New Zealand. She knew that we knew what she had done. It didn't stop her walking in as bold as brass to apply for her visa. The fact was that she was not entitled to one, and she knew that too. She also knew that there was not a thing we could do to prove she had burgled us.

February went out with a bang when O'u told us that she was also pregnant and would be leaving us later in the year. She had been such a pillar of strength to us during all the recent difficulties that this news was a terrible blow. It was a blow to her too since the problems had brought us all very close together and she had neither planned nor wanted this pregnancy. I had, by now, found another housegirl and she was shaping up very well. Her condemnation of the behaviour of her predecessor was such that I thought to myself, "Well, it doesn't look as though *she* will ever behave the same way, thank goodness." For now, anyway, we tried hard to get our lives back onto a more even keel, and by March had even managed to recruit a new cook, a gay Tongan man (called a fakalady), who unfortunately had the same name as our new puppy, which we had called Tao after the cat who had been poisoned. Now we had a puppy called Tao II and a cook called Tao III! The cook opted to be called Lina, but this caused confusion with Nina, so it seemed we couldn't win with his name whatever we did! He didn't prove to be very satisfactory although he was an amusing person and brought back a more relaxed atmosphere to the house.

By early March the new British High Commissioner and his wife had arrived, and we were delighted to meet them and find them such a nice couple. We arranged a dinner in their honour, with our new cook now in charge, but it transpired that he could not cope with food suitable for a dinner. Once again I found myself in the kitchen, the blind leading the blind, and somehow between us we produced a passable meal. However, since I could not be in the kitchen on the night of the dinner, once again it had all had to be done in advance. In the event, what had been a passable meal was presented in a fashion which made it look like something we had scraped out of a tin, and I felt most embarrassed as I saw this sorry mess being brought round. Mercifully the Crown Prince was not present on this occasion, and his sister, Princess Pilolevu, who had been planning to attend, had been taken ill and was, in the event, unable to come. Her absence would mean that we had thirteen at the table, and since I felt we had all the potentials for disaster needed I was keen to avoid asking for trouble! Graeme's new First Secretary was asked to help us out.

At this time we had several other alarming events to contend with, and the most serious of these was being informed by the doctors that Nina had ruptured her eardrum while jumping into a swimming pool. He advised medical evacuation to New Zealand, and the day after the dinner we had everything in place for Nina and me to fly down to Auckland. This panic continued, with the doctor chopping and changing his mind as to whether it was necessary, but in the end he decided that it was not. However, it had frightened us badly and we were left exhausted with all the on/off decisions that had been forced on us. I thought that we had probably had all the excitement we were currently due for and was not therefore prepared for the next one, which arrived in the middle of all the decisions that were being made about whether to evacuate or not. I was using the children's lavatory and when I came to flush the loo I saw, to my horror, that I had been sitting on top of *an absolutely enormous crab*. Yes, *crab*! I froze, not knowing what to do, but in the end decided that if I flushed the cistern, then perhaps the crab would disappear. No such luck; he withstood the gushing water and glared at me from the lavatory pan, filling all the available space. Nobody was prepared to pick up this huge creature, not even my fakalady, nor Graeme come to that. I will spare you the details of how we eventually disposed of it. But, what a surprise, even for Tonga. I was, at least, thankful that it was me who had found it and not the children.

I went out onto the verandah, to restore my shattered nerves with the soothing sight of the Pacific Ocean stretching out for miles around me, speckled with tiny islands which were no more than a dot of sand with a coconut palm standing proudly in the middle. I surveyed the scene, which usually afforded me such calm, but today there was a tropical downpour in progress and the scene was a dark and menacing one. It matched my mood, not changed it.

Chapter Nineteen
Back To Base Camp

By Nina's sixth birthday in April 1987 things had quietened down a little again, which was merciful because both children were having continual ear infections, interspersed with tonsillitis, and seemed to spend their time on antibiotics. We used this lull to try and enjoy regular Saturday evening bridge with the new British High Commissioner, Paul Fabian, and his wife Eryll. They were such cheerful company that we began to look forward to this weekend bridge, to the extent that we felt upset when official functions got in the way. Of course, all the regular annual events came round once more, just as they had in Bahrain, and we were up at four o'clock in the morning for the ANZAC service, but this time the Australians were hosting it so we didn't have to put the children back into the hotel. The coup which took place in Fiji created a lot of extra work in the office. I had been hoping that someone there might have found time to type the Red Cross cookery book, so that we could get it printed and start to make some money for the organisation, but we were in for a long delay before getting it moving again. As it happened I was checking the final proofs with Eryll on the eve of my departure from the country!

The lull was also the impetus we needed to finalise the remaining work which was still outstanding on the house. Almost everything had been attended to, much of it by Graeme and me, but now we needed to get workmen in to re-tarmac the driveway which had become potholed and cracked in the harsh climatic conditions. The men who did the work managed to get about as much tar on the house as they did on the driveway. So once they had finished they went round the house cleaning it up with an oily rag and a jerrycan of petrol. When they were satisfied that they had removed all traces of tar from the house, they went back to their vehicle, left parked by the front door, and before they went they emptied the remains of the petrol onto the newly-completed driveway. The pool of petrol ate its way into the new tarmac and then snaked down the drive, leaving an ugly scar on the road in its wake. The upshot – a new driveway, smeared paintwork on the house, ugly scar running from the front door down to the bottom of the hill! It was just another example of what happens when you try to get things done in Tonga, and rather reminiscent of the tablecloth episode which had ended up being cut up into pillowcases for the laundry workers. It was yet another test of our patience.

Our cook Lina was put to the test, too, when we had a very unexpected visit by one of the Assistant Secretaries from the Ministry. I had decided to try to avoid making the meal the central event of the evening, and so we got out the Trivial Pursuits box and kept the dinner as simple as possible. However, the food was a complete disaster and almost inedible. These dreadful meals were something we had come to accept, but they were not what was needed when Karyn and Nigel paid their usual visit during the May holidays. Karyn was not yet over her anorexia nervosa and it was distressing seeing her playing with the food which was presented. The two of them had to contend with appalling weather as well since most of May passed in stormy conditions which included several cyclone warnings, which meant that we had to really batten down the hatches at the house and place cyclone covers on the roof. We were also back to the endless round of functions during their holiday and at one such do were forced to sit on concrete steps, throughout a howling gale, from half past one in the afternoon until six in the evening. Soon afterwards the Australians were holding a reception for their visiting Staff College course. This commenced at the usual hour of 6.30 p.m., but nobody was able to leave until 2.45 a.m. the following day because the Crown Prince did not leave until then. The Australians now held the record for the 'longest cocktail party', although only by a small margin, since it was common practice for the Crown Prince to stay on at parties. It was not unknown for a dinner hostess to have to prepare bacon and eggs for breakfast the following morning! Indeed, our own lunch time reception after the Opening of Parliament (the High Commissioners took it in turns to host the annual party after this event) went on for so long, for the same reason, that we were late for our evening commitment.

The ear infections continued and we were beginning to become exceedingly worried about Marc in particular since he was still not talking at three and a half years old. It was decided that I should take him to Auckland to see an ENT specialist, and this I did. The outcome was alarming for it transpired that Marc had been sixty per cent deaf all his life, and since he had never heard properly he had never learnt to form words correctly either. Had we been in 'civilisation', where regular health checks on children took place, this would have been picked up long ago. It had also caused him difficulty in concentrating. Since he was not hearing properly he was never stimulated enough to pay much attention to anything. Hence the difficulty they had had at the Mata'aho Kindergarten getting him to stay in one place long enough to get on with what the children were doing. Even today that problem is still with him since his early learning experiences were so muffled. He was operated on immediately, having his tonsils and adenoids removed, and grommets were inserted into his eardrums to drain the blocking fluid. He was in hospital for a few days and then we both returned to the hotel in Auckland for the following month, during which time he made slow progress in his recovery. One of the main difficulties was getting food which appealed to a small boy with a very sore throat. Everything was so fancy, and even when I ordered ice cream it arrived covered in sharp nuts – the last thing he needed in his condition. He was listless and cried a lot, and I wished that we knew people in Auckland with children who could help take his mind off his problems.

One day we were out in the street going to the hospital for one of his post-operative check-ups when a fire engine hurtled past us with its siren going full blast. It was the moment when I knew that Marc could now hear for the noise terrified him and he dashed between my legs with his hands over his ears. Poor little boy. Fancy being in a big bustling city with all these terrifying things happening after spending the past eighteen months in the sleepy hollow of Tonga where the loudest noise he would have heard was the telephone ringing. At least it had demonstrated to me the extent to which he could now hear and I thought that this would result in rapid developments in his progress. We had an appointment with a speech therapist who quickly disabused me of this idea, explaining to me that it would be a long slow process to bring him up to speed in this area.

While Marc and I were spending our time visiting specialists of one kind or another and generally trying to get him well again, Graeme was preparing to leave Tonga to attend a Heads of Mission Meeting in Wellington. This would take place at the end of June and would necessitate leaving Nina behind in Tonga on her own with O'u and the other staff in order to continue with her schooling. The situation had all been explained to Nina before I left for Auckland with Marc and she had been very grown up and understanding about it all. I was proud of her maturity and confident that she was fond of O'u, who would take good care of her. It was far from ideal, but there was little we could do since I could not get back to Tonga until Marc had had the 'all clear' from the doctors. Nor could Graeme fail to attend the meeting. Graeme came to see us briefly in Auckland before flying down to Wellington, and once his meeting was over Marc had been discharged by the hospital and was free to return to Tonga. It was July before the three of us returned together, armed with several presents for the children, who had both been through a difficult time.

Nina was in a very bad way when we got back. There had been more staff problems in our absence and we discovered that Lina had walked out, soon after Graeme left, to go and be a postman in Vava'u! There had, therefore, been nobody around to prepare meals for Nina, although O'u had done her best to keep her fed. The general upheaval, so reminiscent of all the previous ones before it, had clearly upset her along with the realisation that however much she had said that she would be all right without us, the reality had not worked as any of us had expected. She was in a terrible temper and told me that she no longer wanted to have a brother and would I please take him back to New Zealand and leave him there! It seemed to me that there were now several pressing reasons for us all to be back in New Zealand and top of this list was the need to get Marc onto speech therapy. Graeme put our case up to the Ministry with the request that we be released from Tonga early. Regrettably they could not replace him soon enough to get things moving quickly for Marc, and so I had little option but to start making arrangements to leave alone, with a view to getting the children down to New Zealand as soon as possible.

I wasn't out of the new wave of house staff leaving mode yet, though, and another girl left, to be replaced by O'u's sister on a part-time basis. To cover Lina's absence I had promoted the top housegirl into the cook's job (this was becoming fairly common practice!) and she had turned out to be worth her weight in gold. If only I had done this months ago. She was the one who had been so shocked by the events leading up to the burglary, and her attitude gave me the confidence to believe that she would be reliable. Together she and I prepared another meal 'fit for a King' when we had a dinner for the Crown Prince, and also his sister Princess Pilolevu, at the end of July. I had gone down with flu and was running a temperature, but people had already been invited and we could hardly cancel our Royal guests. A week later the cook's Australian boyfriend arrived in Tonga and that evening she left to go back with him. She gave me no notice and didn't come to say goodbye – she simply walked out to be with her man.

Having not been to bed to shake off the flu, I was running even more of a temperature by this time and her actions left me with nobody but O'u to help me once more (O'u having had an argument with her sister, Rose, who had already left as well). There was certainly not going to be time to be ill now, particularly since the packers were coming in a fortnight's time and I had to get everything prepared for their arrival. Nearly two years of coral dust had infiltrated all our possessions, many of which had gone very mouldy in the highly humid climate. It all needed much attention before it could be packed, and O'u and I set to to do as much as we could under the circumstances. The task, for me, was made more difficult having almost severed the end of my finger while opening a tin in the kitchen. I should have had stitches in it but did not have time to attend to it when it happened, and I believed that I could simply bind it into place. It eventually healed but left a scar which would probably not have happened had I attended to it properly. Anyway, the blessed finger made the job of sorting out our things for the packers all the more difficult, and as more and more items came out of the cupboards I saw the extent to which they had become spoilt by the local conditions.

The cook's departure had affected Marc very badly indeed. He had been very fond of her, as she was of him, and after she left he went around saying that he hated her and that she was never going to come to his house again. Another time I heard him say that she didn't love him any more. He began to wet his bed again. Night after night we would be up attending to him and having to bath him and change his pyjamas and put clean sheets on his bed. At seven months pregnant O'u was becoming very large and much less agile than she had been. She could only give me limited help around the place and now I found, as I prepared to leave Tonga, that I was having to put as much time into running the house and doing all the various jobs around the place as I had done during my first months on the island. However, by mid-August I had made all the preparations for the packers and had cleaned everything of mildew and coral dust as best I could. The packing task took ten Tongans two days to complete, and when it was over I flopped into bed in an attempt to throw off the temperature I had been running for so long now.

By the end of August we were giving Marc an early fourth birthday party since he would be back in New Zealand for the real occasion where he would not have any friends to invite. Between us Graeme and I made him a lovely birthday cake, and he was now old enough to really enjoy all the games and activities we planned for his party. Also by this time O'u's sister, Rose, had returned and the two of them stayed until my departure, staying on with the children after I left, but by the time Graeme finally got away there was only Rose, our twenty-second staff member, still at the house, O'u having left to have her baby. Early September was to have seen a string of parties being held prior to my departure from Tonga. All the functions which we had previously attended for the departing British couple were to have been repeated for us too, but in the event none of them happened because, on the third of September, Graeme received news that his father had died. The first of these functions was being held by Paul and Eryll Fabian, and, as it happened, this was the only one we went to because the news of the death in the family only came through a couple of hours before the dinner was being held. We could hardly opt out at that stage, and so went along, but we were both in a state of shock and were hardly sparkling company that night. The next day Graeme flew out, on the first flight available to New Zealand, to attend his father's funeral.

He was away a week, and on his first night back we gave a reception for one hundred and twenty for the visiting New Zealand Staff College course. That was the last function I hosted in Tonga, and as soon as we had returned from a trip to Vava'u for the opening of a new bank it was time for me to leave. My last night in Tonga was spent at the home of the new Bank Manager and his wife, who put on a 'last supper' for me, and after the meal we watched the film *Crocodile Dundee*. It was a good film, and we enjoyed the video, but whenever I have seen repeats of it on television over the years since I have always been reminded of Tonga. The thoughts which are associated with it are not always welcome, and as I flew out the next day I decided that I did not want to be reminded of the place again.

If I had supposed that by leaving Tonga I was leaving my problems (along with my husband and children) behind me, then I couldn't have been more wrong. When I finally reached Wellington I discovered that the keys to our house in Khandallah, which were left for me by the estate agent, were incomplete, and I was unable to get in. Since it was a weekend I was not able to contact the agent until late the following day. When I finally gained entry, I discovered that all the work we had planned on having completed before my return had not been dealt with. The family room wall had developed a crack in the middle and needed to be fixed and repapered. The chimney had also developed a crack and, during a severe southerly storm, water had cascaded down the chimney, soaking the carpet in the lounge with dirty black water. And the landscape gardening had still not been finished in spite of that, too, having been scheduled for completion before my return. These things were such a setback when all I wanted to do was get our furniture out of storage, along with our household effects which were also packed away, and bring about a workable household in which to receive my children home.

The first thing to do was get the wall repaired and a new carpet laid in the lounge. In the process of putting the fridge back in place, the wallpapering men broke the wheel off, and the sharp metal which was now exposed ripped the vinyl flooring in the kitchen. These things simply added to the already long list of things I had to get cleared up and organised in readiness for receiving our crates from Tonga. Once I had cleared up the mess left by all the workmen, it was time to get the furniture and effects from storage in place. There was much to sort out since it had all been packed up six years ago before we left for Bahrain. But more than anything else, I wanted the crates from Tonga, and now I was receiving messages that I would probably not be able to take delivery of them since they had been consigned in Graeme's name! Then I heard that there was a dock strike and it would probably take six months to clear the backlog that was accumulating. It seemed that everything which could delay the children's arrival was put in my way.

I then set about getting Nina and Marc's registrations in schools confirmed. We had applied for them both to go to the Samuel Marsden Collegiate School, a private school in Wellington, but unfortunately they could only take Nina at that time. Marc would have to go to the local kindergarten, which saddened me since he was badly in need of full-time stimulation at a first-rate school. He was already two years older than Nina had been when she went to Una's and had therefore had nothing like the good start to his schooling that she had had. I also needed to get Marc registered for speech therapy but was hampered in my lack of local knowledge (I had only lived in Wellington very briefly before going to Bahrain and really didn't know my way about at all). Eventually I had these things in place and all I needed now was the seventeen cubic metres of sea freight to arrive from Tonga. Finally it was delivered, and I set about the task of unpacking it all and getting the house clean and ready and organised for the children. Several trips to the supermarket, to stock the fridge and freezer and store cupboards, completed the things which I needed to do, and four weeks after my arrival I was able to fly up to Auckland to meet the children who had flown home alone from Tonga.

As soon as I had taken Nina to the school uniform shop and equipped her for school and done the necessary marking of her things, she commenced at Marsden. She was off to a good start, for when I collected her at the end of her first day she was sporting a sticker which read SPECIAL, having come top in a maths test the children had done that day. It was the beginning of what, for Nina, proved to be a very happy and thoroughly successful period of schooling, which was to continue for the next three years.

Marc started at the kindergarten in Khandallah and while he began to talk much more, his speech was still very indistinct. The teachers had much difficulty in understanding him and he made very little progress while he was there. It was with relief that I was told that Marsden could take him at the beginning of the forthcoming academic year, but this would not be until the end of January 1988. In the meantime we had Graeme's return to Wellington to look forward to, and then he would be on inter-posting leave so it would give the two of us some time before Christmas to get things working better in the house. I had begun a list of things which needed his attention long before he eventually returned from Tonga. But it was to a relatively organised house, with all his clothes unpacked and in cupboards and drawers, to which Graeme finally returned. For him it had been the easiest move ever!

Graeme's inter-posting leave enabled us to get on with the various domestic jobs which still needed attention, much of them associated with the damage which had been done to our possessions during their time in the Tongan climate. Pictures and books had suffered in particular and we had to have most of the pictures reframed as a result. Some of the larger books have still not recovered and there are one or two in particular which emanate the damp smell of Tonga even now. We were hampered in many of our tasks because it is difficult to get things done towards the end of the year in New Zealand. Everyone starts to tell you that this material, or that frame, or whatever, cannot be ordered before the long summer holiday period and that we would need to be looking at February next year before things would get going again. We found this not only with domestic items, but with Marc's speech therapy too, which could not be commenced until the new year. It was so frustrating, all round, since everything pointed to it having been a waste of time to come back early to get things moving quickly. I had been back in New Zealand over three months before I was able to get Marc in to see an ENT specialist in Wellington, and it was Christmas Eve when he was finally seen. The news wasn't very encouraging, either, since the grommets had already worked loose and were now out of the eardrum. It was the beginning of what turned out to be years of treatment for Marc, and in the end he had six operations. Nina was checked out too, after all her ear problems in Tonga, and it transpired that she also had 'glue ear' (though to a lesser degree than Marc) and would need to have the same procedure as Marc had had in Auckland.

By the time the children had been at school for a few weeks, prior to their long summer holiday, Graeme's inter-posting leave was over and he returned to work at the Ministry. At first he was put on special duties, which basically meant that they did not have a job for him, but this was mainly on account of having come out of Tonga a little on the early side. It meant that Graeme was not under the sort of pressure which would come later and we welcomed this situation gladly since it was going to take us many months to get things as we wanted them in the house and Graeme was therefore in a better position to help. We celebrated Christmas quietly in our own home, for the first time ever, and thoroughly enjoyed the novelty of having all our belongings in one place, which was another first. By the time the children's long summer holiday was drawing to a close Graeme was able to take a couple of weeks leave and we spent this driving round the South Island of New Zealand. The children and I had never seen it before and it was certainly a very beautiful place to be. However, the weather was not kind to us, and by the time we reached Queenstown we decided to stop travelling and stay put until we had to return to Wellington. I'm told that by doing so we missed some of the most spectacular scenery, further to the south, but it couldn't be helped and that would have to wait for another opportunity to present itself. For most of the time we were driving I had my head buried in the *Highway Code* since I was going to have to take my driving test again once back in Wellington. All around the world my British licence had been adequate, but now I was in New Zealand I found it was not going to be sufficient simply to produce that!

The new academic year was about to begin and we felt that things would start to settle down. Marc was able to commence in the pre-school class at Marsden and we were so happy to have them both there now. His speech therapy classes also got under way and he really enjoyed the individual attention this afforded him. It was all play-orientated and it wasn't difficult to keep his attention on what he was doing. Graeme was also assigned to the position of Director of Consular Division, and so now there was a job for him which he could get his teeth into, so to speak. Things were finally looking up for us and the very best aspect of it all was that we could now live as private people again. Our priorities no longer revolved round the social side of Graeme's job and all that that had entailed in Tonga and Bahrain. At last the children and our home could be the focal point of my attention and I welcomed the opportunity to be a mother and housewife first and foremost for the first time in my life!

1988 was certainly a very domestic period with little of excitement coming our way. We became very attached to the school and always enjoyed the various productions they put on. All the children would be involved on these occasions, to a greater or lesser extent, and it was amusing seeing Marc, who was about the youngest child there, involved too. He thrived at the school, although his development continued to cause us concern for he was very behind his contemporaries, but he was happy. Nina, who celebrated her seventh birthday in April, went from strength to strength, and her academic progress continued to go ahead with leaps and bounds. At the end-of-year prize-giving she was the youngest child to receive a prize. Both children went to the local ballet school which was an exceptionally well-run establishment where the children were highly motivated to do well. Nina took it very seriously, and passed all her exams with 'highly commended', but for Marc it was all just fun. He was there in the hope that he would become more coordinated, having suffered some difficulties in this direction, particularly after he broke his leg in Tonga. It worked for a while, but eventually he lost all interest in pursuing this line of activity and changed to gymnastics!

We made friends locally, and the children in particular enjoyed the unusual pleasure of having other children in the street with whom they could play just whenever they wanted to. Nina's Wendy house, which we first acquired in Bahrain, and which had also travelled to Tonga with us, was now standing proudly in our front courtyard. We lavished a lot of time and trouble to refurbish and repaint it and for the three years we were in Wellington it continued to give the children a lot of fun. It felt like a member of the family, and when the time finally came to give it away (to Marc's kindergarten in Khandallah) when we left, we all felt incredibly sad. But for now "Ma 'Ouse" was still very much a central feature of the play scene in our street. Graeme and I joined a bridge club and so were able to get back to playing again, although never found the club atmosphere nearly so pleasant as our games with the Fabians on those Saturday nights in Tonga.

Towards the end of the year we began to think that perhaps we should sell our house for something smaller. Our finances were stretched to the limit now that we were paying school fees, and we had found a beautiful maisonette overlooking Wellington harbour and fell for the modern design and the spectacular views. However, by December we had still not sold our own house (the crash of 1987 had taken its toll and the housing market was hardly moving), and so sadly we had to let the maisonette go. But by this time we had the excitement of looking forward to my mother's three-month visit to

New Zealand, timed so that she could watch the end-of-year activities at the school, and indeed she stepped off the plane and mercifully was in a fresh enough state, after such a long journey from London, to be able to go immediately to watch Nina perform at Victoria University Memorial Theatre in her ballet school's Christmas production. It was a busy time, with lots going on, and it was lovely for her to see the children in so many things.

However, her arrival also meant that we were bound to discuss the situation with my father. Our relationship had taken a serious turn for the worse during the course of 1988. It had begun in April, when Nina had her seventh birthday, and we discovered that my father had chosen that occasion to inform us all that he was, once again, back with his wife. He had enclosed a photograph of her with Nina's card and, since we had thought they were on the point of getting divorced, it was a terrible shock to find out this way that that was not the case. It would have been much better if my father had written to me about it, rather than placing it firmly on Nina's doorstep. He was trying to manipulate me, through Nina, whose reaction to the whole business was obviously quite different from mine. I had written back telling him that I didn't think much of his methods, and the correspondence had continued all year, rapidly degenerating to abuse on both sides. It had finally come to the point where there was nothing more to be said and I simply wanted to cease this distressing correspondence once and for all.

At the worst point, my father had taken my godfather Cyril, who was by then a very old and ill man, to see my mother in Bromley to get Cyril to tell her what he thought about it all. It was another manipulative move on my father's part, which completely backfired on him since my mother was horrified that my father (having already swayed the opinions of the rest of his family against me) was now resorting to steering Cyril that way too. As it happened, Cyril died before I got back to England to see him and talk to him myself. I was dreadfully sorry to know that he had died having been filled with unpleasant propaganda against me. Anyway, things came to such a pass between my father and me, in the end, with all the old wounds having been aired, that there was absolutely no room for manoeuvre to better ground between us. And there the matter rests.

My mother and I spent so much time talking about all these horrid events, during her first weeks with us, that we had to make a conscious decision to keep the conversation off my father lest the whole matter ruin Christmas for us. As with the year before, we spent the festive days at our Khandallah home and thoroughly enjoyed being able to do so. Another year was drawing to a close and, being the long summer holiday period in New Zealand, it was an ideal time for my mother to be there. Earlier in the year I had, rather to my astonishment, discovered that an old school friend from Farringtons, Sally, (who used to travel to and from Chichester with me at the beginning and end of terms) was also living nearby and her parents would be visiting her at Christmas time too. It was an opportunity for the two families to get together and reminisce over past times, and none of us could get over the coincidence of so accidentally meeting up once more. In January we took the children and my mother to see Torvill and Dean and The Russian Allstars, which was a spectacular show and particularly remarkable since there were no ice rinks in New Zealand! A portable 'big top' circus-style ice rink was used for their tour, and every time that it was dismantled and moved to the next town, Torvill and Dean flew over to Australia to perform there while the 'big top' was moved! Another time we took my mother to Wanganui to meet Graeme's family and she enjoyed the occasion, not least of which was seeing round the beautiful location of Graeme's brother-in-law's farm. But, in the main, the time my mother was with us was spent quietly at home, and after three months she had become so much part of the family that there was a big hole left once she had returned to London in early 1989.

Our social life was quiet, but entirely of our own making, which was just as we wanted it to be. However, one official function we did attend was the annual diplomatic reception at Government House. It was a most interesting experience, being back on the fringe of the 'glittering' society of Wellington, but all in all, we came away thinking that we were glad that we did not have to get caught up in it all too often. We spent Easter in Rotorua, where Graeme and I had spent our short honeymoon, and it was fun seeing the place again. Being such a touristy area meant that there was plenty to do to amuse the children and for us it was a trip down memory lane.

Quiet though our lives were, in the main, there were times when Graeme's job kept him busy round the clock for weeks at a time. His main task was to do what he could for distressed New Zealanders around the world, and the Tiananmen Square massacre was a case in point. Another very busy period involved a New Zealander detained in Somalia, and this particular case hit the media in a big way and consequently involved Graeme being interviewed on television about it quite frequently. His other consular work was of a more routine nature but he never knew what the next crisis would be, ranging from New Zealanders on Death Row in Malaysia on charges of possession of drugs, through to deaths taking place in outlandish parts of the world. All his work involved keeping the families back in New Zealand informed of what was actually being done to help their loved ones, and although Graeme knew that this was always 'the maximum', he still found that both the families themselves and, more often, the press, would hound him for more information. There were times when things were so busy that even at home we could never finish a sentence before the phone would ring again. It was just as well we were living a quiet life and not trying to get out to functions in the evenings, for there would have been many times when we would not have made it.

Chapter Twenty

Tulips, Windmills And Clogs

By and large 1989 progressed much as the year before and our lives continued to revolve round the domestic issues, with the children's needs being our main concern. Another little flurry into the prospective house-purchasing and selling business created a temporary diversion but ended as unsuccessfully as our previous attempt had been. Graeme's job involved an exhausting but nonetheless interesting trip round the world, to several New Zealand Embassies, one of which was The Hague in the Netherlands. It gave him an opportunity to see around both the Chancery (otherwise known as the Embassy or the office) and the Residence there, which was worthwhile since it was starting to look as though this might be our next posting. His absence meant that he missed several of the children's events, such as Marc's sixth birthday and the Open Day at school, but at least we were able to bring forward Marc's party before Graeme left. By Christmas the main Consular 'headache' (the man in Somalia) had reached its conclusion, and we all drank a toast to his return to New Zealand. By now we were as relieved as the family that he was safely back for the case had truly been a long and drawn-out saga.

After another Christmas spent at home, followed by a trip north to see Graeme's family, we went over to the Sunshine and Gold Coast of Australia for our January 1990 summer leave. We loved the place and the weather was beautiful, so it was a very pleasant break away. We tried hard to continue with Marc's speech therapy exercises and on one occasion tried him on the old favourite of "The rain in Spain..." which Marc managed to complete by saying "... falls mainly at the airport"! I suppose he had had a mental image showing rain falling on a *plane* (rather than a *plain*)! But at only six we were quite impressed with the fact that his brain had turned it into something which actually made more sense to him. Anyway, speech therapy or not, the children loved Australia since the holiday consisted mainly of swimming and playing in the sand. We had rented a self-catering apartment in Noosa and this had proved to be both very pleasant and particularly ideal for a family with young children.

By the time we returned to New Zealand towards the end of January the television screen was telling us that "It's Our Country, Our Year"! Right then it seemed to make some kind of sense, and the successful Commonwealth Games in Auckland made a good start to the year. This was followed almost immediately by the main event, New Zealand's Sesquicentennial, when the Queen came to mark the 150th Anniversary of the signing of the Treaty of Waitangi (when the Maori Chiefs had signed the document which handed over administrative control to the British, during the reign of Queen Victoria). In May Sir Edmund Hillary's son, Peter, led the first New Zealand team to the top of Everest, and Peter Blake won the Whitbread Round the World Race in his yacht *Steinlager*. This was all good media stuff, and we were swept up in the feeling that perhaps, after all, it was going to be an eventful year. The international news seemed to be even more spectacular with the end of the Cold War, the tumbling of the Berlin Wall, and the reunification of Germany. But with the demise of the old order in Romania, and the ugly truths emerging afterwards, a less optimistic note seemed to be creeping in. This culminated with the Iraqi invasion of Kuwait, which rocked the whole world on its heels.

By the middle of the year we were becoming very unsettled since the possible posting to The Hague was starting to look more like a definite one to Saudi Arabia. This began to seem even more alarming once Saddam Hussain invaded Kuwait. Not only did we have our own possible future security to consider, but we became very involved with the altogether real situation which many New Zealand hostages were actually facing in Kuwait. This new crisis meant that our kitchen was turned into an Ops Room and all Graeme's off-duty hours were spent on the telephone talking to the families, the press and many overseas contacts who were trying to assist the hostages. Family-speak was now no-speak! If Graeme had been on television a lot through the various other crises, it was nothing to the demand which was now placed upon him. The whole world had been gripped by what had happened in Kuwait and we suddenly found ourselves in the thick of it at the New Zealand end. One day I was shopping in the local supermarket, where the national radio station was being broadcast over the Tannoy system, and my attention was drawn to it because suddenly I realised that I was listening to the sound of my husband's voice!

By the end of August I had had enough of the Gulf Crisis, together with the month-in month-out business of not knowing whether we would be posted overseas, or not, and indeed whether this would be to Europe or the Middle East, so I decided to go back to England to see my mother. After four years away from England I had become very homesick again and had also been unsettled by the events of the past months. So I was glad that Graeme agreed to cope with the children during my absence, although a lot of that time they were on holiday with their grandmother in Wanganui.

The weather was quite glorious during the short time I was home and it did me a power of good to have that break with my mother. I was also able to see a few of my friends again, including, as always, Vicky and her children and, also, Eryll Fabian who was about to depart for St Kitts in the Caribbean! My mother took me on a sentimental journey round Broadstairs, where she had grown up and where I had had so many happy times as a child, and I was so glad to be shown so much which I would never otherwise have known about. Much of Broadstairs had been built by my grandfather, and his father before him, so this was a marvellous opportunity for my mother to show me the buildings of special family note. All the same, had I known then that I would be back in England again by the end of the year I would certainly not have gone that summer. But when I left, we still did not have any firm idea of what was going to happen to us.

Once I was back in New Zealand, though, everything started to happen in quick fire succession and it now began to look as though we would really be going to Holland after all. By the time Graeme's fiftieth birthday had arrived, at the end of November, we had made a start on getting ourselves packed up because the timing seemed to indicate that we would be leaving before Christmas. The first thing to go was "Ma 'Ouse" and to see it disappear down the road on the back of a trailer was a dreadfully sad day indeed. However, we were still waiting for Agrément to arrive (the official consent by Queen Beatrix of the Netherlands to Graeme's appointment), and until it did we would continue to have to make plans without the certain knowledge that we would, actually, be leaving. One of the main difficulties was knowing whether to give the required term's notice to Marsden. In the end we were never able to do so and even when the academic year came to a close, and the children had left the school, we had had to request that they be allowed back the following year if everything fell through. In spite of being so unsatisfactory from the school's point of view, they were extremely understanding of our predicament.

All our plans continued to go ahead, but still without the confirmation that we would definitely be leaving. We were conscious that the change of hemisphere would once again play havoc with the children's schooling. In New Zealand they were about to commence the long summer holiday, and in European schools had only just begun the academic year which Nina and Marc had now completed. In the hope that they would be allowed to slot into their chronologically correct classes (which would mean jumping a term in Europe) we felt that it was imperative that the children be able to commence at school in Holland at the beginning of 1991, and so we were doing everything in our power to see that this would be the case. However, in view of the continued lack of required confirmation we simply had to go ahead on the basis that it would probably all work out. We kept our fingers crossed and proceeded with the packing process, expecting to leave New Zealand by mid December.

In the event two things happened. Firstly, Agrément did not come through until the day the packers were actually packing our sea freight, and secondly by then we already knew that Graeme was not going to be able to leave his job at that time. The crisis in Kuwait was now showing every indication of escalating into war and if this was to happen it would be the wrong moment to change the Director of Consular Division. The plans we had so carefully laid, in order to get the children slotted into their new school at the beginning of the January term in Holland, all came tumbling down when we heard that Graeme was not going to be allowed to leave Wellington at this time. We were too far down the track with our arrangements by now and decided that we would have an early family Christmas together at the end of November, and that the packers would then take our things for shipment to Holland.

The day before our early Christmas, Marc was back in hospital having the fifth lot of grommets inserted. His hearing had fluctuated so much during the year, but at least we now knew he would be hearing again for a while. Once packed up the children and I would go back to Bromley to spend whatever time we had to with my mother until Graeme was free to travel. While we waited it was my intention to get them into a school in Bromley so that they could at least get on with slotting into the northern hemisphere school term. We hoped that this would enable them to have a better chance of being accepted into the right class at their new school in Holland.

By the twentieth of December we had packed the last case, found tenants for our house, and gone through all the various hoops which accompany every move no matter how near or far you are travelling. Our flight to London was exhausting and I discovered what Graeme must have gone through when he flew with the children from Tonga. This was my come-uppance, and I certainly felt by the end of the journey that I had paid in full measure! We were all so tired by the time we got to Gatwick that I had had to separate the children who by this time did not have a civil word to say to each other! The taxi which was booked to meet us was half an hour late arriving, and I began to wonder if we were going to arrive in Bromley without blood being spilt. The thirty-six hour journey had brought us almost to Christmas Eve by the time we arrived, but left just enough time to sleep off the jet lag so that we could enjoy Christmas when it came. Graeme had gone to Wanganui to be with his family there, but we did wish that this turn of events had not come about all the same.

The two months which we spent in Bromley went very well and we crammed as many nice things into the short time available before Nina and Marc began school at Ashgrove, an independent school across the road from my mother's flat. My mother had already approached the school to see if they would be able to take the children and mercifully they had agreed, which was lucky since they had been told that it would be for an indefinite period, but probably not for long. Anyway, there was time first for the pantomime in Bromley in which we saw John Inman playing the dame in *Aladdin* and which the children thoroughly enjoyed. Time spent with family and friends was interspersed with educational trips to London to see some of the sights. During such a trip to the Tower of London I managed to lose the children in the crowd, but eventually found them holding the hand of a Beefeater and very self-righteously telling me that they were doing what I had told them to do if they got lost! I think they both enjoyed all the trips we did together, and for me it was just enormous fun to be back in London again and able to do lots of exciting things with them.

However, all too soon it was time to commence at Ashgrove. The first half of the Lent term passed relatively uneventfully, although Nina distinguished herself by answering the question, "Name the continents of the world" by answering, "Bromley"! No 'special' stickers there! Shame on us too, for somehow this information had not been conveyed to Nina in spite of the fact that she had already been round the world six times. To coincide with Graeme's eventual arrival in early February, the weather changed rapidly and soon we were knee deep in snow. This cramped our style no end, and one particular evening which we had really been looking forward to had to be cancelled. We were to have met up with the girls from the Gloucester Road flat, and their husbands, but this would now have to wait for another opportunity to present itself.

Snow was still around when we flew the fifty-minute flight from Gatwick to Amsterdam, on the sixteenth of February 1991, and it was a very wintry scene which greeted us at our new home. Our arrival had coincided with the beginning of half term at The British School In The Netherlands, the children's new school, and so this afforded me the opportunity to make the final purchases of their uniforms (most of which I had managed to purchase, alter and mark in Bromley) before they commenced there on the twenty-fifth. However, they were not permitted to enter the classes which their peers in New Zealand were now in and, in the end, had to go back to the forms which they had completed at the end of 1990 in Wellington. Oh dear, all those well-laid plans had come to nought!

There are several images of Holland, all of which can be found to a greater or lesser degree. Tulips, Gouda and Edam cheese and windmills spring readily to mind. It is a low-lying country, more than half of it being below sea level, and it is consequently very flat. Sand dunes and a sophisticated system of dykes along the coastline control the sea which is, nonetheless, an ever-present danger to the Dutch, and very modern pumping stations work day and night to drain off excess water. Anyway, I had imagined that this flat terrain would create a rather boring landscape, but this did not prove to be the case. It is an attractive country with an abundance of trees (it is an offence to cut a tree down without permission to do so). One has the impression of it having been landscaped on a national scale. The many small villages are full of character being both quiet and picturesque. Many date from the end of the twelfth century and feature fine old churches and town halls. Traditional Dutch windmills contrast with their modern derivatives – the windmill farms. Canals (with cows nearby!), clogs, tulips, and Delft china are all there, just as we knew they would be, although this rustic image of the Netherlands is actually rather fanciful.

It is a small, densely populated (fifteen and a half million) country situated in northwestern Europe, on the shores of the North Sea and bordering both Germany and Belgium. Its economy is highly developed featuring a strong servicing sector and industrial base, while farming is also an important activity. Cultivation of horticultural goods is intensive with widespread use being made of huge glasshouses for year-round production of flowers and vegetables. Although the Netherlands is commonly called Holland, this is strictly speaking incorrect, as North and South Holland are only two of twelve provinces, each with its own administrative capital. The southernmost provinces are mainly Roman Catholic, while to the north the country is Protestant. Amsterdam is the capital city, Rotterdam is Europe's busiest port, and The Hague is the seat of government and therefore the location of the resident Diplomatic Corps including the New Zealand Embassy.

Many of the diplomatic Residences are located in The Hague but we were rather pleased to find that ours was in the nearby location of Wassenaar, one of the prettiest villages in the country. The seventy year old brick house was large, consisting of three floors, in addition to which there was an extensive basement and loft area for storage. Although it seemed a big house to us, after our own place in Wellington, by the local diplomatic standards it was very modest indeed. Although the sheer size of the place was our overwhelming first impression, it did not take long to realise that it had been allowed to deteriorate badly over recent years. There were holes in the ceilings, walls were cracked and peeling, filthy curtains hung in tatters at the windows, the furnishings and fittings were deplorable and most of the carpets were threadbare. It was quite alarming to see what needed to be done to rectify all this, both in terms of time and money. We seemed to be in yet another of those old familiar situations where we were going to have to give a lot of our time to sorting the place out. We were nothing if not experienced at this but had hoped that one day we might arrive somewhere where others before us had done all the hard work! This was definitely not that occasion, in fact the more we looked the more alarmed we became to see just how bad it all was.

Our first four weeks were relatively quiet, on two counts. Firstly Graeme was not able to present his Credentials to Queen Beatrix until the middle of March (which meant that we were not yet here officially and could not, as such, be out and about at functions) and secondly our sea freight had not arrived. Although the former point was welcome and gave us a chance to focus on our new surroundings, and, for me at least, to attend to domestic issues which would help the children feel more settled, the latter point was quite amazing. Our crates had been packed up in December the year before, and two months later we had expected to find them waiting for us in Holland. The first few quiet weeks before the Credentials ceremony would have been an ideal time to get unpacked and it would have helped us all to feel more settled if we had had our possessions around us. By the time Graeme enquired of the Ministry as to the whereabouts of our sea freight we were astonished to discovered that it had not yet left Wellington. In the end we did not receive it until just before Nina's tenth birthday in April, by which time Uncle Tony from New York had come to stay with us. His arrival had galvanised us to get the crates unpacked and things in place within three days, although there was a lot left behind closed doors which would need our more leisurely attention.

Our first diplomatic event in Holland was when Graeme presented his Credentials to Queen Beatrix. It was a unique experience for us and unlike anything we had done before. We were taken to the Noordeinde Palace in a horse-drawn carriage, accompanied by the Queen's Chamberlain, and greeted by Palace officials and a hundred man Guard of Honour on our arrival. Graeme's seconded staff from Wellington were in the carriage behind us and while Graeme was formally presenting his Credentials to the Queen, the rest of us were entertained by the Mistress of the Robes and other Palace Aides. It was all done beautifully, in simply magnificent surroundings, and was an awe-inspiring experience for both of us. The moment came when I was called to join Graeme in the Queen's presence, where we were offered a glass of champagne to toast the success of our tour of duty in the Netherlands. Queen Beatrix could not have been more charming.

Both amusing, and highly knowledgeable, she ensured that the hour we spent at the Palace was an experience neither of us is likely ever to forget. It wasn't so very long afterwards that we were at the Queen's Palace, in Amsterdam this time, for her annual dinner for the Ambassadors and their wives. It was another glittering occasion, with all the wonderful trappings that one would expect, including liveried footmen, beautiful silver and glassware, and a cordon-bleu meal. It was the first of several such occasions we would experience during our time in Holland.

When we had arrived in Holland we thought that one of the great advantages of being located in mainland Europe would be the ability to get from country to country with relative ease. In fact this did not really prove to be the case, mainly due to insufficient leave to get away, and secondly even weekend trips were hampered on account of the children's commitments. However, we didn't know it would be like this and before we got too sucked up into all the events which prevented us getting away, we made that first trip to Germany which I mentioned earlier. We went to Bad Oeynhausen, armed with my old photograph album, which enabled us to persuade the owners to allow us to look around the house I lived in as a small child. It was a lovely opportunity to revisit the past, something I always do whenever possible. It is symptomatic of being rootless; the scattered remains of one's life have to be harvested as best one can!

Reminiscence was the name of the game, too, when Graeme went to Oslo to present Credentials there (being cross-accredited from Holland to Norway, Sweden, and Israel as well). Norway was the one overseas Credentials trip that I went on with him. We really loved Norway and had a most enjoyable time there. Great interest was taken in Graeme's Norwegian ancestry, and it was quite amazing how effortlessly a person can be found once the bureaucratic machinery is set in motion. In no time at all a relative was traced and we had a most enjoyable trip out to Kongsvinger, north-east of Oslo and an hour away by train, to meet Tove, a distant cousin of Graeme's. Tove was even able to take us to the very house from which Graeme's great grandfather had left to sail to New Zealand a hundred and thirty years earlier. It was a most fitting end to the 'full circle' as it were. Graeme had earlier presented Credentials in Sweden, and several months later in Israel too, but circumstances prevented me going with him on either of those occasions.

Our first five months flew past, filled with old familiar functions such as the ANZAC Day commemoration service, but one thing had changed; New Zealand no longer held National Day functions around the world. But time went so quickly that we were soon caught up in all the end of academic year school functions for Nina and Marc. Marc almost missed one of them, Sports Day, since he found himself once more in hospital having the sixth and final lot of grommets inserted in his ears. However, Sports Day was cancelled, owing to perfectly ghastly weather, so nothing was lost. Anyway he made up for it during the first week of the summer holiday when he and Nina attended a week-long sports course at the Senior School. This kept them out of mischief and tired enough to sleep well, which was good for me too because I was busy trying to get the packing done for our trip the following week to Italy, where we spent our summer holiday.

We arranged our first leave around our wish to see Hedy again, our Swiss friend from Tehran and whose then husband had diagnosed my pregnancy with Nina. Hedy was now remarried, to a delightful Italian, and so we headed first for Siena where she now lived. Hedy and Mario gave us a fascinating time, taking us to see places of much interest, including Pisa (of Leaning Tower fame), Siena, and San Gimignano. They showed us round their magnificent villa, vineyard, and their very own church (which was built one thousand three hundred years ago and is still standing). All these lovely sights were of less interest to two young children (by now seven and ten) than their army of cats! We would have loved to be with Hedy and Mario longer, but were booked into a holiday apartment in Riva for the next fortnight.

From Riva, on Lake Garda in north-east Italy, we made several exploratory trips, the most interesting one being to Venice. However, at the height of the tourist season it was not only dreadfully crowded, but also unbearably hot. We also encountered a thoroughly dishonest gondolier who ripped us off for the gullible tourists that we were. He dropped us at a sightseeing vantage point, saying that he would be back in ten minutes for the rest of the trip we had paid him for, never to return to collect us. Another sour note of our holiday was that I lost my camera, along with most of our holiday photographs inside it.

We had hardly unpacked after the long drive back to The Hague when Graeme was off to Israel, and immediately he returned I left for London in order to attend a WRNS Reunion to be held at the Royal

Naval College at Greenwich. This was to mark twenty-one years since the Course of 3/70 had graduated from the College. Graeme joined me for the reunion dinner, held in the Painted Hall, and it was wonderful to meet again most of the girls I had trained with so long ago. The majority were now married and accompanied by their husbands, but the poor men were left rather to their own devices while we all nattered nineteen to the dozen about all our different memories of the place.

Hardly had we settled back from this trip than we were attending the official Opening of Parliament and then we were off on an official visit to Sweden for a week. Mercifully, I still had house staff at that time with whom I could leave the children. However this situation was not to last for long, as it happened. The children were busy too and since we arrived Nina had started to learn to play the piano and was doing well. Marc had also started to play football at the weekends and Graeme was asked to be the team's coach, so now the whole family seemed to spend every weekend either on the field or on the sidelines. This busy pattern continued for the remainder of the year and our diary became fuller and fuller after Marc's eighth birthday party. Dinners for visiting Ministers, hosting the annual Remembrance Day service and reception and many other functions leading up to Christmas. Then finally it was time to take the ferry over to England to spend the festive season with my mother. The highlight of this visit, for me, was not only seeing family and friends, but to revisit my old Gloucester Road flat after twenty-six years since living there. It was still above the same flower shop and the owner kindly showed us round the flat, which seemed to have changed little in the main. It brought back such happy memories.

January 1992 started badly with me having much trouble with my back. It had been giving me pain for quite some time, but on the day we left England it finally seized up altogether and I really don't know how Graeme managed to get me back to Holland on the ferry. There was no time to take things quietly, however, since we were immediately caught up in a lot of official functions, the main one of these being the Queen's New Year Reception at her Palace in Amsterdam. The highlight of that occasion was a very friendly conversation with the Queen, who was to be travelling to New Zealand shortly on a State Visit. This was to mark the three hundred and fiftieth Anniversary of the Dutchman, Abel Tasman, having been the first recorded European explorer to discover New Zealand.

A few days after this reception I had an appointment at the local hospital for a mammogram, and I left the hospital, two hours later, in a state of shock having had a lump discovered in my breast. The next ten days were, without a doubt, the worst part of all, and Graeme and I couldn't help wondering just what might be in store for us. During this period of waiting the domestic staff problems (which had begun the previous December with the departure of the Portuguese butler) came to a head with the realisation that we were also going to lose the cook. Her appalling behaviour reached its climax on the day we were giving a Reception for over one hundred people and two days before I was due for my operation.

Those two days were hectic and in the event I was called into hospital a day early, which in a way was good because it meant one less day of worry, but in another meant that I was dashing about like a mad thing trying to get everything organised for everyone, particularly since I did not know how long I would be out of circulation. The first day in hospital was for a most unpleasant procedure which involved being clamped to the mammography x-ray machine for half an hour while the doctors poked needles and thread through me in order to find the right place the next day. Once out of the theatre, after the lump was removed, you can imagine my relief to be told that the tumour was benign. I burst into tears of relief, asked for a tissue, and was told that they didn't have one! At the end of that day the surgeon came to see me and tempered my delight somewhat by saying that he thought it would be OK but that further tests were necessary and the results would be through in a week's time.

Once I was out of hospital we needed to turn our attention to giving a black-tie dinner for the Queen's Mistress of the Robes who would be travelling with the Queen to New Zealand. I was still not feeling too good by the time the dinner was scheduled, but luckily it was a happy and successful occasion and the guest of honour could not have been a nicer lady. We went to bed at half past midnight and right after breakfast the following day the Committee of the Australian and New Zealand Women's Club arrived to start organising a lunch party for forty-five ladies. It all passed in a bit of a blur and I was somewhat relieved to see Graeme at 2.30 p.m. arriving to take me to hospital to have the stitches out and to get the final results, which, thank goodness, were a confirmation that all was well.

The search for new domestic staff turned out to be as difficult as it had been in Tonga and so we wondered if we should try to recruit staff from England. Once embarked on that line of enquiry, the number of possible applicants grew from a modest two couples, to an ultimate twenty-three. It was threatening to become a full-time job just sorting through applications, making telephone calls to London to discuss matters with the agency, and simply dealing with the whole process of recruiting. I lurched from excitement at the prospect of having good staff, to worry that the house of cards would collapse. By the middle of February I had done the groundwork and now it was time to go to England to interview prospective staff. The day before I left, the cook departed (no doubt choosing her time for maximum inconvenience), thus leaving Graeme to manage the house, the children and the job alone. A tall order when you are Ambassador to four countries!

Chapter Twenty One
Dutch Courage Needed

As I winged my way to London my mind ran back over our first year in Holland. It had certainly been a busy year. For the majority of that time we had lived with workmen in the house in an attempt to rectify all the horrors we had found on our arrival. It had been necessary to spend many hours selecting materials, paints, and generally working out what we could achieve with the money which was available to spend. The worst of the dilapidation was in the family living quarters, and so consequently it meant that our private areas were frequently in a state of upheaval while first we had repairs done, then painting, then curtaining, and finally, just before we left at Christmas, the entire family area of the house was recarpeted. We also had many rooms which needed to be entirely refurnished. Days were spent selecting these furnishings and many more getting them in place once they had eventually been delivered. Just when it looked as though we were beginning to see the light at the end of the tunnel, the domestic staff began to give us problems.

First the butler had gone, and now this latest difficulty with the cook-cum-housekeeper. The Filipina woman whom we inherited had never been satisfactory. From the generally dilapidated state of the house, and the filthy condition of the kitchen utensils, we had realised from the start that she was not keeping things well. Furthermore, *she* kept telling *me* how things should be done in the house and how our predecessors had wanted her to perform her duties. Since this was now *our* home it had not impressed me much to know how it had been under the former regime. Besides, it had all been in such a state when we arrived that it was hardly likely that I would want to keep it that way.

Throughout the first year I had decided to keep quiet, let her say her bit, but keep my own counsel. However, matters had come to a head just before I went into hospital when I had been speaking to her about how I wanted something done for the reception we were giving that night. She told me that she had neither the time nor the patience to listen to anything I had to say and walked out of the room. It was at that moment that I knew that the two of us could no longer work together with any degree of harmony. We gave her two months' notice, which she did not work, although she continued to live in the staff house for many weeks after she walked out, the day before I left for England. She took us to court for unfair dismissal, and that was now a matter for some concern since the compensation, had she won, would have been enormous. As I flew to London, leaving the family behind alone, I wondered how on earth this mess would end. Now we had no staff, a very busy social life, a huge house to run, and on top of it all we were being taken to court. Furthermore I knew that if I was to recruit staff from England I would need the house she was living in to offer to them. I had no way of knowing how long she would remain living on our doorstep.

The interviewing process did not go too well. The staff presented were not the right sort, some being far too well qualified, others having quite the wrong qualifications, and others simply desperate for a job of any kind at all. However, one couple seemed absolutely ideal, and after all it was only one couple I needed! They were currently working for a titled Member of Parliament but did not yet know when they would be free to leave his employ. There was nothing I could do about it, other than offer them the job and let them know that I needed them as soon as possible. The rest was up to them.

I flew back to Holland as soon as I could and found that Graeme had erected the video camera in one of the bathrooms, monitoring the movements of our Filipina. She had left, in a hurry, ostensibly because she was ill. Her constant comings and goings had indicated that she was in good health, and since we were now needing all the evidence we could get of the sort of person we were dealing with, this seemed like a sensible measure for Graeme to be taking. There was nothing for it, now, but to sit tight, get on with all the domestic chores and hope that the British couple would be able to arrive in Holland soon.

One of the first things we needed to do, however, was to prepare our defence case. Luckily I had kept a diary, over the year, in which I had noted all the times the Filipina had been unsatisfactory and in what way. It saved the day, as it happened, and she was unable to bring a case against us of unfair dismissal. It all took time, though, and we were very concerned throughout the weeks of deliberation. Her lawyer had taken five Ambassadors to court and had won each previous case, so we knew that it was certainly possible for us to lose. Although she didn't win, nor did we – for the legal costs were huge. She, on the other hand, was on legal aid. However, she was eventually out of our hair and we were thankful for that.

During the weeks of waiting for the British couple to make up their minds about whether or not they would take up our offer of employment, Graeme and I set to, as we had done in Tonga, to clean the place up. We started in the kitchen and scraped and scrubbed as much grime off ovens, pots, pans, and utensils of every variety as we had already done in Tonga. Even so, there was a large pile of items which were fit only for the rubbish dump, being beyond salvage. Then we started on the cupboards themselves and went through as much elbow grease as before. Would it never end? Were we destined to go round the world putting government property into good order ourselves? Anyway, while the kitchen was free of staff it was certainly a good opportunity to get the place as we wanted it. We kept our morale up by telling ourselves that we would soon have good staff working there and we should have it as we wanted them to keep it. But as the days passed into weeks we began to wonder if we were kidding ourselves.

One day we received a letter from a Portuguese gentleman, with a Swiss wife, stating that they were looking for work as a domestic couple. It seemed to be the answer to our prayers, since the British couple never did materialise. We invited them for interview, liked them, and decided to employ them forthwith. We were under pressure of a different sort, at this time, because very shortly we would be involved in all the functions arranged for the Abel Tasman celebrations. The first of these was held at the birthplace of Tasman, in Grootegast, where Graeme was to be unveiling a plaque in honour of the commemorations. With the house staff having only just arrived we decided that the only way that I could accompany Graeme to the north of the country would be if we took the children too. They were given leave of absence from school and travelled up with us. It was a most enjoyable occasion, and the children were treated very kindly by the Mayor of Grootegast who gave them nice presents to bring home. The following day Graeme flew with Queen Beatrix, on her official aircraft, to New Zealand. There had been an expectation, in Holland, that I would also be going to New Zealand for the Queen's State Visit, and frequent reference was made to this expectation. It had been a source of considerable embarrassment to me since there were a number of reasons why I would not be able to do so. Firstly, it was not anticipated by the New Zealand Government that I would accompany Graeme, and therefore, had I gone, we would have had to pay my airfare to New Zealand and back. Secondly, though certainly of equal importance, our lack of house staff during the run-up to Graeme's departure meant that there would be no one to look after the children. All in all, there was no way that I could go with Graeme. However, this continued to be a source of much embarrassment for the next couple of years because whenever the subject of the Queen's very successful State Visit to New Zealand was mentioned it was always assumed, by those who did not already know otherwise, that I had gone too. However, during Graeme's absence in New Zealand, the children and I did attend another function, at the Ministry of Foreign Affairs, also in honour of Abel Tasman. It was a lesson to me, however, and demonstrated all the reasons why children are not usually invited to such functions because (unlike his good behaviour in Grootegast) Marc behaved very badly. He is a very friendly and gregarious child, and on this occasion went over the top and started to show off and, to my horror, did so in front of several distinguished guests.

Meanwhile, back at the ranch, we had now got the Swiss/Portuguese couple working for us. For most of the short time they were with us they were living out and travelling in daily by bus since the staff house was still occupied by the Filipina woman. This was far from satisfactory, and although we had given them an advance of salary to cover their initial costs, they appeared to be getting through money with alarming speed. They were constantly asking for more and even (unbeknown to me) borrowed money off the driver which, in the event, they never paid back. Their demands for more money became ever more frequent and ever more threatening to the point when (since I was alone while Graeme was in New Zealand) I thought that I would actually be physically attacked. By the time Graeme returned I had come to the conclusion that they must be needing money to fund a drug dependence. They were not what we needed in our personal lives, and so we saw no alternative but to tell them they had not been successful in their trial period and must leave. Now we were back with no staff again, but one good thing had happened and that was that the staff house had finally been vacated.

We had only had a very brief look inside the staff maisonette, while the previous occupant was living there, since we believed that it was the private domain of the housekeeper and that we should respect her privacy. However, it was part of the property, which belonged to the New Zealand Government, and now that it was empty we had no reason to hold back. Our eyes could hardly take in what we saw on entering the place. The filth and mess was unbelievable. The furniture was broken and shabby beyond further use, the kitchen caked with dirt and the bathroom and lavatory were disgusting. The place needed to be fumigated and professionally cleaned before we could touch anything there, but we knew that there was now a major job to be done to get the maisonette habitable for decent staff. A professional cleaning firm spent a day there removing the worst of the filth, and then the gardeners and the driver removed the majority of the furniture to be taken to the rubbish dump. Graeme and I then spent most of our spare time, over the next several weeks, cleaning, painting, and repairing the entire house. When we had done this we then had new carpet laid throughout, new curtains hung at the windows and we replaced the ghastly furniture with surplus items from departed seconded staff houses. If we had thought that we worked hard on the Residence in Tonga, and Holland too, it was nothing to what the two of us managed to achieve in the maisonette. The finishing touch was to completely equip it with household fittings, crockery, cutlery, bedding, and indeed everything needed to be comfortable there. It was now ready for good staff, although, once more funds were available, the bathroom and kitchen would have to be gutted and new units installed. This we did some months later and the final result was a complete transformation.

Our attempts to get staff continued and we had another brief foray into the British domestic staff market. None of the people I had interviewed were either suitable or available and so we decided to take another couple (sight unseen) who came highly recommended by the agency. Suffice it to say that on their arrival in Holland they turned out to be thoroughly unsuitable in every way. They were both too old for the job, far too set in their ways, and completely unused to the diplomatic scene and unwilling to adapt to it. It took no time at all for both sides to come to this conclusion and they were with us for little more than a week, most of which time we were away in Luxembourg for Easter.

By April we were certainly ready for this change of scene, the year so far having exhausted us. Luxembourg provided a peaceful and beautiful setting in which to restore our spirits (although the weather was simply dreadful – so cold and wet) before returning to Holland to resume the quest for house staff. We didn't know it then but our problems were nearly over, for by early May we had interviewed and employed an excellent Portuguese couple, José and Linda, who stayed with us throughout our remaining three years in Holland. They became good friends to the whole family, the children in particular, and their first babysitting duties were performed after only a few days with us when I made my return to the diplomatic scene by attending the Queen's annual dinner for the Ambassadors with Graeme.

Although I had kept a fairly low profile during these difficult weeks, much of which time Graeme was travelling, not only to New Zealand, but Scandinavia too (he seemed to be away more than he was at home then), there had been several functions which I had not felt able to miss. One such event had been at the home of the Defence Attaché at the British Embassy. He was leaving The Hague and so held a farewell reception at which his successor would be present. My old Naval 'ties' pulled me to the party and, when I asked the newly arrived Defence Attaché where he had been serving, I discovered that it had been at Northwood, my old stamping ground. However, we decided that we had not been there together. Hugh asked me where else I had served, and as soon as I mentioned HMS *Raleigh* his eyes lit up and he immediately knew that I had been the A/Sec there. He had a good memory to recall this after close to twenty-five years, but I think I was forgiven for having failed to recognise him since he was now grey, definitely balding, and beardless. When I knew him, he had had a full head of brown hair, and a 'full set' (Naval parlance for a beard and moustache). One thing had not changed, though – his laugh was as distinctive as it had always been! We both laughed now, rather to the consternation of our spouses, who were apparently wondering if we had, in those long past days, been more than just work colleagues. Such a thought never crossed our minds. We were just delighted to have this strange coincidence occur.

The staff problems had created difficult times for the children as well, and although they had been very good while we were so busy with the staff house and all the other domestic chores, they seemed to react really badly the minute it was all over. Now we had a different set of problems to contend with, and getting the children in a better frame of mind became a priority. This wasn't helped by the fact that the remainder of the year was spent with a new wave of workmen in the house and this situation continued up until our third year in Holland. But by now we were nearly at the end of the academic year and the end of term was marked in the usual fashion, with Speech Day. This year the school had Patrick Moore (of *The Sky at Night* fame) as guest speaker, which made it an interesting occasion. Having had a visit by Helen Sharman (the first British astronaut in space) earlier in the year, the children were well fired up about all things to do with space. Nina was presented with the Asset Cup for Art and Craft, having been chosen out of a group of over four hundred, so we were all pleased with her. And it was nice that we had some other good things to look forward to as well. The first was the visit of my mother at the beginning of the school holidays. The highlight of her visit was to see the Floriade Flower Show. This only occurs every ten years, and it was so lucky that her visit coincided with this beautiful flower event. The children enjoyed a holiday camp through some of her visit, and then the long awaited and much needed family holiday in France commenced.

Although we thought France was lovely, and Paris simply beautiful, we felt uncomfortably hot at a constant thirty-five degrees. It seemed far too expensive too, and it was utterly exhausting being tourists along with several million others. Euro-Disney was a real disappointment as well, and even the children said that they would never want to bother with anything similar again. Quite a verdict from those two! After a week in Paris we headed south to a village in Provence, which was a startling change of scene. Very quiet and very small and just the place to take life very slowly, which we did. In fact our pace slowed to such an extent that we suddenly realised that we were running out of time to see the French Riviera. The next day we got up at the crack of dawn, leaving before breakfast, and headed off to spend the day in Cannes. No sooner had we arrived than Marc announced that he felt sick, and so we had to head back into the hills. Of course, on our return, it became clear that all that was the matter with him was that he needed his breakfast! It was several days before we decided to try again but when we did we thoroughly enjoyed seeing some really spectacularly beautiful places along the Côte d'Azur. We treated ourselves to an unbelievably expensive breakfast at the Hermitage Hotel in Monte Carlo but we all felt that the treat was well worth it, if only from the point of view of the 1930s style of the hotel, the elegance, and, above all, the view. That particular day ended with a drink at a hotel frequented by Dirk Bogarde, along with a swim in the cliff-side pool overlooking Cap d'Antibes. The children were quite awestruck by the beauty and glamour of it all, and, if the truth be known, so were we.

Before we knew it, it was time to head north again. Our journey back was enlivened by being able to call in to see Jean (one of the girls from the Gloucester Road flat) and her family, who were holidaying in southern Holland. We were sorry to have been away during their visit, but at least we were able to spend an hour with them now. As always, before we had properly unpacked on our return home, we were once again caught up in a host of functions. We also had to get Nina installed into her new way of life as a pupil of the Senior School. She found the experience difficult, and consequently so did we. She behaved rather like the red-headed 'typical teenager' in *The Harry Enfield Show* in fact, and "It's not fair" became her catchphrase! She continued to be a model pupil, however, very hard-working and industrious, and soon became the teachers' pet once more. She made out that she was not, to us, and made heavy going of some of her studies – maths in particular. I found out, quite by accident, that she was in the 'A' stream! Marc settled back at school well and was now in a classroom almost next to the one Nina had been in the previous year, at the Junior School. He liked his new teacher and that bode well for the new academic year. However, they were both very badly deaf again, having caught a dreadful cold in France. For a few weeks it looked as if they would each be hospitalised for further ear operations. Marc, in particular, had never been so deaf before.

Within three weeks of our return from holiday, having had continuous engagements ranging from the Opening of Parliament to a black-tie dinner at the Residence, Graeme and I were flying off to Israel for a week. Having missed the previous year's Credentials ceremony, I was glad that I could accompany Graeme this time. It was very busy, but very interesting indeed. We were able to get the Palestinian perspective as well through meetings and also visiting one of the refugee camps. The conditions there were pretty ghastly and we felt very sad for the children in particular. We also managed to fit in some sightseeing both in Jerusalem and Bethlehem, and I took lots of photographs of all the holy places that we saw. Unfortunately Graeme left my camera in a taxi prior to a visit to The Garden Tomb in Jerusalem, and that was the last we saw of it or the film inside!

Once back from Israel we were well and truly into the 'silly season' of the year and were busy most of the time. We also had to say goodbye to our friends from New Zealand, an English couple with Shell who had lived practically next door to us in Wellington. The de Wattevilles had been posted to The Hague a couple of years before us and so we had had to bid them farewell there too, little imagining that we would be following in their footsteps. It was sad to see them go again because they were good friends and they had helped us through our first two years, giving us support and friendship all the way. Two of their children were the same ages as ours, and so Duncan was able to come to Marc's ninth birthday party before he left. This was the best party ever, with a Hallowe'en theme, and all Marc's friends came dressed appropriately. The cake was special too, having been made in the shape of a spider (until some clever clogs pointed out that it had only got six legs!). So it had, and I hadn't noticed when I collected it from the cake shop. Perhaps Dutch spiders only have six legs!

Just before Marc's party we had our main function of the year which was the New Zealand Ceramics Exhibition at the Nieuw Kerk in Amsterdam. The Ceramics had been brought up from Spain where they had been part of the New Zealand Pavilion at *Expo '92* and it had been difficult (and very time consuming) for Graeme to find a location for the exhibition which would be both large enough and also financially feasible. Finally the Nieuw Kerk was able to hold the month-long exhibition and the setting, in the Church where Queen Beatrix had been married, was certainly very beautiful. The Queen attended the opening ceremony and this made it a very special occasion. A Maori Cultural Show was the finishing touch to a most successful official opening ceremony.

Soon the busy year came to a close and it was time to take the ferry over to England again, to be with my mother for Christmas. The journey was passed pleasantly by watching the film *Strictly Ballroom* and, in Marc's case anyway, whiling the time away in the children's activity corner. The Military Attaché at the British Embassy in The Hague had made arrangements for us to view the Changing of the Guard at Buckingham Palace, from inside the railings, rather than outside. This we found ourselves doing on our first morning in England, but the weather was so cold that much of the pleasure was spoilt. Marc distinguished himself by needing to go to the loo (Mr Burshing in action once more) which consequently afforded us the opportunity to go inside the Palace with him. This was before the Palace was open to visitors, and so we considered ourselves rather lucky at the time! Our friend, the Military Attaché, had also made arrangements for a personalised tour of HMS *Belfast*, moored on the Thames in London, and this was another very interesting trip that we did the following day. The other achievement was that we finally managed to have another of our Gloucester Road flat reunions, which this time did not have to be cancelled because of snow. It was lovely to see the girls and their husbands again, and we had a very happy evening at a restaurant in Brompton Road right opposite the flat we moved to from Gloucester Road.

However, no sooner were our feet back on Dutch soil at the beginning of 1993 than we had to snap smartly out of the holiday mode and put our noses to the grindstone once more. The following morning the children were at school, Graeme was at work, and I was wondering if it really was such a good idea to go away after all. There seemed to be sackfuls of mail to attend to and a hundred and one things to do in order to get the show back on the road again. January was the month of saying farewell to those on their way to pastures new and welcoming those arriving in their stead. It felt like one long party all through that month, including saying goodbye to the Dutch Foreign Minister, van den Broek, whom many will have seen on television during the Maastricht debate. The Queen's New Year Reception was one of the earliest functions and, as always, a rather splendid occasion. So was the first night of Britten's Opera, *Billy*

Budd, which we much enjoyed, along with the Gala Concert held for the visit of the Israeli President.

It was also during January that our dining-room table saga began to reach its crescendo, which in essence began some months earlier when it arrived ex-New Zealand Embassy in Athens (where it had become surplus to requirements). From there it had gone to the Embassy in Madrid (where they could find no better use for it other than as a food stall for Expo), to us as our wonderful 'new' dining-room suite! It was so congealed with food remnants and scratches and gouges that on arrival it seemed to be fit only for firewood. However, we knew that we were going to have to make the most of it, and so Graeme and I took it into the garden, along with all the equally filthy chairs, and hosed it all down, soaped it up and scrubbed the filth off with thick sponges. Some of the food was so congealed that it required more drastic measures than this, but eventually we had cleaned it sufficiently to send it away for French polishing. This involved much toing and froing of the table between the polisher and us before we were finally forced to accept that we would not get a better result. It was eventually returned for the last time some three or four days before we needed it urgently for our first function of the year, a lunch for 40 or so Australian and New Zealand women to celebrate the combined National Days of the two countries. It was at this point that we asked José, the Portuguese butler (who joined us the year before) to screw the various pieces together. We still don't quite know how he managed it, but he succeeded in putting the screws through the surface of the table. After returning the table yet again to the polisher for fairly major repair work to be done, we finally got it back half an hour before the first people arrived. Little did the guests know that we nearly didn't have a table on which to set out the buffet lunch!

The Indian National Day was at about the same time as all this, and who should be serving at their reception but the Filipina who worked for us when we arrived and with whom we had had so much trouble – the very one who had unsuccessfully taken us to court. She was the one person I had hoped not to see again but there was nothing for it but to grin and bear it. They say that things come in threes, and so perhaps we should not have been surprised when we were invited to a very splendid dinner given by the Mistress of the Robes, and to which the Queen's sister Princess Christina had been invited. All very nice, you might say, but Graeme's secretary had got the wrong address down on the driver's programme and he delivered us to a quite different location to that where the party was being held! We eventually arrived, but far too late to conform with diplomatic etiquette.

Interspersed between all these happenings Marc was busy with his judo, swimming, and rugby. The latter took him, from time to time, bussing down to Brussels to play against other teams there. He was a bit apprehensive about this at first, but once he realised that there was either a specially nice packed lunch, or barbecue, available on these occasions, his enthusiasm knew no bounds. He was also very excited at the prospect of going to his first disco, but in the event he had to miss it because of going down with flu. I was amazed, for a boy of nine, just how concerned he was about not having anything to wear to it! Nina also went off on some nice trips, but not of the sporting variety, more the disco/sleep-over kind. She also had an enjoyable field trip which took her away from home for a week for the first time. She was certain that she would not enjoy it, but of course she did. She had also developed into a very promising piano player and an equally promising cook. However, she was badly missing her best friend, Rebecca, who had left at the end of the previous year, and she was finding the senior school work-pressure hard.

I found myself getting involved in a magazine article featuring New Zealand and other Southern Hemisphere wines which was to appear in the magazine *Nouveau*. The photo session, involving the wives of the Ambassadors from South Africa, Australia, New Zealand, Argentina, and Chile, was quite an eye opener when somewhere between sixty to eighty photographs were taken for just one picture needed. This little diversion was taking place just about the time we had our Foreign Minister through on a two-day visit which kept Graeme busy for much longer than that. He came to the Residence for a lunch party, and since we were still juggling with the redecoration of the dining-room we had to get the new curtains hung in a temporary fashion for his visit. There had been insufficient time to get the painting and wallpapering done first, on account of all the various functions we held at the house in February. Redecoration began with a vengeance the day after the lunch party, but took longer than expected because the wallpaper was discovered to be from a faulty batch and this did not become apparent until it was actually up on the walls. Perhaps things don't come in threes after all!

Shortly before the Easter holidays, Graeme and I got up to Scandinavia for one of Graeme's routine visits to his 'parish' and we both thoroughly appreciated being able to have time together, something which was so hard to manage in the normal course of events. It was a good visit and we returned a week before the end of term and the start of the Easter break. My mother was able to come and stay with us again for the school holiday, so that made a nice change, and it was lovely for Nina to have her granny there for her twelfth birthday. Lack of normal contact with family and friends is one of the most difficult aspects of living permanently overseas, and so we always put a high priority on seeing people when we can. For this reason we were also delighted to be able to welcome Vicky and her family over for a long weekend in May.

The summer term passed frighteningly quickly on account of the fact that apart from the usual round of functions to think about, we also had a great deal to attend to in order to plan and organise our mid-tour leave back to New Zealand. We did it without the help of a travel agent, since we found they were more of a hindrance than a help and certainly far more expensive. However, we'd never have managed without a lot of practical help and advice from the friends we were planning to visit around the world. We also spent a lot of time organising the purchase of a small flat in South East London. We managed a twenty-four hour stop-over in London on our way back from another official trip to Sweden in order to see the flat and try to decide if it was what we wanted to buy. It was certainly a whirlwind visit, and I wished that it had not been so close to the time of our departure on leave so that we could have spent longer deciding what to do. Within two weeks of our return the children and I were winging our way to the Bahamas to begin our long mid-tour leave back to New Zealand. Graeme was unable to depart until two weeks after us as the Ministry would not permit him to take his full leave entitlement. We eventually met up with him in Atlanta and proceeded together from there.

Chapter Twenty-Two
A New Life On The Horizon

The children and I lazed about in the Bahamas for a couple of weeks, whiling away the time until Graeme could join us. Not that that was difficult for us to do! We would simply have preferred that he was with us. On the other hand, I'm not sure that it would have been his kind of holiday really, but all the same he missed some very interesting experiences. While most of the time we swam or lazed around the pool reading, or sometimes played tennis, we did some exploring too. One day we went into Nassau and enjoyed looking round the shops there. We discovered that the Bahamas is a strange mixture of British and American culture. The American 'larger than life' way of doing things manifested itself, most notable being the massive limousines. Often these were actually taxi cabs and these vehicles were not entirely suitable for the narrow and congested roads. The Governor's Residence was there in all its pink splendour, the very place where the Duke of Windsor came to live as Governor after his abdication of the British throne. At least his American Duchess, the former Wallis Simpson, would have felt at home with the American influence so much in evidence there. But the policemen looked like dusky bobbies! In fact the whole place had an old British colonial atmosphere about it. However, the American influences were still in stark contrast to its colonial past.

Although in July it is very hot we enjoyed seeing some of the incredibly beautiful scenery. This was much in evidence when we sped in a motor launch over the clear turquoise waters to visit Blue Lagoon Island, which had become a dolphin sanctuary. Here the children were able to stand in the water with these beautiful creatures and touch them and watch them perform amazing feats. The island was so beautiful that it was hard to believe it was real and that we had not strayed into some fantasy film set. It was simply there in all its natural splendour and yet somehow seemed too good to be true! Another exciting trip was to go on board the Atlantis submarine to see the coral reefs. Not only was this a first for the children, but for me too, and we saw a shipwreck, divers, sharks, and millions of exotic fish, along with the spectacular coral.

We had been planning to go on an underwater 'walk' but this had had to be cancelled because Nina developed an ear infection. This necessitated several trips into Nassau to see a Bahamian doctor who turned out to be so nice that we almost began to look forward to the repeated visits. Nina's ear troubled her most of the time we were there, which spoilt it rather for her, but once she was on the right treatment it slowly improved. However, she had to be very careful when she swam lest she got water in her ear. Both children suffered problems with their feet which also required treatment. Three times a day our apartment seemed more like a dispensary as ears and feet were treated by Nurse Mummy! Our apartment was self-catering, and so several trips to the supermarket were needed to stock up with food, and one of the things we found was the very best bread in the world! It was quite delicious and the same verdict was given to the plain natural yogurt we discovered in one shop. So breakfasts became our favourite meal for a fortnight.

Our pace of life was slow, and therefore in a way the time did not pass too quickly, but nevertheless it all seemed like a dream which hadn't really happened by the time we found ourselves at Atlanta airport meeting up with Graeme. He had arrived from Holland an hour before us and so had been able to finalise the collection of a hire car which enabled us to get away smartly on our journey to Rome in Georgia, to visit Elizabeth, my American cousin. Elizabeth was seriously ill and we knew that this would be our last chance to see her and, indeed, we had rearranged our journey to fly westwards, rather than eastwards as originally planned. She was far too ill to have us stay with her and so we checked into a hotel for the night before setting off the next day to visit her. In spite of her frailty she was still the lovely person my mother and I had visited fifteen years earlier when I had been on my way back to the Solomon Islands. Her husband, Yancey, had died several years ago and she was missing him dreadfully, but she was fortunate to have a very kindly live-in carer to look after her. They both seemed delighted that we had gone to visit them, but owing to the fragile state of Elizabeth's health we could not stay very long. Elizabeth lived one more year, as it happened, and I don't know how she coped throughout that time. She was so ill with emphysema when we were there that we feared that she would not be with us for long. It was terribly difficult to say goodbye knowing that it would be for the last time.

From Rome we returned to Atlanta to catch our flight to Los Angeles, from where we would change planes to get our onward connection to Auckland. Once in Auckland we were glad to be nearing the end of our journey, with only one more flight to take us on to Wellington. From mid-summer in the Caribbean and the States, with soaring temperatures there, we now found ourselves in mid-winter New Zealand. Fortunately the weather was pleasant, if somewhat cold, and the crisp air was quite welcome after the heat of Georgia. We had taken another self-catering apartment in Wellington and were glad to arrive and get ourselves sorted out.

The first week was going to involve work back at the Ministry for Graeme, and so the children and I set about getting in touch with friends and generally looking round Wellington. Our apartment overlooked the spectacular harbour and we thoroughly enjoyed this lovely view which we had tried so hard to acquire for ourselves during our house-hunting days. On one occasion the children went back to Marsden to spend time with their friends there and none of us could get over how big the children had grown. Yet ours were the same size too but we hadn't seen it happening! It had been such a happy school for Nina and Marc, and I was afraid that they were going to miss it all over again.

However, we kept ourselves busy to try to keep their mind on positive things, and when Graeme was free to join us, we went up to see round our house in Khandallah. This was let to tenants and we were only moderately satisfied with the way it had been kept. However, we consoled ourselves with the knowledge that it could certainly have been worse. Our visit highlighted a number of things which needed attention and these we were able to set in train. It was lucky that we were there then, for one of the worst problems concerned the roof and we were therefore able to make on-the-spot decisions regarding the best course of action. The week in Wellington went fast and soon it was time to go to Wanganui to visit Graeme's family. The weather was glorious, and so the children were able to thoroughly enjoy our visit to the farm which is always such a fascinating place for city children. Eventually it was time to return to Wellington for our flight to Sydney, and just as we were almost running out of time to catch our plane we decided to pay a visit to "Ma 'Ouse" at its new location at the Khandallah Kindergarten. We shouldn't have gone. It was like seeing a dear old friend in her death throes.

It didn't take long for the Sydney 'magic' to lift our spirits. It really is one of the nicest places in the world. Although we only had three days we made the most of them and managed to see Mike and Gail again, along with their yet again increased family. This time we were able to meet their beautiful little girl, Shanna. Keiran, who was just a baby when I visited after leaving the Solomon Islands, was now an exceedingly handsome teenager and it was interesting to see Nina's reaction to this fact. Anthony and Marc were much of an age and got on well, and the only sadness was that we couldn't be with them for longer. We also managed to catch up with the friends who had been our first tenants when we bought the Khandallah house in 1985. The visits left all too little time to see Sydney, but a trip on the Darling Harbour Monorail rectified this to some extent and gave us a bird's eye view of many places of interest. A stop at the Queen Victoria Building, a shopping arcade described by Pierre Cardin as 'the most beautiful shopping centre in the world', completed the visit for me! However, the children were not as impressed by this as they had been at the Symbio Koala Gardens, where we had been taken by Mike when we visited. They had seen so many varieties of Australian wildlife there and had been able to hold koalas and stroke kangaroos which was much more fun than shopping. If only we could have stayed longer, for Sydney has something to offer everyone.

Malaysia was our next stop. For me this was the sentimental journey of a lifetime and for the family as a whole the main part of our holiday with Graeme. To be going back to that beautiful country which I had left thirty years earlier was something I had dreamed of doing for many years past. They say that you should never go back after such a long time because your memories of a place will be ruined by the changes which have occurred. It was a gamble, I knew, but one worth taking, since the changes which had undoubtedly occurred did not interfere with my memories. We arrived at Kuala Lumpur late in the evening and went to a hotel near the airport to rest for the night. Little did we know that this stop in Kuala Lumpur was to be the setting of a credit card fraud which resulted in several hundreds of guilders being illegally extracted from our bank account! But this was something we discovered only on our return to Holland and so the following day we got a hire car and drove down to Port Dickson with not a care in the world! Here was the place where so many happy weekends had been spent; where I had learnt to water ski and where 'the young ones' from Seremban had had so much fun. Yes, I have to admit that Port Dickson had changed. In fact, I recognised so little that I was unable to find anything I had known before. It wasn't too disappointing, though, since it had only been a weekend retreat and after all, the beach was much the same in spite of being ruined in one area by a newly-acquired power station!

The main excitement revolved around returning to Seremban and this we did after a day or two of relaxing by the pool at the hotel in Port Dickson. I knew that I would be unable to find my way about and so we had already decided to head straight for the police station in the hope of picking up some directions to the places I wanted to show Graeme and the children. To my astonishment it wasn't directions they gave us, but a police escort which would lead us to all the places I had had most association with! Such kindness would be hard to find in other countries, but here this friendliness was very typical. The first stop was to the Sungei Ujong Club. This we found to be even better than I had remembered it to be, since the whole place had been refurbished and redecorated beautifully but nonetheless leaving the rooms exactly as they had been. Nothing had changed, just a new coat of paint applied. The pool was as it had been and the surrounding grassy area too. I could look around and see all the old familiar sights of a place where I had enjoyed myself so much. We stayed for lunch, and the very friendly policemen said that they would come back for us in an hour's time.

When they returned we set off in search of the army barracks where my father and I had worked. They took me to a camp which I didn't recognise at all; then on to another with even less success. At this point they told me that they really had taken me to the right place to begin with and so we returned there. It transpired that the entrance was different and that the part I had known was in a secure area, below, which I would not be allowed to visit. I was saddened by this as I would have loved to go in, having been assured that nothing had changed in all those years. However, this disappointment was soon assuaged by being taken to the house we had lived in in Tobruk Road. We were even allowed to go inside and see around. The house was now the home of a Malaysian colonel and all the married quarters previously occupied by the British were now the homes of Malaysian army personnel. I couldn't believe that I was actually walking into that house again. Even harder to take in was the fact that nothing whatsoever had changed. Even the tiles on the floor were the same! We were received very kindly by the colonel's wife, who offered us cold drinks, and as I looked from the verandah I could almost see my mother tending the garden which she had so enjoyed doing. Even that hadn't changed. The only sad thing was that we had been using the video camera all day to record what we saw, and now that we were inside the house where I had lived the battery went flat and so we got nothing whatever on film!

From the west coast we drove over to the east and there we found that even less changes had taken place than might have been expected. It is still beautiful and the turtles still come up to lay their eggs. We spent until two in the morning one night watching two turtles do just that, and in spite of extreme tiredness on the part of the children we returned to the same spot the following morning to watch an earlier batch of eggs (now hundreds of miniature turtles) being released by the wardens into the sea. It was nature in the raw and, as such, a very moving experience indeed. The following day we took a boat trip deep into the Malaysian rain forest slowly winding our way along a jungle river. This was another unique experience for the children and something which we did, luckily, manage to capture on video. We continued with this journey until we reached an aboriginal settlement where we saw a demonstration of how the blowpipe is used as a weapon to survive in the jungle and also a demonstration of rubber tapping. We had spent two wonderful weeks in Malaysia and had found it to be as beautiful now as I had remembered it to be.

We flew from Kuantan on the east coast to Tioman Island (where the film *South Pacific* was reputedly made, and indeed Tioman was Bali Hai in the film). Tioman was magical but we didn't 'find' Bali Hai at all (I think you must have to view it from somewhere out in the South China Sea to see it as it was in the film). I had seen it years earlier and recognised it as it had appeared in the film, and couldn't understand why I was unable to see it now. The island has become very touristy, which is a shame, but nevertheless the weekend we spent there passed very pleasantly indeed. However, our experiences on flying out were certainly different from those normally associated with your average international airport. The children and I even managed to get on the wrong aircraft and were only alerted to this fact after I had handed in their log books to be completed by the Captain!

From Tioman we flew to Singapore for an overnight stop. Once there, we decided to go for a cheap hotel since all we would be doing was getting a night's sleep. We compensated for this by treating ourselves to a little light supper at Raffles Hotel! Like the shopping arcade in Sydney, I've never seen anything like the new Raffles before. The old Raffles was gentle and elegant; the new is indescribable. It is an experience all by itself. It encompasses not only a conventional hotel, with facilities par excellence, but also a shopping arcade displaying the best wares available from around the world. I'm sure you could stay there for a very long time and never need to leave the place for any reason. And yet none of the gentle charm and elegance has been lost, and if you half shut your eyes to all the gleaming new white paint you can see it is still just as it was. The renovations have been done brilliantly. The Sikh Major Domo is still there to greet you at the door as behind you a guest is drawing up to alight from Raffles' very own gleaming London Taxi. And to think that there was some talk of knocking it down. The children's eyes were on stalks all the time we were there, and their only complaint was that we subsequently discovered that we had missed Michael Jackson's stay there by only a few hours!

At six a.m. the next morning we were at the airport for our flight to Bahrain, only to be told that we had been off-loaded, even though we had taken the precaution to re-confirm our flights. Every cloud has a silver lining, as they say, and we were happy with the outcome in that we were upgraded from economy to business class in the end. On our arrival at Bahrain we were greeted at the airport by one of Graeme's former local staff members with the wonderful news that they were lending us a car for the duration of our stay. It really was good news because it was the only way to see Bahrain again. We used it to the full and drove round and round seeing everything that we wanted to see, plus much which had been built since we left.

Marc was able to visit the hospital where he was born and met Mr Hutchings who delivered him, which was very special indeed. We met up with Jessie and Angeline, two of the house staff we had when we lived there. Both these ladies had known the children as babies, and it was an emotional reunion for us all. We revisited everything we could remember as having been part of our lives so many years earlier. We went back to the house we had lived in and that was extraordinary in itself because it was just days away from being demolished. Although it was sad to see it in that barren state, we were so glad that our visit was in the nick of time. In spite of the simply dreadful humidity and heat, we were all so glad that we had returned.

Our final destination was Cyprus. There we stayed at the hotel we had been to ten years earlier during our time in Bahrain. Oh, what a shock! In all the revisiting we had done during the past weeks nothing could compare with what we found had happened to the Park Beach Hotel. It was, in our opinion, quite ghastly. It certainly wasn't what was needed at the end of our long and tiring holiday. The one nice thing, though, was that we were there to see my old school friend, Pene, and her husband Alan, and the welcome and hospitality they showed us was a merciful relief from the hotel. The three days passed in a flash, and before we knew it we were winging our way back to Amsterdam and the end of an incredible journey which would never have been possible had we not had the air fares paid officially for the purpose of home leave to New Zealand.

While we were away, the legal machinery was progressing on the purchase of our flat in Lee and the completion date was less than a week after we returned. The children were bundled off to a new academic year, with all the attendant settling in needed, and I was glad of the new-found peace to concentrate on the things that had to be attended to as the new owners. Graeme was expecting to go to Israel four weeks after our return, but in the event that visit was cancelled, and so we decided to use the opportunity instead to take some of Graeme's still outstanding leave and went to London for a week to redecorate the flat. It really was quite an experience and not one either of us would wish to repeat. We went on the ferry with the car laden down with paint and painting gear, tools, cleaning equipment, and food to last us through thick and thin. (I had spent the previous weeks making endless lists to ensure that we didn't have to leave the flat for a second unnecessarily). We had never worked so hard in our lives and our daily schedule was to be up at 6 a.m. and continue working through to midnight. It seemed as though the only time we had to speak to each other was when either Graeme fell over my cleaning bucket or I fell over his paint! It was a shambles really, but we managed to transform the place and felt extremely proud of our efforts at the end of it all. Graeme's hands were in such a state by the end of the intensive work schedule that he got blood all over things as he loaded up the car at the end. My hands, meanwhile, had developed a very unpleasant rash. What a way to spend your leave! However, the feeling of satisfaction at having achieved so much did go a long way to compensate us. The sad thing was, though, that we were not able to keep the flat empty for our own use (which is what we would have liked to do), but eventually had to get a tenant to make it financially viable. This being the case, we were lucky that the person we purchased from was happy to sell the flat fully furnished, down to the last teaspoon, and so we did not have to buy very much at all in order to make it comfortably habitable.

Our world trip seemed a lifetime away as soon as we were back in Holland and engrossed not only in the affairs concerning our flat, but our hectic diplomatic lifestyle. One of the main demands on my time, however, was the paperwork generated by the lawyers involved in the conveyancing of the flat to our name. All of this was much more difficult to attend to from a distance. Nevertheless, we got there slowly, and in time were able to hand much of the administration over to the agent.

The few weeks which remained before Christmas went in a flash. Graeme seemed to be in perpetual motion, going to Brussels, Oslo, and Stockholm, before finally getting to Israel just three weeks after returning from painting the flat in Lee. Although we had managed to be in Holland for Marc's tenth birthday, we had had to leave for Israel immediately afterwards, and it was not until our return that we were able to give Marc a party. Having lost my camera in Israel the year before, I felt obliged to return to all the main Christian places of worship in order to retake the pictures I had lost. While it was fascinating to see them all again, I very much wished that I had been able to set a different schedule of visits then, but there was simply no time to do more than retrace my steps. One thing I hadn't seen before, though, was the obscenely expensive tomb of Robert Maxwell on the Mount of Olives. The Mount of Olives is a highly prized burial place for Jews, and the area is totally covered with graves, but this particular one of Maxwell's is large enough to be clearly visible from some distance away.

We had barely unpacked our cases on our return from Israel before we were taking the children to the Guy Fawkes night arranged by their school. It was a bitterly cold evening and the icy wind meant that most of us were simply peeping out from under pulled-down anorak hoods to watch the fireworks display. The children enjoyed it, although rather to our surprise Marc was quite frightened by the noise of the exploding fireworks. His reaction was reminiscent of his fear of the noise of the fire engine after his operation in Auckland (although he didn't dash between my legs!), and I wondered to myself if that earlier experience would be with him, subconsciously, for life. The following evening Graeme was due to present prizes at the International Yacht Club, of which he was Honorary President, and the freezing wet weather continued during our drive to the Club House. So much so that we became lost in the small country roads while trying to find the place, and I fear the members would have wondered if there would be an official guest arriving that night. We finally made it, however, and the warm welcome made up for the dreadful weather outside.

It was not until mid-November that we had time to give Marc his birthday party outing with his friends. This was the first year of not having a party at home, but rather an outing to the bowling alley in Scheveningen. They all appeared to be having great fun, and the fact that it was much easier than having them all run riot at home did not seem to detract from the occasion. The final weeks before we left to be in England for Christmas were spent trying to catch up with our official entertaining and we crammed in black-tie dinners and receptions which had been impossible earlier with all Graeme's travelling. Inevitably we were exhausted when the time came to pack the car up for the ferry trip across the Channel to be with my mother for Christmas, but at least we had some leave to look forward to in order to recharge our batteries. Not that it worked like that, of course, since the time was crammed with visits and outings, which, although enjoyable, meant that there was actually little time left over to simply relax.

With the dawning of 1994 we knew that we would have to give serious thought to the children's future education. We were now caught up with the system at Sevenoaks School, and Nina was scheduled to take the entrance exam in February. We still did not know what the Ministry in Wellington had in store for Graeme, which made it impossible to make plans, but felt that for the time being we had little choice but to keep our options open. So on the 7th of February Nina duly took the senior entrance exam for Sevenoaks School. '(That was the day I started to talk to you, my reader! The story took longer to tell than that day when I needed your company to survive. However, you certainly did help me by being there when I needed you.) I picked Nina up at the end of the day-long exams and she seemed a lot happier. I think she knew in her heart of hearts that she had passed, but it is always difficult to judge, isn't it? Anyway, she did collapse at the end of the day and succumbed to the flu, which had been all too apparent in the morning. We had to wait a number of weeks before we heard the results and, during the waiting period, had news from Wellington that we were to be posted to Riyadh in Saudi Arabia. This meant that it was even more important that the children be settled at boarding school, and so it was with relief that we finally got a letter from Sevenoaks saying that Nina had been accepted.

Now we had a problem with Marc, who was not due to go there until September 1995, but with our proposed move this would have meant he would attend three different schools that year if he came with us. So we approached the school to see if there was any chance of them taking him a year in advance and, much to our delight he, too, passed the exam and was accepted. We then had a big rush to tie up loose ends in order to get over to England to attend the Prospective Pupil's Day. Marc had only sat the exam two weeks before and so the cogs were still falling into place as we dashed out of the door to catch the ferry. It was worth it, though, since it gave both children a good opportunity to see around their new Alma Mater.

In the middle of all this exam-taking excitement, Nina went to Switzerland on a school skiing trip, which she thoroughly enjoyed, and Marc also went off to Twickenham, the famous rugby club in London, again with a school trip. They really benefited from these breaks away, and it was good for them to be independent of us for a change. We, on the other hand, did little earlier in the year, except that Graeme had to go up to Oslo for the funeral of the Norwegian Foreign Minister, Johan Jørgen Holst, in January. It was an interesting occasion since Warren Christopher, Yasser Arafat and

Shimon Peres were there as a mark of respect for the man who had been so instrumental in getting the Middle East Peace Process moving.

In between exams and school trips both Nina and Marc began a course of orthodontic treatment to get their teeth straightened out. A very good start was made in Holland and a significant improvement was quickly apparent. However, there is an awful lot more that is going to have to be done for them both and they are not going to see the back of an orthodontist's chair for a few years yet. For me, all of April and most of May was spent getting the children's things ready for Sevenoaks. I sewed on several hundreds of name tapes (Marc's day socks alone required twenty-four) and altered items which had been bought on the large side. Then there were hundreds of buttons to be reinforced (Marc's school shirts required eighty!). There were so many other things to attend to as well in order to get the two trunks ready by late May. Nina made a good start in sorting out her things during the Easter holidays too (stopping only briefly in order to celebrate her thirteenth birthday!), since there would be no time during the summer term for her to get down to this task. Marc and I managed to do the same for him, but in a fraction of the time it took Nina, so things were beginning to look a little more organised for their departure from Holland. The New Zealand Governor General, Dame Catherine Tizard, paid us a visit at the beginning of May, when my mind was far more on what I needed to be getting on with, but she was on a private visit to Queen Beatrix and we felt it would be remiss of us not to host a luncheon in her honour. May also saw us attending the Queen's annual diplomatic dinner, that splendid occasion which we had enjoyed several times already. It was to be the last time that we would do so and was made particularly special by being placed on the top table.

By the time we got to the summer half term Graeme had started a string of meetings across Europe – first in Paris, then in London. It was the London meeting which had been the cause of my May deadline with the children's trunks, which Graeme was able to deliver to the school by driving to England on that occasion. No sooner was he back from that meeting than he departed for another in Helsinki. This pattern continued when he got back just long enough to put his dirty clothes in the linen basket before departing for Oslo and Stockholm. I would love to have done the Paris and London bit of his travels with him, and Helsinki too come to that, but I was just too busy in Holland. I finally caught up with him in Stockholm, though (where I joined him for my annual official trip to Scandinavia), and this proved particularly useful since the then Ambassador in Riyadh and his wife were there on holiday at the same time. This gave us the chance to meet up with them and get lots of first-hand information and advice. It was most worthwhile, although I cannot say I was overjoyed by some of the information they passed on. Graeme had taken the office laptop computer with him, and the next day I typed up seven pages of notes from our talk with them the night before – lest I forgot it all by the time we arrived. A week later it was Nina's turn to travel when she went on a week's school field trip to Altenahr in Germany. The weather was far too hot for enjoyment, and the field trip just about finished the children off at the end of a hard-working academic year.

There were only a couple of weeks left, after our return from Stockholm, before the children left The British School in The Hague. Helen Sharman, the British astronaut who had earlier visited the school, was the guest of honour at Speech Day and her address was really first class. Unfortunately Graeme missed it (being in Oslo at the time) but I was glad the three of us had gone along. It marked the end of yet another chapter in our lives, but also the beginning of the summer holidays which we were all ready for by this time.

It was now time for the final wrapping up of the children's affairs in Holland and much frenzied last-minute packing took place before we all went on holiday. It was time too to cancel milk and mail and newspaper deliveries. Simple things, you'd think, that we all do before going away. Not so in the case of the newspaper, since we had tried to cancel it several weeks in advance of our departure believing that it might not be as simple as we thought. We were right and in spite of writing, telephoning, and faxing the distributor constantly, we could not get them to stop delivering. It went on, week after week, and there seemed to be nothing we could do to stop it coming. Finally Graeme hit upon the idea of removing our mail box (which was situated outside by the road) each night, and only putting it back just in time for the postman's delivery. It seemed like drastic steps to have to take, but, of course, it worked for the few days we did that. But as soon as we thought we had cracked that one, and put the mail box back, the deliveries started up again, along with a week of back issues! In the end we decided we had to get some outside help to stop this ridiculous situation continuing and I rang the Chief of Protocol at the Mayor's office. He was someone we knew well and he sprang into action. I don't know what he said to the distributor, but whatever it was it worked! Two month's later, after I had returned to Holland from being in England, an unrequested newspaper was delivered once more. I had visions of the whole ghastly business starting up again, but mercifully it was a one-off.

We left Holland in a heatwave (which we had had for several weeks), and it was hard to think of packing warm clothing for our camper-van holiday in England. We sailed from Calais feeling thoroughly overheated by the experience of driving four hours in a car which would have been hard pressed to find space for an extra bottle of drinking water, let alone the two school trunks. Thank goodness we had had the foresight to realise that this would be the case and that Graeme had been allowed to deliver them to the school back in May. There was barely room for the children and certainly no chance of Graeme being able to see out of the back window. By the time the ferry reached Dover the summer was virtually over and it was a grey and drizzly day in England. We collected the camper-van from London a couple of days later and set off to see as many friends and family as we could fit in in the time available. It was a rushed schedule, but we managed to keep on course and on time for the following three weeks, but we had really bitten off more than we could chew and the experience was utterly exhausting. Definitely the last time we do that! The fact that we saw so many people, and several items of interest to the children in particular (such as Stonehenge, the *Mary Rose*, Stratford-upon-Avon, etc., etc.) was what it was all about, and, at the end of the day, what made it all worthwhile, but my own shower and my own bed certainly did feel good when I finally got back to Holland six weeks later.

Project 'Sevenoaks' was drawing nearer by the day, by now, but sadly Graeme had to return to Holland and was unable to spend the final couple of weeks of the holiday with us. The children and I spent that time with my mother, and used it, in the main, as a chance to recover from the holiday! On the day we returned the camper-van to Notting Hill we had our final exhausting fling in London. We 'did' the Buckingham Palace tour, the Hard Rock Café, and finally a boat trip down the Thames to Greenwich. Regrettably, Graeme had to return to work the following day, and if he was as tired as I was from the previous three weeks (and I'm sure he was), I don't know how he managed to stay awake, much less cope with the backlog of work. Anyway, for the rest of us, the time soon came to take the children to their new school, and it was as traumatic an experience as I had imagined it would be. I dashed between the two different Houses to which the children had been allocated and did my best to help them unpack and settle in. It was an emotional experience for all three of us and one which I doubt that any of us will ever forget.

I remained in England for a few days more, to see if there might be anything I was needed for, and indeed I was glad that I had. Poor Nina, in particular, was having a really hard time settling and was very unhappy indeed. Although there was little I could do to really ease her pain, at least she knew that I was still there and it also gave me the chance to be in touch with the staff and get to know them a little. As it happened I had to talk to the staff rather more than might have been expected, not because of the children, but because of my father. The years of silence had come to an end. He had been contacted by the school, who had him down as a prospective guardian, and they had written to him at an address which had ceased to be relevant and indeed had been demolished years earlier. However, the good old post office had tracked him down and delivered the envelope to him safely! Now he had written to Nina and this had caused additional problems which we could well have done without. At least it enabled me to get to know the staff rather better than I had expected!

By the time Graeme came over to collect me and the car, I was feeling like a limp rag that had been through the mangle once too often. There was no chance of recovering when I got back to Holland either. Not only was there six weeks of accumulated paperwork to plough through, and a car full of junk from the camper-van to clear up, but also I returned in the nick of time for the fiftieth Commemoration of Operation Market Garden at Arnhem. This was a week-long affair which involved us both from early morning until late at night for the three days we were over there. However, we would not have missed it for anything. We learnt a lot, too, and found the whole event most moving. It was also interesting to have the chance to meet and talk with Prince Charles who, as Colonel-in-Chief of the Parachute Regiment, was there for the commemoration. No sooner were we back in The Hague than a week of frenzied activity followed, including the Opening of Parliament, an annual diplomatic outing, and our own reception to welcome South Africa back into the Commonwealth. It's always busy, between September and December, and this pattern varied little from year to year. However, I managed to escape it for a few days when I went over to see the children for their first exeat from school, and it was wonderful to see them again and be able to catch up with their news. They had made great strides towards settling into their new way of life, and this enabled me to return to Holland feeling better about it all than I had at the beginning.

I didn't have long to mope about without them, for in just over a week from my return I had a 'full house' of ten weekend house-guests who had come over to celebrate my fiftieth birthday. Friends from the Gloucester Road flat were there, principle amongst them was Janet who I had met on board the troopship going to Malaya thirty-two years earlier, and Naval and WRNS friends too. Vicky and George came over and Hugh (my ex-HMS *Raleigh* colleague) and his wife Tricia were there, but it was just as well that we didn't have to find a bed for them as well! The presence of long-term friends meant that it was, for me, a very special occasion indeed. Not being able to see the people who mean most to me, other than on the infrequent occasions which present themselves, is one of the saddest things about our way of life. But these special people ensured that this milestone in my life was passed with the minimum of trauma.

Five days later the children arrived for half term. Luckily this was a long break from school, being eleven days in all. It gave us time to catch up with more of their news and they seemed to be settling down little by little. This was reflected, too, in their grades, which in Nina's case in particular, were excellent. Luckily Marc's 11th birthday coincided with half term, and we were so glad that we could all be together for that occasion and that he was able to celebrate with some of his friends in Holland.

The day after they flew back to school, Graeme and I left for our final official visit to Israel. At first it looked like being a disaster with all the ingredients of a traveller's worst nightmare. Missed flight connections were followed by suitcases which did not turn up until our fourth day, and when they did arrive it was clear they had been searched. Mine had been relocked with items of clothing left hanging over the edge and Graeme's was not even relocked. When he opened his case he discovered that the official gift he had brought to present to the President of Israel had been ripped open during the course of the search.

Mercifully our first two days were spent with the Parkinsons. John was the chaplain to the British Embassy in Tel Aviv and had, years earlier, christened Marc in Bahrain. John and Joan took us to the shops to buy a few essentials and then took us sightseeing. Having our own personal chaplain to guide us round the Holy Land was an incredible bonus and made it all so special. The rest was all official, but I did have one more unusual experience while waiting for a hair appointment and having lunch at the American Colony Hotel in Jerusalem. The dining-room was deserted, with not even a waiter in sight, but for one other person. The man sitting at the next table was Sir Peter Ustinov, and for twenty minutes, while we both waited to be served, I was agonising with myself as to whether I could speak to him. I nearly did, but my courage failed me when I thought how awful it must be to be famous and for ever be accosted by strangers. I will never be alone in a room with Peter Ustinov again, and ever since that missed opportunity I have kicked myself. A few weeks later I was watching television, and the programme was a documentary featuring Peter Ustinov talking with the major players in the Middle East Peace Process! At least my first question (had I spoken to him), "What are you doing here?", had been answered!

Graeme was back from Israel for one week before going off to Scandinavia again, and with Christmas rapidly approaching I was glad that this time I was not travelling too. I needed to get on with a number of things which had been sadly neglected during the course of the busy year. It was not long before we would be departing for England to spend the final Christmas from Holland with my mother prior to commencing our posting in the Middle East. A new chapter in our lives was about to begin. Another story to be told another day!

Appendix

That's My Last Chance

A poem by Nina Ammundsen

That's my last chance – I'll never have another,
To look inside that house in Delmon Avenue, Manama.
50 Delmon Avenue, Manama, Bahrain,
The place where I grew up, had my fun and played my games.

The airport man on our arrival said solemnly to me,
"Take a look now, or it never will be."
To see the house again after eight long years,
Was the highlight of my holiday; but I felt like crying tears.

Driving down the street and stopping by the door,
We looked to see, but couldn't find, the house we all adored.
The reason was, I must explain, the gates were closed and
   black,
No more the guard, who used to be, praying on his mat.

On looking closer, we could see, that this was really it,
How should we know, when all was looking so much like a tip!
We checked the gate and to our glee, we didn't need a key,
So walked inside to take a look – memories came back to me.

The garden, barely looking that, was barren as could be,
Not at all how I remembered it, when cared for by Salim.
He gave me dates, straight from the palms, which tasted good
   to me,
But if my mother ever knew she wouldn't have been keen!

Next I passed the old back door, which led to where had been
My Wendy house which I had called "Ma 'Ouse" when I was
three.
I then turned left and saw once more the front door at the rear,
I never knew why this was so – the gate was far from near!

I turned before I entered to glimpse the swimming pool,
The place where I had learnt to swim and often played the fool.
It was stagnant, green and smelly now, but never had been so,
When I was there it seemed so huge; but that's 'cos I was low!

I tried the door, to see inside, and found that it was open,
It creaked a bit and dust fell off, but there was nothing broken.
So in I went and looked around and though it was a ruin,
My imagination overcame the lack of anyone there living.

The walls were bare, but in my mind, the house was how't had
been,
And then the place was peopled by the ones who cared for me.
Before I knew it, in came Venu, on his head he had my tea,
But then my thoughts dissolved, and I refocused on reality.

On looking round, I could see that nothing had been left,
No wonder it was open; there could be no fear of theft.
Perhaps it was a mercy; had it been filled with other things
I would never have remembered the images it brings.

I looked around, for one last time, and this was really it,
There would not be another chance, not even just next week.
For on Monday morning, sharp at nine, the bulldozer with
noisy sound
Will knock the house, where I grew up, right down to the
ground.

———————

N.B. This poem was written by Nina in 1993 (aged twelve years), having
returned to Bahrain on the way back to Holland from mid-tour leave in New
Zealand. She was able to see the house where she lived from nine months old

to the age of four and a half years, just before the former New Zealand Residence was demolished by developers. That really was her 'last chance'!

A.A.